WHICH? WAY TO
BUY, OWN AND
SELL A FLAT

About the author

Michael Haley is a solicitor and reader in law at the University of Keele, specialising in the law of landlord and tenant, on which he has written extensively.

About the book

Throughout the book you will find the names of helpful organisations marked with an asterisk (*). Their addresses and telephone numbers can be found in the address section at the back of the book.

WHICH? WAY TO BUY, OWN AND SELL A FLAT

MICHAEL HALEY

CONSUMERS' ASSOCIATION

Which? Books are commissioned and researched by
Consumers' Association, and published by Which? Ltd,
2 Marylebone Road, London NW1 4DF

Distributed by The Penguin Group:
Penguin Books Ltd, 27 Wrights Lane, London W8 5TZ

Thanks to: Diane Campbell for the chapter on Scotland; Peter Wilde for
comments on the typescript; and the Leasehold Enfranchisement Advisory
Service for help with Chapter 17.

Index by Marie Lorimer
Typographic design by Paul Saunders
Cover illustration: Ace/Mauritius

First edition March 1996
Copyright © 1996 Which? Ltd

British Library Cataloguing-in-Publication Data
A catalogue record for this book is available from the British Library

ISBN 0 85202 594 7

Typeset by Townsend Ltd, Worcester
Printed and bound by Firmin-Didot (France) Groupe Herissey
N° d'impression: 33497

CONTENTS

INTRODUCTION

SINCE the late 1980s there has been a severe decline in Britain's real-estate market and a major slump in property prices. Many people have been experiencing difficulties in selling their property, but for the first-time buyer it has been – and continues to be – a time of opportunity, particularly while interest rates are relatively low and mortgage finance is readily available. Moreover, prospective buyers nowadays have a wide range of flats to choose from. In addition to new, purpose-built flats, many large buildings (such as former churches, warehouses and office blocks), especially in major cities, are being converted to meet the ever-increasing demand for flats.

Buying a flat has, for many years, been a popular alternative to buying a house for many reasons:

- flats are generally cheaper to buy than houses;
- they are often situated in central areas;
- they are usually smaller and more convenient to live in;
- they are normally laid out on one level and, particularly if on the ground floor, can be a major advantage to the elderly and infirm;
- they can be cheaper to run and maintain;
- decisions and worries concerning external repairs and decoration, and maintenance of communal gardens and common parts are often delegated to the landlord or a management agent/company;
- with new developments, there may be extra facilities such as a gym, swimming pool, underground car park, security system and porterage.

Nevertheless, for the existing flat-owner who seeks to sell, the picture may not be that rosy. Apart from the problems associated with disposing of any property, a new complication has emerged in the guise of the negative equity trap. This arises where the current market value of the property is lower than the mortgage taken on to buy the property. The owner may not be able to afford to sell, or, if he or she can, it may be that part of the debt has to be carried forward.

Flat-owners have been favoured by recent legislation that allows groups of tenants jointly to buy the freehold of their building (a right known as collective enfranchisement), or individual tenants to purchase a new lease on their flats. Other statutory provisions have increased the control that tenants have over the quality and cost of services provided by the landlord. Perhaps most importantly for flat-buyers, the Landlord and Tenant (Covenants) Act 1995, which came into force on 1 January 1996, greatly altered the law relating to lease-hold covenants and abolished the continuing liability of the original tenant. The implications of this Act are discussed in Chapter 9. However, despite the existence of laws designed to protect – and indeed extend – the rights of the flat-owner, unscrupulous landlords have found loopholes enabling them to take advantage of their tenants in various ways. Some landlords have been selling the freehold of their properties to 'ground-rent feeders' – ruthless individuals who milk the tenants by way of exorbitantly high service charges and management fees. This nightmare scenario is discussed in Chapter 17. As we go to press, the government is looking at ways in which the law can be strengthened to prevent such abuses in the future.

In addition, although the Leasehold Reform, Housing and Urban Development Act 1993 has given flat-owners improved rights, it does not go far enough. Tenants who wish to apply to buy their freehold often find the conditions highly prescriptive, rendering them ineligible. Commonhold (examined in Chapter 1), whereby tenants buy the freehold of their individual flat but own common parts with other tenants, could be the solution in that it will do away with leases and landlords altogether. However, proposals to introduce commonhold are still a long way off, and it remains to be seen whether the eligibility criteria for it will be broadened in comparison with those for enfranchisement. This book deals with the law as it stands at the end of 1995 and should provide most flat-buyers and tenants with the guidance they need for some time to come.

CHAPTER 1

AN INTRODUCTION TO LEASEHOLDS

BUYING a flat is for many the first step in home-ownership. This chapter explains the concept of leasehold, terms associated with it and the peculiarities of leasehold conveyancing and ownership.

What is a leasehold?

Conveyancing is the legal and administrative process involved in transferring the ownership of land and/or any buildings on it from one owner to another. Buying and selling a flat is similar to buying and selling a house apart from one crucial difference – the nature of what is bought and sold.

Unlike a freehold, which gives the buyer what is, to all intents and purposes, complete ownership of the land and the buildings on it, a leasehold gives only a limited type of ownership for a fixed period of time. It is essentially permission to occupy property given by the land-owner (known as the freeholder or landlord) to the buyer (known as the leaseholder, lessee or tenant) in return for payment. In a loose sense, leasing can be compared with hiring land for a definite period and subject to a variety of rights and obligations. Nevertheless, a properly executed lease (the document setting out the terms and conditions of the leasehold) gives the tenant a legal estate in land. For reasons that will become clear in the rest of this chapter, people who own flats generally own the leasehold, not the freehold.

A leasehold is carved out of a landlord's freehold estate and can adopt various forms. At one end of the spectrum there is the tenancy of a furnished bedsit, providing short-term accommodation at a weekly market rent. (For all types of short tenancies at market rents see *The Which? Guide to Renting and Letting*.) At the other end is the long-term lease for a fixed number of years – for example, 99, 199 or 999 years. Once a long lease is taken and the capital premium (the purchase price of the property) is paid, the tenant's financial responsibility to the landlord is limited to a small ground rent (payable annually or quarterly) and any service or management charge levied by the lease in respect of the premises. It is with the long, fixed–term lease that this book is concerned.

What you should know about a leasehold

- Mortgage money is not automatically available for the purchase of every type of flat. Banks and building societies are generally unwilling to lend money on freehold flats (see pages 15-16). Even in the case of leaseholds, they will look at the nature and state of repair of the property before making a loan and will usually be reluctant to advance funds on a lease which has less than 60 years to run or on a property which has substantial defects (see Chapter 3).
- All flat-owners have to pay a ground rent (usually nominal) to their landlord. In addition, if the landlord retains control and management of the premises (as occurs with a block of flats), the tenant will be obliged to pay an annual service charge to cover a share of the costs of repair, maintenance and insurance of the entire building, usually to a management company (see Chapters 12 and 13.)
- The leasehold normally imposes obligations (in the form of covenants) on the tenant: for example, to repair and maintain the interior; to take out 'bricks and mortar' insurance if the landlord does not do so; to pay service charges; and to use the flat only for the purposes of a dwelling (see Chapter 8).
- The flat-owner has the right to occupy the flat and can be dis-possessed only on certain grounds. These include defaults on the mortgage agreement (e.g. non-payment of the interest and capital; see Chapter 3) and breaches of the leasehold covenants (e.g. altera-tions carried out without the landlord's consent; see Chapter 9). All these possibilities are regulated by Parliament and offer the tenant some protection against unjust action (see Chapters 9 and 16).

Basic vocabulary

Lawyers have devised a language of technical terms and expressions that is often baffling to the general public. This is certainly true in relation to leasehold conveyancing and, in particular, the wording of leases and the covenants they contain. Coming to grips with some of the terminology is, however, a necessary evil. Some of these basic terms are explained below and a more detailed glossary is provided at the back of the book.

A **freehold** is property held absolutely (until the end of time, as it were). Normally, in the case of a flat, the freehold will be the title owned by the landlord and will relate to the whole building and the land on which the building stands. A **freeholder** is, simply, the person who owns the freehold. When this person creates or grants a lease (i.e. sells a flat) he or she is known as the **lessor, landlord** or **reversioner**.

A **leasehold** is ownership of property for a specified time, the terms and conditions of which are set out in a contract known as a **lease**. A lease may also be called a **tenancy, term of years** or **demise**. A **leaseholder** (or **lessee** or **tenant**) is the person to whom a lease is granted (i.e. the person who buys the flat).

A landlord can **assign** (sell) the freehold and a tenant can usually assign the unexpired period of a lease. This **assignment** can be of the whole or just part of the premises. Although this is unlikely, and is subject to the lease prohibiting this, the tenant can structurally convert the flat and sell off parts of it. The effect of an assignment is that the property has a new landlord or a new tenant (the **assignee**). Assignments can occur any number of times during the course of a lease. At any given time there must be two owners of the property: the landlord, who owns the freehold, and the tenant, who owns the leasehold.

When a lease is granted, the landlord retains the freehold of the property. This is described as the landlord's **reversion** because at the end of the lease the property traditionally reverts back to the landlord.

A tenant can also carve out from the lease a shorter tenancy in favour of someone else, known as a **sub-lease, sub-demise** or **underlease**. The tenant's own lease will then be known as the **head-lease**. This can be of the whole or just part of the premises, so the tenant could sub-let one room in the flat, for example. Unlike assignment, this transaction does not dispose of the entire interest under the lease. The parties to the transaction creating an underlease are often known as the **sub-lessor** and the **sub-lessee** or **sub-tenant**.

A sub-tenant can either assign the existing sub-lease or create a further **sub-letting** (sometimes called a **sub-underlease**) of the flat for a shorter term than the first.

It should be noted that the terms **landlord** and **tenant** can be used to describe various levels of relationship. A sub-tenant will regard the person from whom he or she is sub-leasing as the landlord, in which case that landlord's lessor (in other words, the freeholder) might become known as the **head landlord**. Furthermore, the words landlord/tenant apply equally to both short-term leases, in which a tenant pays a market rent to the landlord, and long-term leases, for which the tenant pays only ground rent. To confuse matters even further, a sub-tenant might in everyday language be referred to simply as a 'tenant'.

The diagram below illustrates the transactions possible for a single flat.

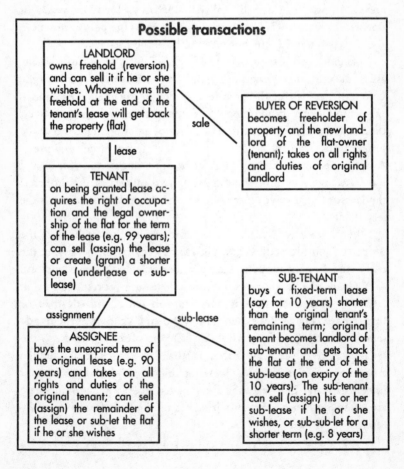

Possible transactions

LANDLORD
owns freehold (reversion) and can sell it if he or she wishes. Whoever owns the freehold at the end of the tenant's lease will get back the property (flat)

sale

BUYER OF REVERSION
becomes freeholder of property and the new landlord of the flat-owner (tenant); takes on all rights and duties of original landlord

lease

TENANT
on being granted lease acquires the right of occupation and the legal ownership of the flat for the term of the lease (e.g. 99 years); can sell (assign) the lease or create (grant) a shorter one (underlease or sublease)

assignment

sub-lease

ASSIGNEE
buys the unexpired term of the original lease (e.g. 90 years) and takes on all rights and duties of the original tenant; can sell (assign) the remainder of the lease or sub-let the flat if he or she wishes

SUB-TENANT
buys a fixed-term lease (say for 10 years) shorter than the original tenant's remaining term; original tenant becomes landlord of sub-tenant and gets back the flat at the end of the sub-lease (on expiry of the 10 years). The sub-tenant can sell (assign) his or her sub-lease if he or she wishes, or sub-sub-let for a shorter term (e.g. 8 years)

Examples

(1) Janet leases a flat in 1970 for 99 years to Sammy. In 1995, Sammy sells the entire lease to Sadek. Janet remains the landlord, Sammy ceases to be the tenant, and Sadek takes the **assignment** of the rest of that 99-year lease, which then has 74 years to run.

(2) Janet leases a flat in 1970 for 99 years to Sammy, who immediately creates a **sub-lease** of 25 years for Sadek. Janet remains the head landlord, Sammy is the tenant of Janet and the sub-lessor of Sadek, and Sadek is the sub-tenant. At the end of 25 years, the remaining 74 years revert back to Sammy and, when that period expires, the premises revert back to Janet.

What you should know about a lease

Leases tend to follow a certain format, although the precise terms will vary according to the nature of the property and the wishes of the parties involved. Whatever form a lease takes, it must satisfy certain conditions.

- The parties to a lease must enter a legally binding relationship. A lease cannot, for example, be a purely domestic arrangement.
- The lease must be for a certain duration which can be calculated precisely. This is why leases are often granted for, say, 99 or 999 years. Such arrangements as 'until the landlord seeks possession of the property for road-widening purposes', 'until the landlord pays off a debt to the occupier', or 'for the duration of the present government' would fall foul of this rule.
- The date when the lease is to commence must be stated.
- The lease will contain covenants (i.e. contractual obligations) between the parties either spelled out or implied into the lease (e.g. to pay ground rent).
- The landlord must retain the reversion.
- The transaction must convey to the tenant what is called 'exclusive possession', which is the legal right to exclude all others, including the landlord, from the property.
- If it is for a fixed period of more than three years, the lease must be created by deed. A deed is a formal document which is signed by the parties in the presence of a witness.

Problem leases

The fact that a lease details the obligations of the landlord and tenant, and that these obligations can be enforced between the parties, does not offer any guarantee that the flat is saleable or mortgageable. Many long leases of flats are problematic. The main points to watch out for are:

- **Insurance** It is imperative that the lease makes adequate insurance arrangements (see Chapter 11 for details). There must be an obligation to insure comprehensively. A block policy covering the entire building, usually arranged by the landlord or a management company with the premium shared among the flat-owners by means of a service charge, is preferable to individual flat-owners taking out separate cover, with different insurers and for differing amounts. In the event of a claim it is easier if a single insurer and policy deals with it. Most mortgage lenders will not lend on flats if the insurance clauses are not adequate.

- **Repairs** Like insurance, it is preferable for one person or company (usually the landlord or a management company) to take on the legal responsibility for the main fabric of the building. The roof, foundations, main timbers and so on must be legally covered. The covenant to repair must be enforceable and workable. The cost of repair is normally shared by means of the service charge. Again, if the lease does not deal properly with such matters, the flat will be difficult to sell or to secure a mortgage on. See Chapter 14 for more details.

- **Management structures** The lease must provide a proper management structure. It is normal for a management company to be formed by the landlord, but it is possible for the tenants to set up a company themselves and manage the property (see Chapter 13). If the tenants do take over management of the building, each flat-owner becomes a shareholder or member of the management company, which will own the common parts of the building and assume the major responsibilities. This way the tenants collectively run the property, and there is one vote per flat. There is legislation to force bad landlords to comply with the lease (see Chapter 14), but having to resort to litigation to do so is hardly the best way to manage a block of flats.

● **Mutual enforceability** It is essential that each tenant can enforce the obligations which the other flat-owners have entered into. The simplest way to do this is to ensure that the landlord or management company is legally obliged to enforce the obligations at the request of each flat-owner. If those obligations cannot be enforced by the other flat-owners, the lease is defective. A clause in the lease obliging such enforceability is the best answer.

Why leasehold flats?

From the freeholder's point of view, selling long leases for the flats in a building will raise capital (from the first tenants of the leases and re-sales at the end of those leases) and income from ground rent. As ground rent for individual flats is very low (never comparable to the market rent for a flat), such income is probably worthwhile only if the freeholder has numerous properties or some other interest in the property: for example, if he or she lives in one of the flats.

Some landlords may view the long-term prospect of a property reverting back at the end of the lease as an inheritance to leave for future generations. However, this notion is now threatened by the recent rights given to groups of tenants to buy jointly the landlord's freehold – collective enfranchisement – and to individual tenants to obtain an extension of their respective leases (see Chapter 17).

From the tenant's point of view, owning a leasehold flat may not seem very different from owning a freehold property. For many purposes this is very near to the truth. The leaseholder can sell the un-expired period of the tenancy for such price as the market will pay. The lease, although declining in value with the passing of time, will for many years be a saleable asset. Indeed, for the greater part of the lease, the tenant has a more valuable interest than that held by the landlord.

Apart from the financial advantages to both landlord and tenant, the main practical reason why flats are traditionally leased out rather than sold freehold is maintenance. Landlords usually wish to retain a high degree of control over the premises. The simplest way to do this is to set up a management scheme covering all the flats in the building, whereby the upkeep of the whole property is ensured. As has been mentioned before, leases generally impose a variety of conditions (covenants) on a tenant. In a block of flats, for example, it is essential that the covenants regulating maintenance, repair and insurance are enforceable against each flat-owner, so that ceilings, walls, floors and other important parts are kept in good repair.

While positive covenants (i.e. to do something, like repair or pay money) are enforceable between landlords and tenants of a leasehold flat, they are not enforceable between the parties in a freehold flat. This is why banks and building societies are reluctant to lend on freehold flats: the security for the loan cannot be protected in the same way as with a leasehold flat. This general unavailability of mortgage finance for freehold flats is an important reason why leasehold flats are the norm.

Disadvantages of a leasehold

A lease becomes less marketable below a certain number of years (usually estimated at 60 years), or marketable only to a cash buyer because of the difficulty of obtaining mortgage finance for a comparatively short lease. New statutory rights allowing tenants collectively to buy the freehold or to obtain a new lease go some way towards overcoming the problems associated with the wasting nature of a lease.

The value of the property may also be depressed by lack of maintenance and unchecked deterioration of adjacent flats. This can be a major cause of concern for flat-owners and give rise to many legal difficulties.

What happens when a lease is assigned?

When the unexpired term of the lease is sold on (assigned), the original tenant, and any intervening assignees, drop out of the picture for most purposes. The first tenant, however, is in an unusual position. As regards leases that were granted before 1 January 1996, he or she will always remain liable on the contractual covenants contained in the original lease.

Sadly, during the past few years and particularly since the recession of the 1990s, there has been an increasing number of legal cases in which action has been brought against an original tenant when a landlord has been unable to sue a current, insolvent, tenant for breach of covenant. This has happened even when the first tenant sold the flat at a market price a long time ago and had nothing to do with the current tenant's breach of covenant.

As a step in the right direction, however, the Landlord and Tenant (Covenants) Act 1995 has altered the law relating to leasehold covenants. With new leases granted since 1 January 1996 the first tenant is automatically released from liability on tenants' covenants when the lease is assigned. When a freehold is sold, the former landlord can apply to the court to be released from landlord's covenants.

The Act does not affect the rules that apply to sub-leases. With a sub-lease, the original tenant should ensure that the covenants in the head-lease, which still bind him or her, will be performed by the sub-tenant.

Proposals for commonhold

It is in theory possible to buy the freehold of a flat which is separate from the freehold(s) of the rest of the building. This is known as a 'flying freehold', but such freeholds are unusual and, as mentioned, mortgage finance for them is almost impossible to obtain. However, many flat-owners would prefer to own a freehold estate rather than a leasehold estate. Pressure for reform of the law has come from both lawyers and consumers and has helped create a concept known as commonhold. Since 1965, there have been repeated calls for change so as to allow the passing on of positive covenants when the freehold is sold on. Positive covenants, as mentioned above, are those that require something to be done (e.g. to repair), whereas negative covenants stop something from being done (such as building into a roof space). Unlike covenants in leases, freehold positive covenants bind only the parties to them and do not bind any new purchaser of the freehold.

Freehold titles of flats can already be found in the USA in the form of condominiums and in Australia and New Zealand in the form of strata-titles. In 1990 the Lord Chancellor's Department proposed the commonhold scheme of freehold ownership of flats and communal management of common parts. In short, commonhold is a freehold development consisting of at least two separate units that share services and facilities. Under commonhold the owner of each flat will own the freehold of that unit with the right to essential and communal services, for example the right to use a common garden and communal facilities. The main legal title will be held by a commonhold association, and regulations will be laid down to govern the mutual obligations between all the flat-owners. The obligations will bind all future purchasers of the flats.

Commonhold has the great advantage of doing away altogether with leases and landlords, and is probably the best method of empowering flat-owners. Legislation on the issue has been promised, but could take years to enact, and details of the scheme have yet to be finalised. The furore over collective enfranchisement (see Chapter 17) may accelerate the process towards commonhold. It remains to be seen, however, whether the rather restrictive eligibility criteria for collective enfranchisement will be relaxed in any new scheme to introduce commonhold, thereby helping more flat-owners.

CHAPTER 2

BUYERS, SELLERS AND ESTATE AGENTS

Types of flats

THERE are various types of flats and, while the law applies equally to all, there are different considerations to take into account depending on the nature of the flat bought. The main descriptions that are applied to flats are:

- **Conversions** This is where the freeholder of a building converts it into a number of dwellings. In most cases each flat will have a separate entrance and there will be no common parts retained by the landlord and shared between the tenants. The tenants will be responsible for maintaining and repairing the interior and exterior of their flats. Maintenance of the roof, for example, will normally rest with the owner of the upper-storey flat. During conveyancing a surveyor's report (see Chapter 5) will indicate how well the conversion work has been carried out and alert the buyer to potential problems. Conversions of older properties can lead to higher risks of expensive repair works and structural problems. Often there will be no service charges payable under leases taken in small conversions.
- **Mansion flats** This term, often used by estate agents, does not have any legal significance, but it does, however, carry a certain prestige. It simply refers to the character of the building in which the flats are contained – normally a large, imposing residential building. In such large-scale conversions, the landlord will retain common parts and, as with purpose-built blocks of flats, enter into a series of mutual covenants with each tenant. A service charge will be payable to reimburse the landlord's costs of managing the premises.

- **Purpose-built blocks of flats** In purpose-built blocks, the legal relationship between the landlord and the tenants (and between the tenants themselves) is close and there is a greater degree of inter-dependency between them all. The individual tenant has little direct control over the external structure of the building, and the quality of life and the value of the flat are influenced by the actions of the landlord as well as those of the other tenants. The tenants will pay the landlord an annual service charge (which can be sub-stantial) to finance the costs of managing the premises. The problem with purpose-built blocks is that they may not be well constructed. To detect any structural problems the whole building may have to be surveyed, thus adding substantially to the surveyor's fees. If the block falls into serious disrepair, the tenants may be faced with hefty service charges and a flat that cannot be sold except at a knock-down price. Moreover, banks and building societies will not lend money to buy a flat in a block that is rundown.

- **Studio flats** These are essentially one-room flats (the living room normally doubles as a bedroom) with a separate kitchen and bathroom. Some studios, however, may have a galleried balcony to accommodate a bed. Obviously, studios are cheaper than one-bedroom flats, but tend to be more difficult to sell. It is often worth spending a little extra to acquire a separate bedroom.

- **Basement flats** These are, as the name suggests, flats that are below ground level. Such flats may have problems with damp and lighting. Generally speaking, they are not as easy to sell (and do not retain their value as much) as flats on the ground (or higher) floors.

- **Maisonettes** Generally speaking, maisonettes are similar to flats, but they have their own entrance and are on two floors, with their own internal staircases. They may have a common garden or shared water tank in the roof space. Maisonettes could be in purpose-built blocks or in houses which have been divided up. The law applies similarly to leases of property whether horizontally or vertically divided.

- **Pied à terre** This expression sometimes finds its way into estate agents' particulars. It applies to flats in cities and large towns, and means that the flat would make a small and convenient second property (a stop-over) for those who live outside the city/town.

- **Newly constructed flats** Whether such flats are in a large block or a small development, the buyer has some protection offered by the National House Building Council (NHBC)★. This is a non-profit-making body with a register of some 25,000 builders and developers who undertake to build flats and houses to a set of standards drawn up by the Council. NHBC inspectors will have examined the property and, if the builder is registered with the Council, will issue a ten-year Buildmark warranty. This offers the buyer some protection if faults emerge (see Chapter 7 for details). It is also generally easier to raise mortgage finance on a newly constructed flat than on an old property. Clearly, the newer the building, the less likely it is that it will require repair or maintenance in the short term.

- **Local authority flats** Tenants who have lived in council property for a certain number of years have the right to buy at a substantial discount (up to 70 per cent of the value; see Chapter 18). Ownership of such flats is the same as that of any other flat, except that there is a clawback of the discount if the flat is sold on within three years. Problems may arise, however, on buying a flat in a council block. Often, such blocks fall into severe disrepair. If that happens, the tenants could face service charges beyond their means, and, more importantly, the property will become 'red-lined', which means that no prospective purchaser (if one can be found) will be able to obtain mortgage finance. Consequently, the tenant will have to sell at auction at a considerable loss.

- **Housing association flats** Housing associations exist to give people the opportunity to buy their own home. The development projects are financed by government grants and the properties are normally situated in poorer housing areas. In essence, housing association properties are subject to the same 'right to buy' rules as council properties (see Chapter 18).

- **Repossessed flats** Flats which have been repossessed by the mortgage lender can be bought in the same way as any other property. The lender will not, however, be able to supply comprehensive details about the property and will not know whether the previous tenants had any disputes with the neighbours. Sales of repossessed homes often take place at a public auction or by tender, and there is no doubt that the lucky buyer can snap up a bargain.

Buying a flat

Flat-hunting

Once you have decided to buy a flat the process of looking for one can begin. You may even have chosen the area in which you would like to live. This choice can be influenced by a combination of factors such as: closeness to work, public transport or family and friends; price; safety; or general attractiveness in terms of amenities and natural beauty. If you have not yet selected an area, it might be helpful to compile a checklist of features that you are looking for and check out different locations.

Estate agents

By far the most common way of finding a flat is the use of an estate agent. Contact estate agents in the area you have chosen, give them your specifications (the number of rooms you want, whether you want a garage or garden, how much you are prepared to pay, etc.) and ask to be put on their mailing lists. This will ensure that details of suitable properties ('particulars') are sent to you at regular intervals.

Although estate agents are prevented by law from actually misdescribing property that they are trying to sell, you should remember that they tend to use the most flattering terms possible in their particulars. Do not get carried away by their use of adjectives. 'Desirable residence', 'deceptively spacious', 'conveniently situated', 'luxury kitchen', 'exceptionally well presented' and similar expressions adorn many agents' descriptions. They have, however, no legal significance and are merely designed to get the prospective buyer into the flat. Photographs of properties will also tend to flatter.

When you want to view the properties that seem attractive, the estate agents, who act as negotiators between the seller and you, will arrange appointments for you to do so, and very often will accompany you there. Estate agents can also offer advice about mortgages, surveys and solicitors. As a buyer, you do not have to pay the agents: they get their commission from the seller.

Many estate agents are members of professional associations and will have agreed to abide by the codes of practice set out by those associations. The codes offer tight regulation of the estate agency business and usually offer an informal arbitration scheme through which any dispute may be settled. An estate agent may also be party to the Ombudsman for Corporate Estate Agents★, especially if it is part of a large group. If your complaint of unfairness, inefficiency or delay is upheld against an agent who is party to the scheme, the Ombudsman has the power to award you compensation.

If you have genuinely been misled by the estate agents' particulars, or have another grievance against the agents, complain first to the firm and then, if necessary, contact the association of which the estate agent is a member or the Ombudsman (if relevant). General and legal advice may be sought from the Citizens Advice Bureau or a solicitor. Recourse to the courts should be viewed as a measure of last resort.

Other sources

There are other ways in which a buyer can find out what is on the market. Flats for sale are advertised in specialised property magazines and local and national newspapers. It is also useful to drive or walk round the area chosen, looking for 'For Sale' signs and to ask friends and acquaintances about any properties they might know of.

What to look for

Apart from the dimensions and the internal layout of the flat – which are arguably the most important considerations when choosing a flat – there are a variety of other factors that a prospective purchaser should bear in mind. It is worth writing down a list of the features that are important for you in a flat, so you know what to look out for when viewing. Compromising on some of them will almost certainly be called for – no single flat will provide all you want – so it would help to decide before you start viewing which factors are absolutely essential and which you can forgo. Some of the more important things to look out for are listed below. Many of them are specific to flats, so even an experienced house-buyer will find the tips useful.

The exterior

● Notice the state of decoration and repair of the outside of the building: as far as possible, look at the condition of the roof, pointing, chimney stacks, down pipes and gutters. As regards any common parts of the building – the stairways, gardens, parking areas – examine whether they are clean, reasonably decorated and well lit.

- In a block of flats, check whether there is a lift and examine the width and incline of the stairways. If possible, ask other residents about the reliability of any lift fitted. If there is no lift, imagine facing the daily climb up to the flat carrying shopping, children, etc. It is also advisable to find out about rubbish disposal and window-cleaning facilities.
- Check on the rights to use (and the obligation to maintain) access areas and gardens, and verify what the price does and does not include.
- Note how close the building is to the road, schools, pubs and railway lines etc. These factors are potential irritants. Conversely, check on how conveniently located the flat is with respect to public transport and amenities which are important for you – parks, banks, shops, medical facilities.
- Check whether there is a garage (large enough for your car) or parking space which comes with the flat. A garage, in particular, can add to the selling price and make the property more marketable. You should also check on where visitors can park.

The interior

- Inside the flat look for any tell-tale signs of damp: for example, a musty smell, crumbling plaster, stained ceilings and mould around the windows. With ground-floor or basement flats, ask if a damp-proof course has been fitted. Look also for cracks in the ceiling and bulges and cracks in the walls, which may indicate settlement problems.
- A number of factors which may seem trivial at this stage could prove to be problematic later on. Check, therefore, on things like how well the doors and windows fit and whether they open and close easily; how many telephone and television points there are; how old the central heating boiler is; what state the bath and other sanitary facilities are in; and whether the storage space and loft space available are adequate.

Check whether there is central heating and double or secondary glazing. It is always wise to ask the seller to turn on the central heating to see if it is in working order.

One of the most important tips is that if you are interested in a flat you should visit it more than once and at different times of the day. By doing so you could discover, for example, loud neighbours, barking dogs, noisy lifts or increased traffic. If you can, talk to the neighbours to settle any queries you may have about the area. It is also likely that one visit might leave a more favourable impression about the flat than is deserved. For example, you may not realise on your first visit that the carpets are stained or that few rooms benefit from natural light. A second or even third visit may be necessary for you to put your doubts at rest.

Selling a flat

Although there are alternative means of finding a buyer (e.g. placing an advert in a local newspaper), employing an estate agent is the most effective and efficient means. An estate agent (or a valuer working with one) will help you fix a price for the flat based on the local market. The agency will conduct negotiations with prospective buyers, advertise and market the flat, and arrange (conducted or unconducted) viewings of your property.

Estate agents work for the seller of the property. They have a duty to obtain the best price reasonably available and an obligation under the Estate Agents Act 1979 to disclose offers made in respect of the property. Choosing an estate agent to sell your property can, however, be perplexing: there are likely to be numerous firms in your area. It is possible that one may be personally recommended to you or that you have used a particular agent before and were satisfied with the service provided. It could be that, when looking for a property to buy, you have come across an agency which impresses you by its professionalism. A local agent might have a special expertise in selling flats in your area – you can tell if you see many more 'For Sale' signs from one particular firm than any other outside flats being marketed. What an agent is prepared to do to advertise and sell the property (and at what price), and whether it can help arrange a favourable mortgage or put you in touch with other professionals (e.g. a solicitor) might prove decisive.

An agent's right to payment will depend on the contract entered with the seller. Some require a fee to be paid at the outset and most require the seller to pay a percentage of the purchase price (or, alternatively, a fixed fee) when a buyer is introduced. The contract may provide that if a willing buyer is introduced, but the seller decides not to proceed, the fee still remains payable. It is also possible that the agent will operate on a 'no-sale, no-fee' basis, but beware of this ploy as some agents require the payment of expenses even if a buyer is not found.

Two types of arrangement with estate agents are commonly found: 'sole selling rights' and 'sole agency'. The sole selling rights agreement means that, even if the flat is sold privately without the agent's involvement, the fee becomes payable. The sole agency agreement, however, allows a private sale without fee. It also allows other estate agents to be employed in addition to the original agent. However, if one of the other agents finds a buyer, the seller must pay double commission (that is, to the original agent as well as to the selling agent).

Other arrangements that might be encountered are the 'joint agency' (whereby two agents are instructed and they agree between them as to how the commission is to be split) and the more expensive 'multiple agency' (whereby the seller chooses how many agents to employ with the commission being paid to the one who finds the buyer).

CHAPTER 3

MORTGAGES

THE majority of residential purchases are financed by a mortgage, which is a major form of credit. Strictly speaking, the word does not mean a loan; it refers to the security provided by the borrower to the lender. A loan helps you (the mortgagor) buy a flat, which you pledge as security for the loan – i.e. you cannot sell the flat without repaying the loan, and if you do not keep up your repayments, the lender (the mortgagee) has the right to go to court to repossess the flat.

The major characteristics of a mortgage are:

- a person borrows a sum of money for a fixed period of time – usually between 20 and 30 years – from a lender to buy a property;
- the borrower gives the lender a legal right over the flat, but retains legal ownership of it;
- the borrower has a right to redeem the mortgage – that is, he or she can repay the capital and interest (and any redemption fee, see page 37) and so terminate it at any time during the mortgage;
- if the borrower defaults, the lender has certain rights and remedies through which the security for the loan may be safeguarded and enforced;
- if the borrower becomes insolvent, the lender has priority over other creditors and is entitled to be repaid in full.

Home-ownership: dream or nightmare?

A mortgage is the largest financial commitment in the lives of millions of people. By offering a flat as security for the loan, the buyer can borrow a substantial sum which is normally repayable over

20, 25 or 30 years. The attraction is that the borrower has the opportunity to become an owner–occupier, which would otherwise not generally be possible. The borrower not only acquires a place to live but also makes a speculative capital investment: even though the buyer owes the lender the amount borrowed, if the flat rises in value then the increase belongs to the buyer and does not affect the amount owed.

In recent years, however, there has been a dramatic and disturbing rise in the number of mortgage defaults. The recession, characterised by high rates of inflation, fluctuating interest rates and rising levels of unemployment; reductions in the availability of tax relief on interest payments; and increasing numbers of divorce are among the main causes of the problem. Although the lender has wide powers of enforcing the debt (particularly taking repossession, see page 38), the substantial decline in property values means that, often, selling the property will not recoup the value of the mortgage. The borrower remains liable to the lender for any excess outstanding, plus interest. This concept of a 'negative equity', that is, where the value of the flat is less than the amount initially borrowed, has become a common feature. This is particularly so with regard to property purchased during the property boom of the late 1980s.

Therefore, the best advice to a potential borrower is not to over-extend yourself financially. If you are seeking a mortgage it is imperative that you should find out exactly how much it is going to cost you each month and be sure that you can meet those payments in the longer term. Taking out insurance (home loan protection) against being unable to make mortgage repayments is generally advisable (see Chapter 11 for details). If you do face problems about repayments, it is advisable to contact either a solicitor or the Citizens Advice Bureau and let them undertake debt negotiations (see page 39).

Kinds of mortgages

Repayment and endowment mortgages

When you have a mortgage you have to pay back the money you borrowed (the capital) and the cost of borrowing the money (the interest). This is done by paying regular monthly payments over the life of the mortgage. There are two main types of mortgage: repayment mortgages and investment-linked mortgages, the most popular of which are endowment mortgages.

With a **repayment** mortgage, interest and capital are repaid over a set number of years (e.g. 25) by monthly payments. In the first few years of the mortgage the repayments go almost exclusively towards paying off the interest. The proportion of the monthly repayment being used to pay off capital gradually increases over the years. The borrower might be obliged (or at least advised) to take out separate life assurance cover, so if he or she dies during the life of the mortgage the balance owed will be repaid.

With an **endowment** mortgage, two separate payments are made each month. First, and this is the bulk of the repayment, is the money which goes to the lender towards repaying the interest. The second amount goes into an investment administered by a life assurance company, and also acts as the premium for a life assurance policy. There are many kinds of policies available; many lenders are 'tied' to an assurance company and so will encourage borrowers to take a policy with that company. The idea is that the money paid into such a company – which will invest it for you – will build up over the years to enable you repay the capital outstanding in one lump sum when the policy matures. A simple **non-profit endowment** policy is designed to pay out just enough to pay off the capital borrowed, but no more. A **'with profits' endowment** policy is also designed to pay enough to cover the capital borrowed, but, in addition, if the company invests your premiums well and profits from it, you will get a share of the profits when the policy matures. The premiums on the former type of endowment mortgage are cheaper than on the latter. The possibility of getting a surplus amount on maturity, and the benefit of built-in life assurance (so that the mortgage is paid off by the assurance company should you die during the period), are the usual reasons for choosing an endowment mortgage.

The amount paid monthly on both endowment and repayment mortgages usually changes when interest rates go up or down (see page 33).

Repayment versus *endowment mortgages*

The question of which type of mortgage to choose must vex most first-time buyers. Although endowment mortgages have come in for some criticism recently because there is no guarantee that the maturity value will be sufficient to discharge the whole mortgage, there is no simple answer: thinking about your circumstances now and in the future is the best way to come to a decision.

A **repayment** mortgage is probably better for you if:

- you are unlikely to move house every few years. Under the repayment system, when you move house, the mortgage is (it is hoped) paid off with the proceeds of the old property and a new mortgage is taken out on the new property. This means that if you move every few years the debt will not significantly decrease throughout that time, because the first few years will be spent primarily paying off interest rather than capital;
- you come into a lump sum of money that can be used to pay off all or part of the debt outstanding: it is relatively easy to arrange this on a repayment mortgage;
- you start experiencing difficulties in paying the monthly amounts. Under the repayment scheme, the overall mortgage term can be increased more easily so that those payments are reduced;
- you are not likely to stay in the UK housing market for the whole 25 years – with an endowment mortgage the benefit arises only when the policy matures;
- for the same reason as above, you want a mortgage term of less than ten years.

On the other hand, an **endowment** mortgage is better for you if:

- you are likely to move house every few years. When the flat is sold, the same policy can be used for the next endowment mortgage: if a larger loan is needed for the next flat, an additional policy is taken out, so endowment mortgages give you more flexibility to move more easily;
- you are willing to take a small risk – if the investment (made by the life assurance company with your premiums) performs well you could end up paying off the capital and have a tax-free lump sum left over. As a general guide, an endowment is likely to be more beneficial than the repayment method if the returns on the investment exceed the interest rate by at least 2 per cent per year (see below on how to check on this). On the down side, and as

indicated above, there is no guarantee that the policy will provide a surplus lump sum on maturity, or even that it will be enough to cover the capital.

It is, of course, possible to switch from an endowment mortgage to a repayment mortgage and vice versa. If you have an endowment policy, at the end of every year you will receive a statement telling you how your investment is performing. If you find that it is not doing very well, you could cash in your policy early and change to a repayment mortgage, but you will get very low returns on your policy and will have to spend some money in converting from one type of mortgage to another. It might be that if you are having difficulties meeting the mortgage repayments, you will benefit from switching to a repayment mortgage and making a lower monthly repayment.

In any event, it is important that if you want an endowment mortgage you must shop around for an assurance company with a proven track record for investment: do not rely on the company recommended by the lender (unless the lender is an independent adviser under the Financial Services Act 1986).

Pension mortgages

This type of mortgage is normally relevant only for self-employed people above the age of 35 years. With a pension mortgage, the borrower arranges for a mortgage loan alongside a suitable pension policy (and sometimes a life assurance policy as well). During the term of the mortgage, the borrower pays the interest due each month and regular premiums to a pension plan. There is no capital repayment. The premiums under the pension scheme generate a (tax-free) cash sum that is ultimately used to pay off the mortgage debt and also provide a pension for life which is then taxed as earned income.

Although somewhat similar to an endowment mortgage, a pension mortgage is more tax-efficient because of the relief on the premiums paid into the pension scheme. The borrower should, however, be aware that the lump sum used for repayment of the mortgage loan reduces the capital upon which the pension is based, so that the pension will be a reduced one.

Council housing: right-to-buy mortgages

Various statutory provisions give local authorities the power to sell freehold or leasehold council housing stock to tenants. Since 1993 tenants no longer have the right to a mortgage from public funds in order to finance the transaction. The traditional local authority mortgage is repayable over a period of up to 25 years. Each prospective buyer has an individual income limit, although a local authority may, if appropriate, advance a sum greater than this income would normally warrant. The detailed calculations of the income limits are in accordance with regulations prescribed by the government.

Drip mortgages

This is a method of home-buying more properly known as a rental purchase. It is technically not a mortgage but a scheme akin to buying a home on hire purchase. In essence, it consists of a contract for the sale of the property, with the buyer occupying the premises and paying the purchase price to the owner by instalments. Legal title to the property is conveyed to the borrower only on the final payment.

This form of credit is generally used in the context of low-quality, low-priced housing. The borrower is particularly vulnerable as the protection afforded by the law to the mainstream mortgagor is unavailable. An occupier can be evicted for non-payment, losing both a home and the rental payments already made. The drip mortgage is often used by landlords to avoid statutory protection afforded to tenants of rented property and is, potentially, the source of much abuse. It should be treated with great caution.

Other variations

Other types of mortgage include:

● **Unit-linked endowment mortgages** The borrower pays interest along with regular monthly payments which are invested in unit trusts. At the end of the mortgage the idea is that the units are cashed in and the proceeds used to discharge ʰe capital borrowed. This a risky venture because unit values can go down as well as up and so it is possible that the units when cashed in do not discharge the mortgage debt.

- **Personal equity plan (PEP) mortgages** As well as making interest repayments, the borrower subscribes to a PEP scheme (the maximum contribution being £6,000 per year per individual). The proceeds of the scheme are then used to pay off the mortgage. There is no guarantee that the proceeds will be sufficient, but it can be tax advantageous for higher-rate taxpayers.
- **Interest-only mortgages** The borrower pays only the interest on the loan and discharges the mortgage debt when the necessary funds are obtained (e.g. on the sale of the flat). This is advisable only when the sum borrowed is a low percentage of the market value of the flat.
- **Annuity mortgages** This is a scheme aimed at older borrowers who already own a home. The borrower mortgages the flat and with the proceeds purchases an annuity which provides an annual income for life. This is an expensive way of generating income, particularly if interest rates rise, and is not to be recommended.
- **Fixed-rate mortgages** These mortgages guarantee that interest rates will not increase for a set period (e.g. three or five years). Fixed-rate offers have proved popular, but their value hinges on the economic climate prevailing through the period of guarantee. If interest rates are both low and stable, then the fixed-rate method can prove more expensive. If interest rates are unstable and likely to rise, a fixed rate can produce savings. Some lenders require an extra payment (an arrangement fee) to secure the availability of such a mortgage and charge a penalty if you change mortgages within the fixed period.
- **Variable-rate mortgages** Most mortgages have a variable interest rate which can move upwards or downwards. All major lenders offer similar rates, which are dictated by national economics.

Tax relief

Tax relief of 15 per cent is allowed on interest payments made under a mortgage to purchase the taxpayer's only or main residence. Only interest on the first £30,000 of the mortgage is deductible. In the case of couples, the allowance of £30,000 is shared between them. If the mortgage is from a building society or bank then the mortgage interest relief at source (MIRAS) scheme operates. The borrower makes the repayments to the lender net of basic-rate tax, and the latter claims the balance from the Inland Revenue.

How to apply for a mortgage

Choosing a lender

If you want to buy a flat – and you need a mortgage – you will have to decide who to borrow from and find out how much you can get. With the emergence of the high-street banks into the mortgage market and the recent decline in the number of mortgage applications, competition has become fierce. Home-buyers not only have a wide choice of institutions from which to borrow, but also face a bewildering range of schemes, discounts and incentives to tempt them towards a particular lender. It is advisable to shop around and check out the various offers available. There are frequent *Which?* reports dealing with mortgages. See below for a checklist of what to ask a lender.

Building societies and banks are the two main kinds of mortgage lenders, and there is often little to choose between them. Some societies may have a policy of lending only to people who already

---

Checklist: what to ask a lender

- What interest rate does it charge for the different kinds of mortgages?
- If you are a first-time buyer, does it offer you a special interest rate?
- Does it have fixed-rate, variable and capped interest rates?
- What happens when interest rates change?
- What is the maximum it will lend you?
- What percentage of the valuation (see page 36) will it lend you?
- How easy would it be to switch from one type of mortgage to another?
- What types of insurance (see Chapter 11) will you have to buy as a condition of the loan?
- Is the advice the lender gives completely independent: is the firm trying to sell you the products (say, insurance) of the company it is tied to or are you free to choose the best for yourself?
- Will there be a redemption charge if you pay off the mortgage early?

---

have accounts with them, so check first. Another consideration is that banks can decide at any time not to offer further new mortgages. There are other, less important, lenders: some insurance companies, local authorities (to buy council flats, see page 32), some employers, builders of new flats, and finance houses and credit companies. Many estate agents are owned by building societies, banks or insurance companies and may offer to arrange a mortgage for you.

How much can you borrow?

Most lenders have a formula for working out how much they will lend you. This calculation is usually based on your annual income before tax. If you are buying a flat on your own, you will probably be able to borrow up to 3 times your annual income; if it is with a partner (no distinction is usually made between married and unmarried couples), the amount will be around 2·5 times your joint incomes. However, some lenders are more generous than others in this calculation, so it is possible you could be offered different amounts by different lenders.

Most lenders will advance between 90 and 95 per cent of the purchase price, subject to valuation of the property. If you need 'top-up' finance because the loan you can get is not sufficient, you may be able to get it from an insurance company or a bank. You may have to pay a higher interest rate on this top-up loan than on the mortgage itself, and may have to take out another insurance policy to cover it, so think very carefully before you do this.

It is important to realise that just because a lender will advance you a sum it does not necessarily mean that you can afford the repayments. Do not stretch yourself by borrowing the absolute maximum you can. You may well have other financial commitments – like children or elderly relatives – now or in the future. Moreover, bear in mind that you will need money to equip and run the flat (buy furniture and curtains, pay the council tax, service charges, etc.) and for other stages of the conveyancing process (e.g. solicitor's fees, survey, etc.).

Getting a mortgage certificate

It is possible, in many cases, to obtain a so-called mortgage certificate, even before a property is found, which states how much the lender is willing to advance you (subject to the value of the flat you want to buy). The buyer will normally approach only one lender for a certificate, but there is nothing to stop a number of certificates being obtained from different lenders. Nevertheless, there is little advantage in approaching more than one lender unless you anticipate difficulties in obtaining a mortgage at all or for the amount sought.

You apply for such a certificate usually by filling in a form giving details of your income and commitments. The lender will almost certainly check with your employer, bank and present landlord whether you are a credit-worthy and reliable person to lend to before giving you a certificate. A mortgage certificate is usually valid for a limited period, but it could be useful if you need to persuade a seller that you are a serious buyer who will have access to the finance required.

The certificate is not, however, an absolute guarantee that the lender will advance the money on the preferred property. Whether the money is forthcoming will depend on factors like:

- the results of the survey (see Chapter 7);
- the length of the lease on the flat (anything less than 60 years could be problematic);
- the age and location of the flat.

Arranging the mortgage

When you have found a suitable flat and have put in an offer on it you can apply formally for the mortgage. You have to provide the lender with information on the flat you want to buy, including the price. You will have to say how much you need to borrow, and probably also where the rest of the money (say, for the deposit) is coming from.

The lender will then arrange to have the flat valued by means of a survey, which you have to pay for. This is a basic survey (see Chapter 5 for details), but most lenders will ask if you want a home-buyer's report or a full structural survey done at the same time. If the lender decides not to give you a loan based on the valuation (see Chapter 7) – or if you decide to pull out of the purchase – the fee you pay for having the valuation done will not be refunded.

It should also be borne in mind that the borrower will have to pay the lender's legal expenses as well his or her own fees in connection with the purchase of the flat. To keep costs down, the borrower's conveyancer will usually act for the lender as well.

Mortgage covenants

The lender imposes various obligations on the borrower in addition to the one on repaying the loan. These will be listed in the mortgage deed, which will be kept in the custody of the lender throughout the mortgage. A copy of the deed will be provided to the borrower. The obligations may include:

- keeping the property in good and sufficient repair ;
- carrying out repairs and remedying defects as specified by the lender;
- obtaining the consent of the lender before structural alterations and extensions are carried out;
- sub-letting the premises only with the prior consent of the lender; complying with all the provisions of the lease;
- keeping the premises insured (see Chapter 11).

In the case of non-payment or breach of any other obligation, the lender may seek, and will have the right, to take possession of the flat (see page 38).

The mortgage debt can be paid off prematurely only if written notice is given to the lender, who may then ask for a 'redemption fee'. Penalties for early redemption may be the equivalent of three or six months' interest, regardless of notice given, but such a fee is the exception rather than the norm.

The borrower's rights

The borrower is given certain powers and rights in relation to the mortgaged property. These include the following.

Redemption

The right to redeem (repay in full) the mortgage at any time after the date stipulated for redemption in the mortgage deed (normally six months after the date the mortgage is created) cannot be excluded, unreasonably postponed or unduly restricted by any other contractual terms.

Possession

Subject to the lender's right to possession (see page 38), the borrower is entitled to possession of the property.

Sale

It has been recently decided by the courts that, even if in default, a borrower can sell his or her flat to a buyer against the wishes of the lender. Until then banks and building societies routinely took possession of a flat belonging to a defaulting borrower and sold it themselves, often at a price lower than the mortgage amount, and claimed the remainder of the debt from the borrower. The decision to allow the borrower to find a buyer is important, as a private sale will often command a higher price than a sale by the lender.

Leasing
The borrower will have the right to sub-let or otherwise rent out the flat, but this may be regulated by the mortgage deed.

Lender's remedies

The lender has a number of remedies which can be used against a borrower who is in breach of the mortgage agreement.

Breach of contract
The lender may sue the borrower for breach of contract to pay the money due or to perform any other covenant in the mortgage deed.

Taking possession
The lender has the right to take possession of the mortgaged property from the date the mortgage is entered. In theory, this right exists even if there has been no default by the borrower. In reality, however, lenders take possession only on default and as a means of obtaining vacant possession as a preliminary to exercising their power of sale.

Sale
The lender has a right to sell, which can be exercised only if the following conditions are met:

● the borrower has failed to repay the loan following three months' notice to do so; or
● the borrower is in at least two months' arrears with the repayment of interest; or
● the borrower is in breach of any other covenant in the mortgage deed (e.g. to insure or to repair).

Foreclosure
Foreclosure is an order of the court which terminates the mortgage and transfers the title to the lender. It requires a court order.

Staving off repossession

The most common reason for a lender wishing to obtain possession of a flat (or repossess it) is default on mortgage payments by the borrower. Although the number of repossessions has been rather high so far this decade, it does not mean that if you have difficulties in repaying your mortgage the flat will be repossessed immediately.

If you become unemployed or fall ill, and when you have taken out such cover, your home loan protection insurance (see Chapter 11) may help to make the mortgage repayments. Where no insurance is taken out, if you become unemployed, the Department of Social Security (DSS) can make payments to cover interest due under a mortgage. At the time of writing, in such circumstances the DSS will pay the mortgage interest, but not the costs of an endowment policy. However, recent proposals by the government advocate a tightening-up of income support, and so things could change.

You could lessen the chances of a repossession order being granted by the court by:

- raising the necessary money and paying off the arrears;
- requesting the lender to accept a short-term reduction in the monthly repayments;
- sub-letting the flat (with the lender's permission) to generate some income to repay the mortgage debts;
- persuading the lender to allow a switch from an endowment mortgage to a repayment mortgage if the monthly premiums for the latter are less. This would involve surrendering the endowment policy and using the proceeds to repay mortgage arrears;
- asking for an extension of the term of the mortgage (e.g. from 25 to 30 years) in the case of a repayment mortgage;
- finding a buyer who can pay a more favourable price than would be obtained by the lender. If legal action is being undertaken at the time, the court may deny the lender possession and allow the sale to proceed.

Remortgaging the flat (i.e. taking out another mortgage for a greater amount) is emphatically **not** advised. The risks in doing so are great – you may face higher interest rates, be forced into the clutches of the back-street credit agencies and end up owing more money than before. The only reason for considering this bleak possibility is that it could delay homelessness.

CHAPTER 4

A SUMMARY OF THE BUYING AND SELLING PROCESS

THERE are normally two distinct phases in the creation or transfer of a lease: preliminary negotiations and checks, followed by the formal contract after which the lease of the property is conveyed to the buyer. This chapter gives buyers and sellers an overview of the process, with some indication of how long the procedure takes and the types of costs that are involved. The two chapters following this one go into the details of the pre-contract and post-contract phases respectively.

Different kinds of conveyancing

The process involved in buying/selling a flat varies according to whether the title to the land is registered or unregistered (see pages 41-2). There are also some differences between the purchase of a new lease and that of an existing lease.

New lease, old lease?

The differences between the creation of a new lease and the transfer of an existing one are fairly minor. The buyer of a new lease can attempt to negotiate the terms of the lease, whereas the buyer of an existing lease has to be content with terms which have been negotiated by others. There is also a difference in terminology in the two situations: the sale of a new lease of a flat is normally called a 'grant' and the buyer may be termed a 'grantee', but the sale of an existing lease is described as an 'assignment' and the buyer referred to as an 'assignee'.

In the granting of a (new) lease by a developer of flats there is the normal contract stage followed by completion. However, in most sales of new flats, the developer provides a comprehensive package, and the terms are, largely, non-negotiable. The lease is prepared and engrossed in deed form and completed by the developer's solicitors. The Law Society's* protocol (see below) is not normally applied when the sale is by a developer.

Usually, such a lease contains all the relevant clauses and the developer adopts a 'take it or leave it' attitude. Unless there is something fundamentally wrong, no negotiations are possible. In addition, National House Building Council (NHBC)* cover (see Chapter 7), planning permission and building regulations are far more important with a new flat than with a second-hand flat.

In contrast, selling an existing flat takes the normal conveyancing format and usually the protocol is used, but the emphasis for the buyer is on matters such as service charges, insurance premiums and existing breaches of leasehold obligations.

The Law Society's protocol

The pre-contract conveyancing process, particularly for the sale of existing leases, has been simplified, since 1990, by the introduction of a standardised procedure. This procedure is known as the 'protocol'. The protocol includes a standard type of contract and a checklist of steps to be taken in order to ensure that the conveyancing goes ahead smoothly and quickly. A distinctive feature of this new scheme is that as soon as the seller notifies a solicitor that a potential buyer has been found, the solicitor prepares a bundle of documents ('the package') to be sent to the buyer's solicitor. These documents include a draft contract, 'office copy entries' (if registered land), outline of title deeds (if unregistered), property information form, a fixtures, fittings and contents form, and a copy of the lease with details of service charges and insurance. Although preferred practice, the protocol is not compulsory, and there remain many solicitors who stick to their own tried-and-tested methods. It might be a good idea to ask your conveyancer to use the protocol. Those solicitors who already use the protocol will normally show a TransAction sign and logo on their office windows.

Registered or unregistered land?

The system of conveyancing used also depends on whether or not the title to the land is registered. In practice, however, the distinction between registered and unregistered land crops up only in sales of existing flats. All new flats will almost certainly be on registered land (from 1990 the whole of England and Wales has been designated a compulsory area of registration). Although the detailed implications of the distinction between registered and unregistered land are examined in Chapter 6, the main differences lie in how the seller's title to the land is proved and the way in which the transfer occurs.

Possible ambiguities

There are several phrases and terms which can cause confusion and need to be explained at this early stage.

- **Contract** This is the document which makes the sale legally binding. It is usually in two identical parts, one signed by the buyer and the other by the seller, and has to be exchanged.
- **Lease** A lease is the document which transfers the legal title to the buyer and details the premises leased, the number of years for which they are let, the ground rent payable and all other conditions on which the lease is held (i.e. the covenants).
- **Exchange of contracts** Most contracts will be drafted by conveyancers in two identical parts. One part will be left with the buyer and the other with the seller. Each will sign their own part and then swap them. This act of swapping parts is the exchange, and at that point the contract is binding.
- **Completion** This stage follows after the contracts are exchanged and is when the lease or assignment is 'engrossed' in deed form and signed by the parties. This completes the transaction.

A typical transaction

The process

- An offer is made on a flat privately or through an estate agent.
- The buyer and seller instruct their respective legal advisers.
- The buyer arranges mortgage finance.

- The seller's legal adviser obtains proof of the seller's ownership of the flat. If the flat is unregistered, this will be a chart of how ownership passed to the seller (an 'epitome' of title). If the land is registered, this will be a copy of the Land Register (known as 'office copy entries'). A copy of the lease will also be obtained.
- The seller's legal adviser prepares a draft contract which describes the property to be sold and the rights and obligations that go with it.
- If the conveyancing protocol is used, the seller will have conducted a local land charges search and forwarded (with the documents mentioned below) the certificate showing the buyer the results of that search. Otherwise, as also shown below, the buyer will have to conduct an official or personal search in the local land charges register maintained by the local authority.
- The contract, the draft lease, assignment or sub-lease, and proof of the seller's ownership are sent to the buyer's adviser.
- The draft contract is approved by buyer's legal adviser.
- The buyer arranges for a survey of the property and obtains the mortgage offer.
- The buyer's legal adviser makes formal enquiries of the seller about the property; and traditionally either the buyer or his or her adviser makes enquiries of the local authority about the surroundings, as well as making a local land charges search.
- Both the buyer and the seller agree to the contract as drafted and are ready to enter into a legally binding written contract to buy and sell the flat.
- The contracts are exchanged and the buyer provides a deposit, equal to either 5 or 10 per cent of the price of the flat.
- If the title is unregistered, the buyer's legal adviser will examine recent conveyances of the property; if it is registered, the buyer's legal adviser inspects the Land Register.
- If anything needs clarification, the buyer's adviser makes enquiries of the seller.
- If there is a mortgage offer, the adviser for the lender (usually the same one as acting for the buyer) also investigates the seller's title documents.
- The buyer's legal adviser makes searches to discover any rights of third parties over the property. For unregistered land, search is made of the land charges register; if registered, search is made at the district land registry.

- The final version of the lease, sub-lease or assignment is drafted, embodying the relevant terms as agreed and, when approved by both parties, the final copy is typed up in deed form.
- If mortgage finance is involved, the lender prepares the mortgage deed to be signed by the borrower.
- Completion takes place. The buyer pays the balance of the purchase price and the seller provides the title deeds (if unregistered land) or the land certificate (if registered land). The lender takes the documents and the signed mortgage deed in return for providing the mortgage funds.
- In unregistered conveyancing, the buyer acquires legal ownership of the flat on completion. If the title is registered, the transaction has to be registered at the Land Registry before legal ownership passes to the buyer.
- The lease, sub-lease or assignment is shown to the Inland Revenue by the buyer's legal adviser, so that any necessary stamp duty can be paid.

A rough timetable

A typical transaction from beginning to end is often estimated as taking between two and three months. This is a rough and ready rule and can act merely as a guide: the exact period can be shorter or longer. There are many reasons why it takes this length of time:

- it can take up to a month to obtain the results of a local land charges search from the local authority;
- obtaining a mortgage offer can be delayed by the time it takes to investigate the buyer's financial standing and to survey the flat to be bought. The application for a mortgage can and should be made as soon as a flat is found. Contracts will not be exchanged before a mortgage offer is made. It can take several weeks for a bank or building society to confirm the availability of funds for the transaction;
- it is common for there to be a chain of transactions, with each separate transaction needing to be synchronised with the others. For example John is buying Ted's flat, Ted is buying Diane's flat and Diane is buying Doris' house. Diane cannot proceed until everyone else in the chain is able to exchange contracts at the same

time. Problems arising in one link of the chain (e.g. Ted cannot easily obtain a mortgage) can hold up all the other related transactions.

Costs involved

Buying and selling a flat can prove costly. The buyer will have to pay:

- **Solicitor's fees** These can vary enormously and it is wise to shop around for the most attractive quote. A buyer will have to pay higher fees than a seller. As a rough guide, expect to pay by way of solicitor's fees somewhere between 0.5 per cent and 1.5 per cent of the value of the property.
- **Search fees** The buyer will have to pay for searches of the local land charges register (estimated to be between £35 and £75) and the land charges register or the Land Register.
- **Lender's legal costs** These will be kept down if the buyer's solicitor acts also for the lender. The figures are prescribed by the individual building society or bank, but will normally fall within the £70 to £100 band.
- **Costs of survey** The amount will vary according to the thoroughness of the survey commissioned. The lender will also require a valuation report for which the buyer must pay.
- **Deposit** The buyer will have to pay a deposit (usually between 5 and 10 per cent of the value of the flat) when contracts are exchanged.
- **Stamp duty** A duty of 1 per cent of the total value of the flat if it exceeds £60,000 and land registration fees (payable on a sliding scale), where relevant, will have to be met by the buyer.
- **Hidden costs** These include the costs of moving house, buying new furniture and appliances, and redecorating.

The seller will have to pay:

- **Estate agent's fees** These vary between 1 and 2.5 per cent of sale price. The costs of advertising the flat will also have to be met.
- **Solicitor's fees** The seller will have to pay for the services of a solicitor for selling the flat.
- **Hidden costs** These include removal expenses and, if buying another property, the expenses incurred by any buyer.

CHAPTER 5

'Subject to contract': the first stages

Having found a suitable flat, a potential buyer has to embark upon the process of acquiring it. This may appear to be a rather daunting task, but it has to be remembered that the great majority of leasehold transactions proceed smoothly to the satisfaction of both buyer and seller. Moreover, most of the legal work (and paperwork) is done by legal advisers and other professionals, so the buyer and seller do not have to be involved at every stage. This chapter starts at the point where a potential buyer is in a position to put in an offer on a flat and explains what happens at each stage until just before the contracts are exchanged. Owing to the sometimes drawn-out nature of negotiations, the wide range of enquiries that need to be made and the length and complexity of the standard lease, it is not unknown for errors, mistakes and misunderstandings to arise. Some of the more common pitfalls are dealt with in Chapter 7. Although both sellers and buyers of flats will find the current chapter useful, it is assumed that 'you', the reader, are a first-time buyer.

Agreeing terms

Considerations before making an offer

Before making an offer on a flat you have seen and like, you must consider a few practical details.

- Check that the seller is able and willing to move out when you want to move in. This is particularly important if either of you is in a chain and is waiting to buy/sell other property.

- Find out if there are any 'sitting tenants'; i.e. if the flat or part of it has been sub-let to other people. If it has, you should get legal advice before you go any further.
- Check informally if there are any restrictions on the use of the flat – for example can you keep pets? Although they will come to light in the draft contract, it may help to know before then.
- Ask the seller what the annual service charges are. It may be that every three years or so an extra charge is made for painting the exterior, so ask to see copies of bills over a few years.
- Find out what council tax band the flat falls in.
- Ask the seller what the price includes in terms of fittings and fixtures. There may be some items that he or she is willing to leave (e.g. cooker, fridge, washing machine) for which you have to pay separately. These details will be formalised in the contract later on.

Making an offer

When you have decided that you want to buy a flat, put in an offer for it without delay. If the seller is going through an estate agent, contact the agent to make the offer.

If you can, make the offer orally. It is still standard practice (although technically unnecessary) to make it clear that your offer is 'subject to contract'. Until the contract is put into writing and signed, you are covered if:

- you are unable to obtain a mortgage or loan;
- a survey advises you against going ahead with the purchase;
- you change your mind for some other reason.

When making an offer remember that most sellers will expect some bargaining. A buyer can bring the asking price down a little unless there are other potential buyers who are likely to pay the full price. Once you have made an offer, either it will be accepted straight away or you will have to wait until other potential buyers have made their offers. Problems that could arise at this stage include 'gazumping' and 'gazundering', and are dealt with in Chapter 7.

The seller will decide whether or not to accept the offer made and this decision will be influenced, for example, by how near it is to the asking price, the state of the housing market, the length of time the property has been up for sale and how desperate he or she is to move.

Moreover, the problem of a 'negative equity' might put pressure on the seller to hold out for the advertised selling price for the flat. In other cases, it might be advantageous for a seller to get rid of the flat at a lower-than-expected price so as to be free of liabilities to meet mortgage repayments, service charges and other obligations under the lease (e.g. to redecorate). Any 'loss' incurred because of a depressed market might balance out if the seller is then able to buy a new property at a reduced price.

Estate agents' deposit

Some estate agents request a deposit from you to demonstrate your commitment to buy. This is not the same as the deposit you will have to pay on the flat when contracts are exchanged (see Chapter 6). There is no legal significance in this payment to the estate agent, and, if the transaction does not go ahead to contract, the deposit can be recovered. Under no circumstances should you pay more than a nominal sum (e.g. £25) to indicate good faith. Make sure that you receive a signed receipt for any deposit you pay. If you refuse to pay any deposit, the estate agent will still be desperate for a sale and will probably not bother too greatly about the absence of a deposit.

Instructing legal advisers

Do-it-yourself or use professionals?

There has never been anything to prevent 'do-it-yourself' conveyancing, but it is a difficult and risky business. At its most complicated, the process demands a knowledge of land law, trusts, planning and contract law. Moreover, although it is not beyond the abilities of the average person, leasehold conveyancing is more complicated than its freehold counterpart. The covenants concerning repair and maintenance, the rights of the tenant to use common areas, services provided and the liability to service charges, for example, are crucial matters that need to be considered extremely carefully. Once the transaction is completed, the parties are, to all intents and purposes, bound to it, so they have only one chance to get it right. Obviously, even professionals sometimes make mistakes, but at least they are insured and will be in a position to compensate for any loss that arises (see Chapter 7).

Who can do the job?

Until 1987 conveyancing for payment could be undertaken only by a qualified solicitor. It is now lawful for 'licensed conveyancers' to undertake conveyancing work on a professional basis. Licensed conveyancers can set up in business alone or work for solicitors' firms, estate agents, building societies and the like. This erosion of solicitors' monopoly on conveyancing (and the increased freedom of solicitors to advertise) has produced cut-price competition. It is worth shopping around for the best deal.

Legal advisers are obliged to charge only what is 'fair and reasonable', but this excludes stamp duty and Land Registry and other unavoidable fees. It is prudent to ask about such 'hidden extras'. A mere estimate of costs does not bind the adviser to the figure quoted. The Law Society* recommends that any estimate should be put in writing by the adviser (see Chapter 4 for a rough idea of costs).

The vast majority of purchases of residential flats will take place with the aid of a mortgage. This means that the lender (the building society or bank) will require a conveyancer to represent its interests. This may involve a third solicitor, but often your legal adviser will be allowed to act for the lender as well. In any event, this will increase the overall cost to you.

To find a conveyancer, you could ask a legal firm you have used in the past if it has members specialising in conveyancing. If you are going through an estate agent, the agent may be able to suggest a legal adviser. Alternatively, ask friends, relatives and colleagues, check with your local Citizens Advice Bureau or look for an advertisement in your local paper or *Yellow Pages*.

Tell your legal adviser as soon as you wish to put in an offer on a flat and give him or her the name and address of the seller and that of the latter's legal adviser. The seller will provide the equivalent information to his or her legal representative.

Arranging a mortgage

It is more than likely that you will need to borrow at least part of the cost of the flat you want to buy. Loans to people buying property are usually in the form of long-term mortgages, and are made by banks, building societies or other institutions like insurance companies, local authorities or finance houses. Chapter 3 explains in detail how and when to apply for a mortgage, what kinds of mortgages there are and what rights borrowers and lenders have.

The draft contract

At this stage in the process the seller's legal adviser prepares a draft contract which describes the property to be sold and the rights and obligations that go with it, which is approved by the buyer's legal adviser.

Preliminary documents

The buyer and seller are unlikely to become involved in preliminaries involving proof of title, but there will be a flurry of activity between their advisers and banks or building societies.

Before the contract is drafted, the seller's adviser will obtain title deeds to the property (if it is unregistered land) or an up-to-date copy of the Land Register (obtainable from the district land registry) and copy. of the filed plan depicting the land to be bought (if it is registered land). See Chapter 6 for the distinction between unregistered and registered land, and its relevance to the flat-buyer/seller. The title deeds will normally be in the custody of the seller's bank or building society, and will be released by them to the solicitor subject to certain conditions.

Preparing the contract

The contract, prepared by the seller's adviser, is commonly typed on a standard form (usually the Standard Conditions of Sale), which contains a large number of provisions. It incorporates both the **particulars** and **conditions** of sale. The particulars include a description of the property, the nature of the lease to be sold, and the rights which the owner may exercise over other land (benefits such as a right to use someone else's driveway) and rights which other people may exercise over the land to be sold (burdens such as the right of someone to use the driveway of the property to be bought; any charges on the land; and any freehold covenants which restrict the use of the land).

The conditions state the terms on which the property is to be sold, for example, provisions as to the deposit, covenants, vacant possession, the date for completion and insurance.

For the professional, it takes only a short time to fill in the details in these standard contracts, delete irrelevant provisions and add any special terms required for that particular transaction. In the case of a new lease (or sub-lease) being granted, the draft of that lease may be annexed to the contract. If the lease is being assigned, as well as a copy of the lease to be bought, there may be a draft deed of assignment attached.

Fixtures and fittings

One important issue the contract deals with is that of fixtures and fittings: it sets out what is included in the flat as part of the purchase price. Items often mentioned include fitted carpets, curtains, mantelpieces, gas fires and light fittings. Generally speaking, if the articles are attached to the building (screwed in, nailed down or plumbed in) they will be regarded as fixtures and left in the property (but see below). This rule of thumb is not, however, conclusive, because if fixing an item to the building is the only way that it can be enjoyed (for example, a large painting), it will remain a moveable (a 'chattel' or fitting) and not become a fixture. Fittings may be taken away at will unless the contract specifically mentions them as being left behind.

In addition, the purpose for which an article is on the premises is a key factor in determining whether it is a fitting or a fixture. If it is intended to be an improvement of permanence, it is likely to be considered a fixture rather than a fitting. The only fixtures a tenant may remove during or at the end of the lease are those that, despite being attached to the building, are ornamental or domestic in nature. This category would normally include cookers, pictures, mirrors and mantelpieces. If, however, an item is part of the architectural style of the room (e.g. curtains specifically designed for a room) or if its removal would cause major damage to the fabric of the building, it must not be removed. When an article is removed, any damage caused to the property should be made good and this may involve some redecoration work. The seller may otherwise be liable to compensate either the buyer of the lease or the landlord.

The seller is rarely entitled to remove fitted wardrobes, kitchen units, showers and doors. Such items are clearly intended to be fixtures and cannot be classified as either ornamental or domestic. As a general rule, fitted carpets, light fittings, gas fires, attached towel rails, soap fittings and tap fittings also fall into this category.

Unless the contract states otherwise, the fixtures are paid for in the purchase price for the flat. The seller can insert a contractual provision whereby the buyer pays an extra sum for items which the seller would be entitled to remove but is leaving behind.

Because the rules concerning what is and is not removable are confusing, it is important for both seller and buyer to know what is to be included in the purchase price, what will be removed and what will be left behind at extra cost. It is useful to have an inventory annexed to the contract detailing the items to be paid for by the buyer, and their prices. A well-drafted contract should mention any doubtful items (for example, fitted shelves, satellite dishes and wall lights) and not simply trust that they are covered by the term 'fixtures'. Under the conveyancing protocol, there is a fixtures, fittings and contents form designed for this purpose.

Approval by buyer's adviser

The draft is forwarded, with an identical copy, to the buyer's adviser for amendment or approval. The terms of the contract may be further negotiated at this stage, and it is not uncommon for the final agreed draft to be quite different from that originally proposed. There may be much 'to-ing and fro-ing' between the advisers to sort out such issues as the date of completion, the amount of deposit to be paid and, where it is a new lease or sub-lease which is being created, the wording of the covenants.

Once agreement has been reached, the buyer's adviser retains one copy of the draft and returns the other to the seller's adviser, who types out the contract in its final form and then sends one copy back to the buyer's adviser for checking.

The survey

As the seller gives no guarantee as to the condition of the property (the principle of *caveat emptor* or 'let the buyer beware' applies), the buyer should commission a survey of the flat. The contract usually

Auction contracts

If the flat is being sold by public auction, the contract should be prepared by the seller's adviser in collaboration with the auctioneer. Although the law does not require this contract to be in writing, in practice the contract is drafted in written form. It is concluded on the fall of the auctioneer's hammer, and any documentation will be signed subsequently.

An auctioneer is in a somewhat odd position because he or she initially acts as the seller's agent and can sign a contract on the latter's behalf. On the fall of the hammer, however, the auctioneer becomes, through implication, the agent of the buyer and can sign the contract also on behalf of him or her. An estate agent does not have the authority to sign a contract on behalf of the seller, unless given express instructions to do so.

states that the buyer takes the premises in the condition they were in when the contract was entered into.

The Royal Institution of Chartered Surveyors★ and the Incorporated Society of Valuers & Auctioneers★ can provide details of suitable surveyors and valuers, but it is easy to find one from looking in *Yellow Pages*. It is generally advisable to hire a surveyor who is independent of the estate agents who are selling the property. Some problems that could arise at this stage of the process are dealt with in Chapter 7.

Valuation

If part of the money needed to buy the flat is going to come from a bank or building society, the lender will insist on a surveyor's valuation of the property before agreeing to grant a mortgage. The fee for this valuation has to be paid by the borrower. This valuation is, however, carried out on behalf of the lender and is simply to find out whether the property is adequate security for the loan. It is based on a visual inspection and takes on board only the age, size and type of the property; the location and amenities; and the general state of repair of the premises. This type of valuation is not a structural survey and is, moreover, no guarantee that the property is worth the price asked for it.

Home-buyer's report

Most lenders allow the borrower to see a copy of the valuation report, but that is not the same as having your own structural survey carried out. Fortunately, the surveyor who carries out the valuation for the lender can be asked to produce a home-buyer's report or carry out a full structural survey for you at the same visit. As the surveyor is going to visit the property anyway, this can save time and money.

The home-buyer's report is more extensive than a valuation. It should detect any subsidence and damp but it will cover only those areas that are reasonably accessible and visible.

Full structural survey

The full structural survey is more detailed than the home-buyer's report and will cover all the main features of the property. This should be undertaken if the property is old. As many flat-owners have to contribute (via a service charge) to the cost of repair and maintenance of the whole building, such a survey is the safest option. A ground-floor tenant may, for example, be expected to contribute to the replacement of the roof. The survey should, therefore, encompass as much of the building as is possible including the roof, foundations, gutters, and communal services such as water, gas and electricity supplies. If a serious defect emerges, you might be better advised not to proceed with the purchase because the cost of putting it right will usually be yours (perhaps shared with other tenants). The mortgage lender may also decline to make a full advance and retain sums until the repair work is carried out. If the survey identifies a potential defect, such as damp, it might be necessary to call in an expert company to confirm what remedial work will be required and at what cost. It might be useful to discuss the report with your surveyor for direct advice as to whether the flat is worth purchasing.

Making enquiries

Preliminary enquiries

The buyer's legal adviser makes what are normally described as 'preliminary enquiries' of the seller. This is done by sending a standard printed form containing a set of formal questions together with any additional queries that have arisen from an inspection of the property or the title documents. These enquiries are important because the seller is under only a limited duty to disclose defects in the property. Unfortunately, the questions are not always plainly worded and can be difficult for the lay person to understand.

Examples of preliminary enquiries

The enquiries made at this stage usually cover matters concerning the ownership of boundary walls, rights of others to cross the land, planning problems, mains services and disputes involving the property, among other issues. In the case of a flat, several specific questions appear on the form:

- does the seller own the freehold of the land or a leasehold estate?
- what is the name and address of the landlord(s) and to whom is ground rent payable?
- is the landlord's consent necessary for the sale and, if so, has it been obtained?
- have any covenants been broken?
- what service charges are payable?
- is there an insurance policy currently governing the property and, if so, what are the full details of the policy and coverage?

There is space on the form to allow extra questions to be asked (for example, concerning services provided, drainage, access to the flat and cost of past works on the premises).

If the Law Society's protocol is used by the seller, these enquiries are made via a Property Information Questionnaire. This form is divided into two sections: one is to be completed by the seller and the other by his or her legal adviser. The buyer may then make additional enquiries on an Additional Property Information Form. As always, the responsibility of deciding whether any further enquiries are necessary rests with your adviser.

Whether or not the protocol is used, the seller is not obliged to answer these preliminary enquiries, but responses that are deliberately untruthful may make him or her liable for misrepresentation and/or give rise to liability in negligence on the part of his or her legal adviser. It is, therefore, usually the case that the answers are not guaranteed to be accurate (in fact it is common for an exclusion of liability clause to be inserted), but some standard form contracts used by legal advisers expressly allow the buyer to rely on the replies. In any event, mistakes and non-disclosures are unlikely to be discovered until after the lease or the assignment has been completed. Compensation may then be the only remedy for the disgruntled buyer (see Chapter 7).

However, it is common for the answers to these important questions to be very circumspect and unhelpful: 'inspection will show', 'please search', 'we cannot say' and 'not to the seller's knowledge'. The whole point of the exercise can be defeated by non-committal answers.

Local searches

There are a number of matters that need to be clarified with the local authority before a contract is entered into. This is usually done by submitting a standard form to the authority, paying a fee and asking for details of any local land charges entered against the land. A personal search may be made by actually calling at the offices of the local authority and, on the payment of the fee, conducting the search then and there. This does not, however, protect a buyer to the same degree as an official search, but it is a quicker alternative than waiting for the results of an official search. This search of the local land charges register is traditionally made by the buyer, but under the Law Society's conveyancing protocol the task falls on the seller. If the protocol is used, the seller sends the form to the local authority before finding a buyer. A document detailing the results of the search (the official search certificate) will be provided by the local authority. This speeds up the process and avoids delays. The cost of the search will be

---

Why a local search should be done

Matters which emerge from a search of the local land charges register include:

- planning enforcement notices;
- conditional planning permissions;
- tree preservation orders;
- some compulsory purchase orders;
- whether the property is a listed building;
- financial charges for expenses incurred by the local authority (e.g. for street works or repairs to a dangerous building).

charged to the seller, but will be normally passed on to the buyer when contracts are entered. The cost of a search varies between local authorities as does the time taken to complete the search.

Because the results of a local search are valid for only approximately three months, it may be that the search is out of date by the time the parties are ready to enter a binding contract. Rather than wait the two or so weeks that it takes, on average, to obtain an official search certificate, it is possible to take out insurance (a search validation scheme) to cover the risks associated with the search being out of date. In conjunction with the protocol, the Law Society offers solicitors, on the payment of a small premium, insurance cover up to the amount of £500,000 provided that the search is no more than six months old.

Additional enquiries

The buyer's adviser also makes additional enquiries of the local authority for matters not covered by a local search. There is a standard form for enquiries which deals with a variety of issues including:

- any road works proposed within 200 metres of the property;
- possible diversion or closure of roads or footpaths;
- roads and paths maintained by a local authority;
- public footpaths;
- proceedings pending as regards an infringement of building regulations;
- noise abatement orders;
- sewers and drainage.

The replies will give the buyer information that the seller is under no duty to disclose and that would not be revealed on a survey. The local authority may be liable for any negligent replies.

Other searches

Other searches may be appropriate depending on where the property is situated. These may include:

- a search of the public index map to see whether the title to the building in which the flat is situated is registered;
- a British Coal search to check if the land is within an area of past, present or future mining;

- enquiries of British Rail if the property is near a railway line (to discover whether there are any adverse rights of way relevant to railway workings);
- enquiries of planning authorities to discover whether the proposed development of other land might affect the flat to be bought.

Agreeing the contract

The buyer and the seller will receive from their respective advisers a copy of the contract (which will be identical) in readiness to exchange them (see Chapter 6). The copy should be checked carefully to see whether it reflects the agreement actually reached between the parties (e.g. price, extent of the premises, duration of lease and ground rent). Any changes must be negotiated and agreed between the parties and their advisers, and the copies altered accordingly.

Summary of initial steps to be taken

- Buyer selects a flat and makes 'subject to contract' offer.
- Buyer employs surveyor and obtains mortgage offer.
- Buyer receives draft contract and outline proof of seller's ownership.
- If protocol is used, seller forwards property information form and local land charges search certificate to buyer.
- If protocol not used, buyer makes a local land charges search and preliminary enquiries of seller.
- If satisfactory survey and search obtained and a mortgage advance secured, the parties are ready to sign and exchange contracts.

CHAPTER 6

EXCHANGE OF CONTRACTS AND COMPLETION

THE contract, which contains all the terms of the transaction and which is signed by or on behalf of both seller and buyer, is not binding until the exchange has taken place. Once that has happened, the conveyancing can proceed to completion. This chapter covers this final stage of the process, at the end of which the lease of the flat passes from the seller to the buyer.

Exchange of contracts

This stage in the process cannot proceed until the buyer's building society, bank or other lender (the mortgagee) has made a mortgage offer (see Chapter 3). This is because, on exchange of contracts, the buyer is committed to the contract and to pay the full purchase price to the seller.

There are three primary methods by which exchange can occur. With **personal exchange** there is a meeting of the legal advisers of buyer and seller in one office (usually that of the seller's adviser) and the signed contracts are physically passed between them. This type of exchange is suitable where the advisers work close to one another or where (which is not to be recommended) one of the parties does not have an adviser.

Exchange by post is a common practice. This normally involves the buyer's adviser sending his or her client's part of the contract (accompanied by a cheque for the deposit – see pages 60-1) to the seller's adviser, who then posts back the seller's part. It is, however, uncertain when the precise moment of exchange arises. Some argue that the contract becomes binding when the seller's part is put into the post, whereas others contend that it is when the seller's part is received. It is better to have the position clearly spelt out in the contract as, for example, with the Standard Conditions (i.e. the *pro forma* terms that advisers incorporate into most contracts), which stipulate that exchange occurs when the last part is posted.

Most exchanges, however, take place over the **telephone.** The contracts are approved over the phone and it is then deemed that the documents have been passed between the parties. This is not a foolproof method and the courts have expressed the wish that it be undertaken only by partners of a conveyancer's firm and that clear and detailed notes of the telephone discussion be taken by (and agreed between) the conveyancers. The Law Society* has produced formulae for use in exchange by telephone, fax and telex.

If you are in a chain of transactions, it is necessary to synchronise all exchanges on the same date. It would be disastrous to exchange contracts for the purchase of a flat and then discover that the potential buyer of your present property is withdrawing from the transaction.

The effect of the contract

Once a valid contract is in existence (normally on exchange), the seller is usually regarded as holding the flat on trust for the buyer. Although the legal title remains with the seller until the lease is passed to the buyer on completion, the 'beneficial' or 'equitable' ownership (i.e. real ownership, not merely paper title) is regarded as having passed to the buyer. The consequences of this somewhat mystifying notion are dealt with in Chapter 7.

Deposits

It is customary for the buyer to pay a deposit when the contracts are exchanged. (Note that this is different from the optional deposit paid by the buyer to the estate agents: see Chapter 5.) Traditionally, this is either 5 or 10 per cent of the purchase price (less any preliminary deposit paid to an estate agent). The deposit demonstrates that the buyer is committed to the transaction; amounts to part payment for the flat; constitutes a guarantee to the seller; and provides the buyer with an incentive to keep to the bargain. That the seller is not expected to pay a deposit so as to show good will is illogical and unfair, because if he or she withdraws the buyer could lose money (e.g. what he or she has already spent on legal costs). See Chapter 7 for potential problems at this stage of the process and their effect on the deposit.

Deposits: stakeholder or agent?

Most deposits are held by the seller's legal adviser, as stakeholder or agent for the seller.

From the buyer's perspective, it is generally better to ensure that the deposit is held as **stakeholder** because then the deposit cannot be transferred to the seller prior to completion and the funds must be kept in a deposit account. Subject to agreement, however, the stakeholder will be able to keep the interest earned. If the money is held as an **agent** for the seller, the deposit normally must be paid over to the seller on request. Any interest that accrues while the money is in the agent's hands must be paid to the buyer. The question as to whether the deposit is to be held as a stakeholder or as an agent needs to be resolved during the drafting of the contract. The parties should be consulted on this matter, but they can, in any event, give their instructions to their advisers.

Most sellers prefer the deposit to be held as agent. One advantage of the agency system is that it makes it easier for a chain of purchases to be negotiated: a single deposit provided by the person at the bottom of the chain may be used as a deposit for all the other linked purchases in that chain. If the circumstances are such that the seller cannot recover the deposit passed on under a linked purchase, the first buyer can sue the seller personally for recovery of the initial deposit. The Law Society's protocol endorses the agency system.

However, a major disadvantage of the agency system for the buyer is that he or she may have difficulty recovering it if the seller becomes bankrupt before completion. A partial means of protection for the buyer is to get an undertaking, from the seller's adviser, that the deposit will be released only for the purpose of providing a deposit for the seller to buy a replacement property. The buyer will then have the security that the money is still 'in the system' and has not simply been paid over to the seller personally.

Transfer of ownership

As shown earlier, there are two systems of land transfer in operation, depending on whether the flat is on unregistered or registered land.

You do not have to be personally involved in the process of land transfer, whether you are the buyer or the seller – your legal adviser will handle it for you.

If the protocol is used, the package of documents forwarded initially to the buyer will include unverified details of the seller's title. The responsibility of finally establishing good title lies with the seller and, subject to contrary agreement, this must be done within a reasonable time (e.g. two weeks) of exchange of contracts. In practice, however, title is proved when the contracts are drafted.

Given that unregistered land is gradually being phased out, it is likely that the flat will be within an area where the registered system is either in operation or will become operational when the lease is bought. The main difference between the two systems lies in the manner by which the seller's title to the property is proved. The actual mode of transferring legal ownership is also different. In unregistered land, the transfer is done by a traditional conveyance and the passing of title deeds to the buyer. In registered land, the title passes by a transfer certificate and the registration of the buyer as the new registered proprietor of the flat.

Unregistered land

In the unregistered system, the process of what is called deducing the seller's title is by an examination of the title deeds (i.e. past conveyances) of the property. The prospective buyer should secure from the seller evidence of the latter's title to the property. In relation to either the freehold or leasehold title of the seller, this will take the form of title deeds which disclose all dealings with the property during, at least, the preceding 15 years. Lawyers usually provide a summary of deeds (called an 'abstract of title' or 'epitome of title') and, in practice, this normally consists of copies of a few conveyances ending with the last conveyance to the seller. The buyer's mortgagee will also check the seller's title.

Registered land

The registered system is more efficient and straightforward: ownership is guaranteed when the seller's name appears on the official register of title. The buyer's legal adviser needs only to make a search at the Land Registry and check that the seller's name is entered as registered proprietor. An office copy of the entry on the register (and filed plan) should have already been forwarded to the buyer with the draft contract, but it is possible that it is out of date. A further inspection of the Register must, therefore, be made to ensure that there have been no changes since contracts were exchanged.

Since 1990, the Land Register has been open to public inspection, and the authority of the registered proprietor (e.g. the landlord) is not required for the prospective buyer to inspect the registered title to the property. This means that the buyer is in a much better position than his or her counterpart in the unregistered system and can easily verify who has claim to the land.

If the title is registered as 'absolute freehold' or 'absolute lease-hold', the titles are guaranteed by the Land Registry to be perfect. If the title is 'good leasehold', the buyer should be wary because this does not offer a guarantee that the freeholder had the right to grant the lease, is not an attractive proposition to mortgagees and does not reveal whether there are adverse rights affecting the freehold.

Checking previous owners

After contract, but before completion, the buyer's legal adviser will make a search of the land charges register (unregistered land) against the names of all previous owners of the land or at the Land Registry (registered land) against the title number of the land. This type of search is to discover whether there are any adverse rights (e.g. undischarged mortgages, rights of way or restrictive covenants) affecting the property which are protected and which will bind the buyer following completion of the transaction. If such entries exist, the buyer will purchase the property subject to them. The search will also reveal whether there is any bankruptcy petition registered and a receiver appointed.

Completion

As described in Chapter 5, the new lease (or sub-lease) will have been drafted by the seller's adviser and approved by the buyer before contracts are exchanged. As regards an assignment, it is the old lease which will pass to the buyer and this will also have been examined before a contract is entered.

Prior to completion, a statement will be prepared by the seller's adviser and sent to the buyer's adviser. This will disclose the exact sums to be paid on completion. Service charges, ground rent and insurance premiums are matters that will be calculated up to and beyond the completion date and, if appropriate, liability will be apportioned accordingly between the seller and the buyer.

Completion (i.e. the conveyance of the land) takes place when the buyer pays over the balance of the purchase money and the seller hands over the relevant title deeds (for unregistered property) or land certificate (for registered property) and the lease or assignment in deed form. Although the date of completion can be negotiated, it occurs normally within four weeks of exchange of contracts. It takes place at the office of the seller's adviser. If keys are being held by an estate agent, the seller will authorise their release at this stage. Should the completion date be delayed by reason of default on the part of the buyer, the seller can claim interest on the balance of the purchase money.

If the land the flat is on is unregistered, the buyer becomes the legal owner of the flat at this time. In the registered system of conveyancing, the legal title passes to the buyer when his or her name substitutes that of the seller's as registered proprietor on the Land Register. To do this, the buyer's adviser has to send to the Land Registry an application form with the relevant documents.

Mortgagees and completion

Completion involves, essentially, the buyer paying the money for the flat and receiving in return the documents of title and the lease. Generally, however, the situation is complicated because the flat being sold will be subject to the seller's mortgage and the buyer will be assisted by a mortgage advance. The mortgage deed will be signed by the buyer prior to completion. The seller's mortgagee will have possession of the title documents and lease and will release them only when the existing mortgage is paid off. The buyer's mortgagee will hand over the money only on condition that it receives the title deeds or land certificate and the lease. At the end of the completion process, the following will usually occur:

- the seller's mortgagee has a banker's draft to clear the seller's mortgage and has to give an undertaking to do so within a couple of weeks;

- the seller's adviser has a banker's draft for the balance of the sale price which will be paid over to the seller;
- the buyer can go home to a new flat;
- after the formalities of the stamp duty (see below) and registration have been attended to by the buyer's adviser, the buyer's mortgagee takes custody of the title deeds (or lodges the land certificate at the Land Registry), the lease and the mortgage deed.

Stamp duty

Stamp duty is a tax payable to the government on some deeds and documents, including leases, deeds of assignment and other conveyances. A sale of a flat may, therefore, attract stamp duty, to be paid by the buyer. At present, property up to and including the value of £60,000 is exempt. To take advantage of the exemption, a certificate of value must be incorporated into the lease. This certifies that the value paid for the property does not exceed £60,000. On property exceeding £60,000, stamp duty of 1 per cent has to be paid on the **whole** sum. For example, the stamp duty on a flat costing £70,000 will be £700. Deeds and documents cannot be used in evidence or registered at the Land Registry unless they are properly stamped.

The rate for the duty changes from time to time. A solicitor should have up-to-date information about the current rate.

Excluding fixtures

As fixtures are deemed to be part of the land itself and, therefore, included in the price of the flat, it is possible to depress the value of the lease (for stamp-duty purposes) by the seller severing the fixtures from the land and selling them separately to the buyer. This could produce some saving on the duty payable. The sale, however, needs to be genuine and not at an inflated price. The Inland Revenue might challenge the agreement and, if so, it could prove a somewhat unpredictable exercise. Any items which are not fixtures can also be sold separately and do not attract stamp duty.

Example

A flat is worth £62,000 and will attract stamp duty on the whole amount at 1 per cent. The flat contains carpets, curtains, fireplaces, etc. which in total are valued at £2,000. If the contract stipulates that the buyer is to purchase those items at £2,000, the value of the flat falls to £60,000 and is, therefore, exempt from stamp duty. The buyer saves £620.

Implied covenants of title

Unless excluded or modified explicitly, there are several covenants of title implied into every contract and conveyance. These differ slightly according to whether the lease was granted before or after 1 July 1995, but in general terms they are:

- a covenant for title known as quiet enjoyment. This guarantees to the tenant that possession will not be interrupted by any acts of the landlord or of persons acting on the landlord's behalf;
- good right to convey. This does not guarantee that the seller has a sound title, but does guarantee that he or she has not done, nor omitted to do, any act which will prevent the buyer from getting a good title (e.g. there remains an undischarged mortgage on the flat or there is an undisclosed right of way over the land on which the flat is situated);
- further assurance. This covenant imposes on the seller a duty to do anything which is necessary to vest the property in the buyer;
- that the lease is valid and subsisting. This covenant guarantees that the lease being assigned has not been forfeited by a superior landlord;
- that the rent has been paid and the covenants in the lease have been duly performed. Where, for example, the lease contains a covenant to keep the flat in good repair, the seller is impliedly covenanting with the buyer that the flat is in good repair.

CHAPTER 7

Rights, wrongs and remedies

As has been pointed out earlier, the great majority of leasehold transactions proceed smoothly to the satisfaction of both buyer and seller. However, given the nature of the conveyancing process, there is scope for errors, mistakes and misunderstandings to arise at virtually every stage. This chapter deals with some of the most common problems that you could come up against both during and just after

---

Legal remedies

There are a variety of legal remedies which can be used when things go wrong:

- **Rescission** This remedy allows a party to withdraw from the contract if there is misrepresentation, a mistake or breach of a contractual term (see page 71).
- **Repudiation** This is where an important breach of contract is accepted by the other party as putting an end to the contract. This would be relevant where there has been a major misdescription of the premises or the seller had a defective title to the flat.
- **Damages** Compensation is available for any breach of contract and is designed to put the aggrieved party into the same position he or she would have been in had the contract been fully performed.
- **Specific performance** This is an order of the court which compels a reluctant party to perform the contract as agreed.
- **Rectification** This is the power of the court to re-write the contract so as to give effect to the true agreement reached between the parties. It is particularly useful when there has been a typing error or mistranslation in to the written contract of what was agreed.

---

the process, whether you are the buyer or the seller of a flat. It discusses the issues at stake and indicates where the law stands on them. Wherever possible, practical courses of action that you yourself could take are suggested. However, there are some issues that only your legal advisers are qualified to deal with. In such cases this chapter arms you with enough (jargon-free) information to understand what your advisers are saying and know what they should be doing on your behalf.

The offer stage

Gazumping and gazundering

In a buoyant property market it is common for a potential flat-buyer to discover that he or she been out-bid by a rival buyer. As well as losing the desired flat, the unlucky victim of **gazumping** may have already incurred considerable professional expenses: surveying costs, legal fees and fees for preliminary enquiries and local authority searches. It is, however, possible to take out insurance for financial loss arising from gazumping (for details contact your solicitor or an insurance broker).

There is nothing to prevent gazumping from happening, because until the contract is signed there is only a 'gentleman's agreement', under which neither party need act as a 'gentleman' and from which either party can withdraw at will.

In a depressed property market, the danger lies with the buyer refusing at the last minute to go ahead with the purchase unless the price is reduced. This has been called **gazundering**. Alternatively, the buyer may have found a more suitable property or had a change of heart. As with gazumping, there is nothing that the other party can do about it.

Proposals have been put forward that a pre-contract deposit should be taken from both parties and that this deposit should be forfeited if a party withdraws from the transaction without good cause. Another possibility is that the parties could enter into a written contract (a 'lock-out' agreement) preventing the sale to anyone else for, say, 14 days.

In a so-called **contract race**, the seller's adviser sends a draft contract to the advisers of several would-be buyers, and, simply, the first one to return it, signed and with the necessary deposit, gets the flat. The Law Society★ has attempted to regulate this practice by obliging the seller's adviser to disclose the existence of other prospective buyers to all the contestants. Not all advisers fulfil this obligation and, in any event, it does not prevent gazumping, but it does give notice of the possibility to all the parties involved. The 'contract race' is generally limited to when there is a booming market.

Professionals and professional liability

Estate agents

Whether you are a buyer or a seller the chances are that you will be using the services of an estate agent. It is important that the agent acts in your best interests right through the conveyancing process. If you feel you have a genuine grievance against the agent, say, he or she does not keep you informed of progress in your conveyancing, or has misled you about the property itself or the date of completion, there are various ways of seeking a remedy as discussed in Chapter 2.

Other professionals

Professionals become involved at various stages in the process of buying and selling a flat. The price is worked out by a valuer, the structural soundness and state of the premises are assessed by a surveyor, and the title to the flat is checked and later conveyed by a solicitor or licensed conveyancer. You may even have dealings with the architect or builder of the flat. If your professional gets it

---

When professionals get it wrong

Examples of problems with professionals that could arise include:

- shoddy workmanship by the builder or architect of a new building;
- over-valuing or under-valuing of the flat by the valuer;
- failure by the surveyor to pick up major structural flaws (e.g. dry rot, woodworm and death-watch beetle);
- failure by the legal adviser to discover a defect in the seller's title or a restrictive covenant inhibiting the use of the flat.

wrong, possible avenues for legal action are breach of contract and/or negligence.

Contract and negligence

Legal proceedings for **breach of contract** must, generally, be commenced within six years of the date of the contract, but only a party to that contract can sue or be sued. This means that only the people employed directly by, for example, the buyer can be sued by that buyer. A buyer will, therefore, be able to sue only his or her solicitor, surveyor or valuer.

Negligence, however, is of wider scope and has developed to protect the rights of the consumer. The essence of negligence law is that a person must take reasonable care so as not to injure **anyone** who is a reasonably foreseeable victim of that person's actions. It covers victims who have no contractual relationship with the negligent party. The seller's adviser will, therefore, owe a duty of care to the buyer; the lender's valuer will owe a similar duty to the buyer.

The general rule is that action must be brought within three years (personal injury) or within six years (other damage) from the negligent act. Negligence occurs when a person who has a duty of care to someone (e.g. a surveyor to a flat-buyer) breaches that duty and a loss results from the breach.

Your solicitor will advise you as to your rights to sue a professional, and legal aid may be available to assist your claim. Note, however, that if you win and recover compensation the legal aid costs may be clawed back from your winnings. If you wish to sue your solicitor, the Solicitors Complaints Bureau★ will provide a list of solicitors in your area who would be willing to bring an action against another solicitor.

Latent defects

Of particular relevance to flat-owners is the Latent Defects Act 1986, because it tackles the problem of when time begins to run for the purposes of when to bring an action in negligence. As a general rule, time begins to run from the date of the negligent act, but in some cases the damage does not arise until much later. In the case of a negligent construction, for example, there may be difficulties in ascertaining when the time limit commences. Is it the date when the damage appears? Is it the date that the plaintiff (the person bringing the legal action) acquires the flat? Is it the date when the plaintiff first discovers the damage? The Act provides that:

- as regards latent damage not involving personal injury, the relevant period is either 6 years from the negligent act or three years from the date on which the plaintiff knew, or ought to have known, of the damage, whichever is the later. There is, however, a ceiling of 15 years from the date of the negligence beyond which the action will be out of time;
- where the building is acquired by successive owners, a fresh right of action arises and time starts to run from the date the property is bought;
- similar time limits apply also where the plaintiff suffers financial loss by relying upon carelessly given advice (e.g. from a solicitor).

Fraud, misrepresentation and mistake

- **Fraud** A lease which gives effect to a contract induced by fraud can be set aside if the defrauded party so chooses. However, he or she is free to stick with the contract and then sue for damages. The contract can be set aside provided the parties can be restored to their original positions (e.g. the buyer can recover the purchase money).
- **Misrepresentation** Either party can withdraw from the contract following a negligent (i.e. careless) or innocent (i.e. genuinely mistaken) misrepresentation or misleading statement. The court retains a discretion to award damages in lieu of withdrawal.
- **Mistake** When a mistake is discovered after completion, the aggrieved party might be able to withdraw from the contract. For example, if the contract has totally failed (e.g. the premises had been destroyed before contract).

Surveys

When the survey detects a major defect
If during a survey a defect is discovered, the buyer is, at the very least, forewarned and, bearing in mind the cost of repair, can decide

whether or not to proceed with the transaction. The surveyor's report should be read carefully and may also be used to negotiate a reduction in the asking price for the flat. It should be appreciated, however, that clear surveys are not an absolute guarantee that the premises are without fault. If you are aware of a defect and still choose to proceed with the contract, you will not be able to sue the surveyor. The responsibility then rests at your door.

A negative report from the surveyor or an under-valuation of the property might mean that the mortgage lender will refuse to proceed, reduce the amount to be loaned or retain a sum from the advance until the remedial work has been completed.

Guarantees offered on flats

The National House Building Council With newly built properties, the builder may be registered with the National House Building Council (NHBC)*. If so, the property will fall within the NHBC insurance scheme, which provides protection for certain structural defects arising within ten years of the property's first sale and up to a maximum liability of the original purchase price (taking into account the effect of inflation).

Under the scheme the builder agrees to make good any defects (except for wear and tear, lifts and fences) within the initial two years. Central heating systems are covered only for one year.

The NHBC agrees to the following:

- to compensate for any loss arising from the builder becoming insolvent before the building work is complete;
- to make good any failure of the builder to remedy defects arising within the first two years;
- to cover the cost of major structural damage during the remaining eight years of the guarantee. This does not extend to wiring and plumbing, and the defect must be severe (for example, failure of damp proofing, dry rot and collapse). Minor defects, such as ill-fitting doors and defective gutters, are outside the guarantee.

Repair firms In the case of an existing flat which has been treated for woodworm or damp, or has had some other kind of major repair in previous years, the firm that carried out the works may have given a long guarantee. The seller may be able to produce the relevant documentation, which should cover the buyer. If the documentation has been lost, however, it is unlikely that any claim would be entertained by the firm. It is also sometimes the case that the firm has subsequently ceased trading and that the guarantee is worthless. However, it is always worth asking the seller about guarantees if repair work has been undertaken.

The enquiries stage

As discussed in Chapter 5, the buyer has to make a search of the local land charges register and make enquiries of the seller before contracts are exchanged. If the search produces a result which indicates, for example, proposed road works in the vicinity of the flat, then it is up to the buyer to decide whether to proceed or not. If the response to the enquiries is inaccurate, but the transaction goes ahead, it might be possible to sue the seller or the seller's adviser for misrepresentation or negligence. Some contracts, however, state that the buyer cannot rely on the replies given to such questions. Unless the reply was a deliberate lie, this clause will normally prevent a successful legal action.

Other pre-exchange complications

If the buyer is unhappy with the draft contract or the proposed lease, then it is up to the parties to negotiate further to resolve the problem. If this cannot be done, then the seller's attitude will be to 'take it or leave it'. It should be remembered that prior to exchange of contracts either party can withdraw from the transaction at will. If a chain of transactions is involved, the withdrawal of one buyer before contract can frustrate all other sales and purchases in that chain.

Post-exchange complications

The parties are always liable to perform the contract or face being sued for compensation. The buyer should, however, take the precaution of protecting the contract against third parties (that is, to stop the seller granting or assigning the lease to someone else). Unless certain steps are taken, the contract will not be binding on that third party. Protection can be achieved by entering a land charge at the land charges registry (if the title to the flat is unregistered) or a notice or caution at the Land Registry (if the title is registered). If this occurs, then the contract can be enforced directly against the intervening purchaser.

Once a valid contract is in existence (normally on exchange), the seller is usually regarded as holding the flat on trust for the buyer. Although legal title remains with the seller until the lease is granted or assigned, the 'beneficial' or 'equitable' ownership is regarded as having passed to the buyer. Lawyers call this the 'doctrine of conversion' and its consequences include:

- the seller must still manage and preserve the property and is liable to the buyer for any failure to carry out necessary repairs or maintenance. There is, however, no obligation to make improvements;
- the seller has the right to retain possession until the flat is conveyed to the buyer and remains liable for all running expenses until that time;
- under the Standard Conditions (i.e. the *pro forma* terms that advisers incorporate into most land contracts), the property should be conveyed in the same general condition as it was when contracts were exchanged. If not, either party is given the opportunity to withdraw;
- if the Standard Conditions are not used, and the flat is damaged or destroyed, the loss lies on the shoulders of the buyer and not the seller. It is, therefore, crucial that the buyer insures the premises from the day that contracts are exchanged (see Chapter 11 for details);
- if the property is damaged by fire, there is an ancient piece of legislation called the Fires Prevention (Metropolis) Act 1774 which might offer the buyer some protection;
- increases in value of the flat after contract – for example, if there is a rise in house prices or an increase in the market value because planning permission has been obtained; or where the flat is bought at a depressed price because of a sitting tenant, who then dies unexpectedly between the stages of contract and completion – benefit the buyer.

Bankruptcy or death

Sometimes, once the contract is entered, either the seller or the buyer becomes bankrupt or dies. With respect to bankruptcy of the seller,

Breaches of contract

Once contracts have been exchanged, either party may fail to meet his or her respective obligations under the contract: for example, the buyer may be unable to come up with the purchase money, the premises might have been misdescribed or the seller may fail to show a good title to the property. Breaches of contract can occur both before and after completion. Often breaches after the lease has been bought will be breaches of the contractual covenants. General points to be understood about breaches of contract include:

- until a binding contract has been entered, either party can withdraw from negotiations at will;
- once the contract is entered, both parties are bound by its terms;
- if the buyer is in breach of contract before completion, the seller may forfeit the buyer's deposit and sell elsewhere (see below);
- on the understanding that there is a breach of contract, there are a variety of remedies available to the innocent party (see page 67).

completion can and should still take place, though delays will undoubtedly occur. If it is the buyer who becomes bankrupt, it is likely that completion will not take place, though the deposit will be retained by the seller.

On the death of the seller, the personal representatives of the deceased can demand that the sale goes ahead or can themselves be forced to complete the transaction. (Any purchase monies received will be held for those who inherit.) The contract can also be enforced if it is the buyer who dies, with the purchase monies to come from the deceased's estate. Note that the estates of the deceased seller or buyer can, if necessary, be sued for breach of contract.

Losing the deposit

Generally, if, after paying a deposit on the flat, the buyer withdraws from the transaction without good reason, the seller may seize the deposit. Although there is a provision in the Law of Property Act 1925 which gives the court discretion, when it is fair and just, to order the repayment (only in full) of the cash deposit even if it is the buyer who is at fault, this is unlikely to occur in the context of a long residential lease. If it is the seller who is in default, the buyer can sue for return of the deposit. If the buyer withdraws because of a breach of contract on the part of the seller, the deposit can be recovered.

An adverse search of land titles

If there is a right of a third party protected on the land charges register or the Land Register, the buyer may have to have it cleared before proceeding with the conveyance. Certainly, as will also be the case if any defects in title emerge, the buyer will make further enquiries of the seller (known as 'requisitions'). The seller may not be able to solve the problem (for example, where the rights so protected are those of third parties). Often the buyer may, in such a situation, be well advised to withdraw (i.e. rescind) from the dealings and claim back any deposit paid.

Notices to complete

A delay in completion constitutes a breach of contract, and any loss incurred can be recovered from the defaulting party. Nevertheless, delay in itself does not allow the innocent party to withdraw from the contract. Such action can be taken only when the delay is unreasonable or when 'time is of the essence' to the contract. This will be so only if time is made of the essence expressly within the contract (it is rarely implied) or a notice to complete is served on the other party. The Standard Conditions provide that, if completion does not go ahead on the agreed date, the innocent party can serve such a notice any time after that date. It then becomes a term of the contract that completion will occur within ten days of the notice and that time will be of the essence for both parties. The time limit does not have to be ten days; in fact, any reasonable period can be set by the notice.

If the notice is not complied with, and the delay is on the part of the buyer, the seller can seize the deposit and is free to sell elsewhere. Any loss on re-sale can be recovered from the delaying party. If it is the seller who does not comply with the notice, the buyer can recover the deposit (and interest) and sue the seller for loss. Where there is a delay in completion, the injured party can recover for bridging finance and extra legal and removal costs, for exanple.

Funds unavailable

If the buyer exchanges contracts, but does not obtain a mortgage offer and cannot then buy the lease, the seller can sue the buyer for breach of contract and/or seize the deposit. The seller will claim compensation, essentially, for the loss of profit on the transaction.

Calculation of damages

The following points provide some guidance as to how damages are calculated:

- where the seller refuses to honour the contract, the buyer can recover for the loss of the property. This includes the difference between the purchase price and its market value. If vacant possession of the premises cannot be obtained, the buyer could claim for the market-price difference in the value of the property; payments for temporary alternative accommodation; and, if relevant, the legal costs of buying another flat;
- if there is no loss of bargain (i.e. the market value does not exceed the agreed purchase price), the buyer can recover the expenditure incurred by entering into the contract (e.g. legal fees and surveyor's costs);
- the injured party is under a duty to take reasonable steps to minimise the loss: he or she cannot recover for more than the loss that would have been incurred had reasonable steps been taken to reduce or to avoid the loss.

Post-completion remedies

The following remedies can be used even after the flat has been bought.

- **Damages** Once the contract has merged with the lease, damages are not usually recoverable, but there are limited exceptions to this general rule: misrepresentation, breach of an assurance (e.g. as to freedom of the premises from dry rot), and a breach of the covenants for title (see Chapter 6).
- **Rescission** In order to rescind the contract after completion, a court order is necessary. The court may make such an order only on limited grounds: fraud, misrepresentation or mistake. If the purchase has been financed by a mortgage, then rescission is unlikely to be granted because it would prejudicially affect the building society or bank. It would be considered unfair to remove

the security for the loan. Therefore, if the term to give vacant possession has been broken, then the buyer would have to be content with compensation which will be measured to reflect the difference in value between the value of the flat with vacant possession and its value with a sitting tenant.

- **Rectification** Subject to any obvious and minor corrections being made to the lease by judges, when a mistake occurs in the final version then the lease as drafted (with the inaccuracy) will stand. An important exception to this applies where the lease fails to state accurately the terms of the real agreement between the parties (e.g. the lease omits to mention certain covenants which were agreed). In such a case, the court can re-write the lease so as to reflect the true bargain struck. This remedy is, however, at the discretion of the court.

CHAPTER 8

THE LEASE

IT IS often said that lawyers have two major failings: one is that they do not write well and the other is that they think they do. Nowhere is this clearer than in conveyancing documentation. A lease is a highly technical document littered with expressions which are carefully chosen but which are often unintelligible to the lay person. The tradition of not using punctuation adds to the confusion.

The lease is important because it states the rights of the landlord (the freeholder) and the tenant (the buyer) at the start of the tenancy and governs the future relationship between them. The clearer the terms of the lease, the less is the scope for disagreement. The tenant needs to be sure that the premises can be used as intended and that the obligations imposed by the lease will not outweigh the enjoyment of living in the flat. The landlord needs to make sure that the tenant will not cause any nuisance or annoyance and will look after the premises.

The creation of a lease or of an underlease, and the assignment of an existing lease, all follow a similar format.

The drafting of a lease

Although in limited circumstances leases can be created in the form of an ordinary written document or even orally, all legal leases for a fixed term exceeding three years must be created or assigned by deed (that is, a formal document which makes clear on its face that it is a deed). Since 1989, the need for a seal has been abolished, but it is necessary that the following conditions are satisfied:

- the deed must be delivered, which means that the person signing it must, by an act or statement, adopt the deed as being finally executed. Physical or actual delivery is not necessary;
- it must be signed by the individual in the presence of a witness who attests the signature; or, if signed by another but at the individual's direction, the signature must be made in the presence of the individual and two attesting witnesses.

The lease, sub-lease or assignment is initially drafted by the seller's legal advisers and will follow one of the many standard formats available, but will be tailored to the individual case. This means that one lease is rarely identical to another. The draft lease is submitted to the buyer's adviser for approval, comment and negotiation. Amendments will be made (in red ink by the buyer and green by the seller) to the draft if appropriate – about rent, covenants and other terms of the transaction – and, after a certain to-ing and fro-ing between the parties, the final form will be agreed. The lease or assignment will then be put into deed form ('engrossed'), duplicated and provided to each party. Once signed, the deed has legal validity and the transaction is completed.

The wording of a lease

The language used in most leases is, as has been mentioned earlier, archaic and not easily comprehensible. Some recommendations have, however, been made to make them more modern.

- A lease should be clearly expressed in straightforward language and be structured in an accessible and logical fashion.
- It should include a definition section which explains the precise meanings of key words and expressions employed.
- Punctuation should be used properly, bearing in mind that misplaced punctuation can give a sentence a meaning that was not intended.
- Each section of the lease should be as short and to the point as possible. Each clause should deal with a distinct issue – the use of numbered paragraphs and sub-paragraphs is recommended.
- The lease should include a schedule or list at the end in which the lengthy and complex provisions regarding covenants can be set out.

- It should state the basic terms of the agreement right at the beginning: the parties, commencement date, duration, permitted user and ground rent, for example.

Rules of construction

'Rules of construction' are used to resolve difficulties arising from ambiguities and uncertainties in leases. The main rules are described below.

If there is a dispute over what the parties intended, the actual words employed in the lease and the circumstances in which it was made (e.g. nature of the property, background to the transaction, market considerations and purpose of the lease) are looked at.

Ordinary words, such as 'fire', 'repair' and 'damage', are given their strict and ordinary meaning. Technical terms, like 'covenants' and 'provisos', are interpreted in a technical, narrow sense.

Some words used in leases have a statutory definition. For example, month means calendar month; person includes a company; the singular includes the plural (and *vice versa*); and the masculine includes the feminine (and *vice versa*). The definitions of many other words used have been determined by Parliament.

It is important that the lease is read as a whole. Any uncertain expressions or clauses should be interpreted in the context of the rest of the lease and the purposes for which it was granted. Because the meaning of a word or phrase used in one part of the lease may govern the intention expressed in other parts, the need for consistency of expression is crucial.

If a covenant is ambiguous, the *contra proferentem* rule is used, whereby the covenant is interpreted in a manner unfavourable to the party who inserted it (usually the landlord) or, with respect to other terms, to the party who benefits from them. This is an arbitrary way of dispelling ambiguity and is a measure of last resort.

Certain terms will, in the absence of expressions to the contrary, be implied by law. The most important of these is the covenant for quiet enjoyment, which allows the tenant to occupy the premises without unlawful interruption by the landlord.

The structure of a lease

A lease normally spans several pages and traditionally consists of five sections: premises, habendum, reddendum, covenants, and provisos and options. At the end of many modern leases, schedules or lists will appear and set out in detail provisions relating to, for example, service charges and other covenants.

Owing to the length and complexity of the standard lease, it is inappropriate to set out a specimen lease in its entirety. Even the standard schedules to the lease normally describing covenants in detail, giving particulars of the rights and obligations that go with the flat, are too long to reproduce. The specimen lease below, therefore, looks at only the most important features of a typical lease.

> **The Lease** made the 4th day of January 1996 **Between** Janet Clarke of 37 Lenton Road Newcastle (hereafter called 'the landlord' which expression shall where the context so admits include the person for the time being entitled to the reversion immediately expectant on the determination of the term hereby granted) and Zoe Rogers of 19 Poolfield Road Newcastle (hereafter called 'the tenant' which expression shall where the context so admits include her successors in title)
>
> **Witnesseth** as follows:
>
> In consideration of the sum of £75,000 paid by the tenant to the landlord (the receipt thereof the landlord hereby acknowledges) the rent reserved and the tenants' covenants hereinafter contained the landlord **Hereby Demises** unto the tenant **All Those** premises known as Flat 3, 44 The Covert Newcastle **To Hold** unto the tenant from the 4th day of January 1996 for a term of 99 years **Yielding and Paying** thereafter during the said term the yearly rent of £160 by equal quarterly payments in advance on the usual quarter days the first of such payments being due proportion thereof to be made on the date hereof for the period to the 25th day of March next.

The premises

The premises part of the lease will, as shown in the specimen above, include the following details:

Parties to the lease This will provide the names and addresses of the parties and a short description of their respective roles (e.g. 'landlord' and 'tenant' or 'lessor' and 'lessee').

Date on which the tenancy starts The commencement date of the lease may be earlier, later or at the same time as the date of the deed which creates the lease.

Price paid for the lease and the ground rent The expression 'Yielding and Paying' in the specimen lease signifies that it is the responsibility of the tenant to seek out the landlord to ensure that the ground rent (here £160) is paid.

Intention of the parties to create a lease There is no set formula to be used, but the more commonly found expressions are 'demise', 'lease', 'let' and 'grant'. They all mean the same thing and demonstrate the necessary intention. They are called 'operative words'.

Brief description of the property This is known as the 'parcels' clause and defines what property is being leased. For the lease of a flat, the precise boundaries of the flat should be stated. This will involve mention of which walls, floors and ceilings are to be included. A scale plan prepared by an architect or a surveyor is frequently attached. The lease should make clear whether the plan or the verbal description is to prevail if conflict arises between the buyer and the seller. A more detailed verbal description is often to be found in a schedule to the lease and may read something like:

'All that flat known as Flat 3, 44 The Covert Newcastle **Together** with the ceilings and floors of the said flat and the joists and beams on which the floors are laid but not the joists and beams to which the ceilings are attached unless those joists and beams also support a floor of the said flat **And Together** with all cisterns tanks sewers drains pipes wires ducts and conduits used solely for the purposes of the said flat but no others **Excepting and Reserving** from the demise the main structural parts of the building of which the said flat forms part including the roof foundations and external parts thereof but not the glass of the windows or the window frames of the said flat nor the interior faces of such of the external walls as bound the said flat.

All Internal Walls separating the Premises from any other part of the building shall be party walls and shall be used and repaired as such.'

The description states exactly what the buyer is getting and is relevant in connection with the tenant's repairing obligations.

Boundaries

Boundaries are often a source of contention for flat-owners. Where the lease does not say anything specific about boundaries, there are certain rules of thumb. First, the lease of the top flat carries with it the air space and roof space above it. This means that the tenant is responsible for the repair of an entire roof of a building and can extend upwards into it. Second, the tenant acquires the space between the floor of the flat and the underside of the floor of the flat above and so is allowed to run cables and wires through the ceiling space. Third, where the flat has an outside wall, the tenant has both sides of that wall, and so can attach objects to the outside wall.

Exceptions and reservations These are appropriate where the landlord seeks to exclude some part of the building from the lease (stairways and passage, for example) or to reserve a right of way over some part of the premises leased (e.g. a garden or path). These exceptions and reservations may be contained in a separate schedule in the lease and might read as follows:

'All those gardens drives paths and forecourts and the halls staircases landings and other parts of the building which are used in common by the owners or occupiers of any two or more of the flats...All those main structural parts of the building including roof foundations and external parts thereof...cisterns tanks sewers drains pipes not used solely for the purpose of one flat'.

Other rights and obligations The lease might also grant to the flat-owner various rights known as 'easements' over other flat-owners' properties in the same block. These could include, for example, rights of access, support and entry to carry out repairs. Correspondingly, the lease will give similar rights over the tenant's property to the other flat-owners. Generally speaking, and as there is no contractual relationship between the flat-owners themselves, these rights can be enforced only via the landlord and not by the other tenants.

These rights are often set out in separate schedules within the lease along the following lines:

'Rights included in the demise

1) The right in common with the lessor and occupiers of other flats and all others having the like right to use for purposes only of access to and egress from the premises all such parts of the reserved property as afford access thereto.
2) The right of passage and running of gas electricity water and soil from and to the premises through the sewers drains wires pipes ducts and conduits forming part of the reserved property.
3) The benefit of any covenants entered into by the owners of other flats with the landlord so far as such covenants are intended to benefit the premises of the tenant.
4) All rights of support and other easements and all quasi-easements rights and benefits of a similar nature now enjoyed or intended to be enjoyed by the premises.
5) The right to use in common with the owners and occupiers of all other flats and their visitors the gardens drives paths and forecourts forming part of the reserved property.
6) Such rights of access to and entry upon the reserved property and the other flats as are necessary for the proper performance of the tenant's obligations hereunder.'

The tenant will also be subject to certain obligations imposed by the lease, for example:

'Rights to which the demise is subject

1) All rights of support and other easements and all quasi-easements rights and benefits of a similar nature now enjoyed or intended to be enjoyed by any other part of the building over the premises.
2) Such rights of access to and entry upon the premises by the landlord and the owners of the other flats as are necessary for the proper performance of their obligations hereunder or under covenants relating to other flats and similar to those herein contained.
3) The burden of any covenants entered into by the landlord with the owners of other flats so far as such covenants are intended to bind the premises or the tenant.'

The habendum

This part of the lease states the length of the tenancy (in the specimen example 99 years). It is common for the term and the commencement date of the lease to be stated in the introduction to the lease and then repeated in the habendum. In the specimen lease the habendum begins with 'To Hold unto the tenant from....' The term normally starts at midnight after the commencement date stated (in the specimen on 4–5 January) and will expire at midnight on the last day of the period specified (in the example 3–4 January 2095). It is necessary that the beginning of the term is set out with certainty and that the end is specified or can be calculated.

The reddendum

The habendum is usually followed by the reddendum clause, which states the rent to be paid by the tenant. In the example, the reddendum commences with the words 'Yielding and Paying thereafter....' As regards a long residential lease, only an annual ground rent is payable. Ground rent is a rent for the 'bare site' of the land (£160 in the specimen lease) and is substantially lower than the full market rent for the premises. The ground rent is in addition to the purchase price of the lease (in the example £75,000) and is traditionally payable in instalments on each 'quarter day'. The quarter days are 25 March, 24 June, 29 September and 25 December. The lease will make it clear whether the rent is payable in advance or not.

The covenants

The covenants strike at the core of the landlord-tenant relationship. They state the rights and obligations of the parties under the lease. Covenants can be positive in nature (i.e. they can compel one party to do something, for example, to pay rent or to insure) or negative (i.e. they can restrict one party from doing something, for example, using the premises for certain purposes).

Both parties usually enter into a series of **express** (i.e. explicitly stated) covenants, with the heavier burden normally falling upon the tenant. Certain covenants may also be **implied** by law and these are not normally stated explicitly in the lease. Examples of covenants commonly found in leases are illustrated below. The covenants relating to insurance, repairs, alterations and service charges are considered in more detail in separate chapters.

A tenant's covenants

Against assignment and sub-letting In the absence of any explicit restrictions to the contrary in the lease, a tenant can assign, sub-let, part with possession of, or share possession of the premises. It is uncommon for long residential leases to impose restraints upon this freedom. Nevertheless, sometimes such restrictions do appear (e.g. where the freehold is owned by a common employer of the tenants). The lease may also require the tenant to give notice to the landlord of any dealings with the premises so that the landlord will always know in whom the lease is vested and whether any underlease has been created.

To pay the ground rent This might appear in the lease as:

'The tenant shall pay the reserved rent on the days and in the manner above specified.'

To repair An example of such a covenant is:

'The tenant shall to the satisfaction in all respects of the landlord keep the premises and all parts thereof and all fixtures and fittings therein and all additions thereto in a good and tenantable state of repair decoration and condition throughout the continuance of the lease including the renewal and replacement of all worn or damaged parts and shall maintain and uphold and whenever necessary for whatever reason rebuild reconstruct and replace the same and shall yield up the same at the determination of the lease in such good and tenantable state of repair decoration and condition and in accordance with the terms of this covenant in all respects.'

Against alterations This covenant prohibits alterations without the landlord's consent. It could be drafted thus:

'The tenant shall not make any alterations in the premises without the approval in writing of the landlord to the plans and specifications and shall make those alterations only in accordance with those plans and specifications when approved.'

To insure Such a covenant might be worded:

'Insure and keep insured the premises against loss or damage by fire [other perils] in the full value thereof in the names of the landlord and the tenant through such agency as the landlord shall from time to time specify and whenever required produce to the landlord the policy of such insurance and the receipt for the last premium for the same and in the event of the premises being damaged or destroyed by fire [or other insured risk] as soon as reasonably practicable lay out the insurance moneys in the repair rebuilding or reinstatement of the premises.'

On the use of the flat A covenant will normally be included which obliges the tenant to use the premises as a private residence only. This will not normally prevent people working at home, but is aimed at stopping the premises being used, for example, as a hotel or shop. Such a covenant might read:

'The tenant shall not use the premises for any purpose other than a residence.'

An additional express covenant will normally be that the tenant must not do, or permit to be done, on the premises anything which may become a nuisance or annoyance to other occupiers or the landlord. This might read:

'That no act matter or thing which shall or may become or grow to be a public or private nuisance or a damage annoyance grievance or inconvenience to the landlord or any occupier of adjoining neighbouring or other land or buildings or which may lessen the value of any such land or buildings shall be carried on or done or suffered on the demised premises.'

There may be specific prohibitions: no musical instruments to be played after 10 p.m.; no washing to be hung outside; no pets except dogs and cats; or no pets at all. Sometimes there is a whole list of regulations about use and behaviour with which the tenant must comply.

To permit the landlord to enter and view Because the tenant is granted exclusive possession of the flat (which means that, subject to provisions to the contrary, the landlord can be excluded from the premises) this covenant is often included so that the landlord can inspect the state of repair of the property. This might be drafted as:

'The tenant shall permit the landlord to have access to and enter upon the premises as often as may be reasonably necessary for the landlord to do so in fulfilment of the landlord's obligations hereunder or under covenants relating to other flats and similar to those herein contained.'

To leave the premises The tenant will undertake to quit the premises at the end of the lease, for example:

'That the tenant will at the expiration or sooner determination of the term hereby granted surrender and deliver up to the landlord or successors in title peaceable and quiet possession of the demised premises.'

This does not, however, prevent the tenant from taking advantage of any rights afforded by Parliament to stay in the flat (see Chapter 16).

A landlord's covenants

The landlord will give comparatively few covenants to the tenant. The following do, however, regularly find their way into a lease.

To quiet enjoyment This is always implied into a lease, but often it will be stated explicitly that the tenant will be granted the quiet enjoyment of the premises. This means that the landlord has good title and will allow the tenant possession and peaceful enjoyment of the premises. This prevents the landlord (or agents) from interfering with the tenant's possession of the flat. This covenant might appear as:

'The landlord covenants with the tenant that the tenant shall have quiet enjoyment of the property as against the landlord and all persons claiming through the landlord.'

To repair and decorate Although the burden of repair will fall heavily upon the tenant, the landlord might undertake to repair and decorate the outside of the premises and common parts (i.e. the parts reserved by the landlord). An example of this type of covenant might be:

'The landlord shall keep the reserved property and all fixtures and fittings therein and additions thereto in a good and tenantable state of repair decoration and condition including the renewal and replacement of all worn and damaged parts.'

Maintenance of common parts The common parts of the building (lifts, stairways and passages, for instance) will usually be in the control and under the responsibility of the landlord. This obligation might be expressed as:

> 'The landlord shall keep the halls stairs landings and passages forming part of the reserved property properly carpeted cleaned and in good order and shall keep adequately lighted all such reserved parts of the property as are normally lighted or as should be lighted.'

Implied covenants

In addition to express covenants in the lease, there are a few obligations imposed by law. These include the covenants:

- for quiet enjoyment given by the landlord (see page 89);
- not to derogate from the grant. This imposes upon the landlord an obligation not, at the same time as granting to the tenant a lease, to do anything which is inconsistent with that grant. The covenant would be breached if, for example, the landlord did something which would make the premises less fit for habitation; interfered with light which reaches the tenant's windows; or created an excessive noise;
- not to disclaim the landlord's title. This is a covenant by the tenant not to deny the landlord's title or act in a way inconsistent with being a tenant. This prevents the tenant from doing something which prejudices the landlord's title (e.g. by claiming to be the freeholder);
- not to commit waste. This is a covenant by the tenant not to alter the physical character of the premises through any action or inaction. Waste may be voluntary, that is, a positive act which diminishes the value of the property. It can also be permissive, which covers failures of maintenance and repair, leading to dilapidation of the premises. Due to this implied obligation, even if there is no express provision for repair, the tenant is still required to undertake basic repair and maintenance of the flat.

Other implied covenants relate to repair and are considered later (see Chapter 15).

The 'usual covenants'

A lease may, instead of containing a long list of covenants, expressly be made subject to the 'usual covenants' without detailing exactly what they are. This is rare in a long lease, but the 'usual covenants' include:

● covenant by the tenant to pay rent;
● covenant by the tenant to keep and deliver up the premises in repair and to allow the landlord to enter and view the state of repair of the flat;
● covenant by the landlord for quiet enjoyment;
● covenant for re-entry (technically called a 'proviso') which allows the landlord to forfeit the lease on the non-payment of rent or breach of other covenant. This will, however, normally be spelled out in the lease.

What other covenants are to be included in the description 'usual' depends on the nature of the premises, their location and the purpose for which they are being let. In cases of dispute, it might be up to a court to decide what covenants are 'usual' in the circumstances.

Provisos and options

The **provisos** part of the lease will usually consist of the explicitly stated right of the landlord to end the lease if the tenant fails to observe any of the covenants. This is called a right of re-entry or a forfeiture clause. Forfeiture is considered in Chapter 9. A forfeiture clause will read something like:

'**Provided Always** and it is hereby agreed that if the rents hereby reserved or any part thereof shall be unpaid for twenty one days after becoming payable (whether formally demanded or not) or if any covenant on the part of the tenant herein contained shall not be performed or observed then and in any such case it shall be lawful for the landlord at any time thereafter to re-enter upon the demised premises or any part thereof in the name of the whole and thereupon this demise shall absolutely determine but without prejudice to any right action or remedy of the landlord in respect of any antecedent breach of any of the tenant's covenants.'

In the case of a residential lease, a clause permitting forfeiture for bankruptcy would not normally be found. This is because lenders will not advance mortgage funds on the security of a lease containing such a clause.

The lease may give the tenant an **option** to purchase the freehold (i.e. the landlord's reversion) or a right of pre-emption (which offers the tenant first refusal if the landlord wishes to sell the freehold). As discussed in Chapter 17, both can be made available for a specified period or remain open throughout the lease. The option may extend only to a named tenant or be available to subsequent tenants. Similarly, it may be exercisable on the payment of a stated sum or at a price to be determined. Much depends upon the clear drafting of the clauses.

Assignments, underleases and sales of freehold

When an existing lease is assigned, the tenant sells the whole of the interest in the flat. It is similar to creating a new lease, but instead of opening with 'The Lease made...' it will begin: 'The Assignment made....'

There is normally an account of the original lease: its date, the parties, the term, the rent and the property involved. This shows how the present seller came to own the lease. If the original lease contains a covenant against assignment without the landlord's consent, the assignment will state that the consent has been duly obtained.

The operative part of the deed of assignment will be something like:

'...the seller as beneficial owner **Hereby Assigns** unto the buyer **ALL THAT** property described in the schedule hereto and comprised in and demised by the Lease **To Hold** unto the buyer for all the residue now unexpired of the term of years created by the lease **subject** henceforth to the rent reserved by and to the lessee's covenants and conditions contained in the Lease.'

The property is usually identified in the schedule by reference to the original lease:

'The property is more fully described in a lease dated 4 January 1996 and made between Janet Clarke and Zoe Rogers.'

Normally no new covenants are introduced: the assignee (the buyer) is bound automatically by the existing covenants on a 'take it or leave it' basis. The original tenant of a lease granted before 1 January 1996 remains liable, even after the lease is sold on, for the fulfilment of existing covenants. Accordingly, an indemnity covenant is implied (it does not have to be spelled out in the assignment) that the assignee will reimburse the seller for any non-payment of rent or breach of the other covenants and conditions. There is also an implied covenant that the seller has complied with the terms of the lease. As regards leases created after 1 January 1996, under the Landlord and Tenant (Covenants) Act 1995 the original tenant ceases to be liable on the covenants following the assignment of the lease, and the indemnity covenants have no application. See Chapter 9 for more details.

Grant of an underlease

The grant of an underlease (also known as a sub-lease) is not an assignment of the tenant's whole interest in the property. Underleases of residential property are common in the case of new housing estates in some parts of the country. In such instances, the freeholder leases the land to the developer for, say, 999 years at an annual rent of £500. On the land the developer builds five blocks of flats, for example, and sub-lets each individual flat for a term of, say, 990 years at a capital premium (the purchase price) plus a ground rent of £50 per year. This practice is known as a 'building' or 'letting' scheme.

The conveyance is similar to the grant of a lease, as described earlier. It is important to ensure that the sub-lease imposes an obligation to observe covenants at least as onerous as those contained in the head-lease. In order to achieve this, the sub-lease normally states verbatim the relevant covenants appearing in the head-lease or incorporates them by reference.

An underlease too should contain an indemnity covenant. This is not implied by law and must, therefore, be expressly stated. This would read along these lines:

'...by way of indemnity only to perform and observe such covenants and restrictions contained in the head-lease as are still effective and relate to the property and to indemnify the sub-lessor against any liability resulting from their breach or non-observance.'

Sale of reversion

If the freeholder sells the reversionary interest (i.e. the freehold, sometimes described also as a 'fee simple'), the buyer of that freehold acquires the landlord's title subject to the existing lease(s). The conveyance will normally read:

'**To Hold** unto the purchaser in fee simple subject to but with the benefit of the before recited lease.'

This entails that the buyer of the freehold can enforce the tenant's covenants contained in the lease and, similarly, will be bound by the landlord's covenants contained in that lease. The original landlord will, if the lease was created before 1 January 1996, remain liable on the original covenants. If the lease is granted after that date, the original landlord can apply to the court (if necessary) to be released from the original covenants.

If the buyer of the reversion is the existing tenant (see Chapter 16), a term that the lease will merge with and be extinguished by the freehold will usually be incorporated into the conveyance. This will avoid questions being raised subsequently when the property is next sold on. A specimen of such a term is:

'The purchaser as the owner of the fee simple estate and of the leasehold estate in the property declares that from the date of this deed the lease shall no longer continue in force but shall be merged in the fee simple.'

Under the Landlord and Tenant Act 1985, tenants have the right to be informed by written notice when the landlord sells the freehold reversion and be given the name and address of the new owner. This notice must be provided either within two months of the sale or by the day after the next payment of ground rent is due. Failure to give such notice is a criminal offence. The incentive for a landlord to observe this requirement is that, whether or not the Landlord and Tenant (Covenants) Act 1995 applies, he or she remains liable (jointly or otherwise with the new buyer) on the covenants until the notice is served. The Landlord and Tenant Act 1987 offers 'qualifying tenants' the limited right of first refusal when the freeholder decides to sell the freehold (see Chapter 17).

CHAPTER 9

BREACHES OF COVENANT

MOST people who buy flats appreciate that they are acquiring a temporary ownership of a property during the life of the lease. It is also generally understood that the lease represents a contract between the landlord (owner of the freehold) and the tenant (buyer) and that the terms and covenants of the lease must be complied with. The covenants remain enforceable throughout the existence of the lease.

What constitutes a breach of covenant?

Covenants impose obligations on both landlord and tenant either to do something or not to do something. Examples of breach of a tenant's covenant are:

- not paying ground rent promptly (breach of the covenant to pay rent);
- using the flat for bed-and-breakfast purposes (breach of the user covenant).

  Examples of breach of a landlord's covenants are:

- letting the premises fall into disrepair (breach of the covenant to repair);
- attempting unlawfully to evict a tenant (breach of the covenant of quiet enjoyment).

Parties bound by covenants

The issue of who can enforce a covenant and against whom is of particular importance when a tenant assigns the lease (i.e. sells the flat to someone else) or creates a sub-lease (i.e. creates a lease for a lesser duration than that of the tenant), and when a landlord sells the freehold. Following the Landlord and Tenant (Covenants) Act 1995, how this issue is settled in assignments of leases and landlords' reversions depends on whether the lease was granted before or after 1 January 1996. The Act, however, leaves largely unaffected the law relating to sub-leases.

The landlord can easily discover who the current tenant is, but it is not always as easy for the tenant to discover the identity of a new landlord. Nevertheless, it is crucial for the tenant to be able to identify the landlord in order to enforce the latter's covenants. To overcome this problem, and unless it is obvious from the lease, the tenant must receive notification of the landlord's name and address. If the freehold is subsequently sold, the old landlord must furnish the name and address of the new landlord by the date the next ground rent falls due or, if later, within two months of the sale. Until that occurs the tenant can sue either or both of the landlords for breach of covenant.

Pre-1996 leases

Privity of contract and estate

It is important to realise that the original parties to the lease will, even if they sell the freehold or leasehold, remain liable on their covenants for the duration of the lease. This is because 'privity of contract' exists between them. So when the lease or the freehold reversion is sold on or a sub-lease is created, there is no contractual relationship between the original landlord and the new tenant; or the new landlord and the original tenant; or the head landlord and the sub-tenant. Accordingly, in those situations the covenants cannot be enforced by or against the newcomer simply because of the contractual relationship between the original parties. The only means by which the new party can sue or be sued is if the covenants run with the land. If so, the benefit and burden of the leasehold covenant will pass to successors in title of the original landlord and tenant.

The mechanism by which this is done is known as 'privity of estate'. The idea here is that the covenants become imprinted on the estate and run with the lease. Privity of estate exists between those who currently stand in the position of landlord and tenant. Accordingly, once the original tenant assigns the lease, he or she no longer has privity of estate with the landlord. Privity of estate will now be between the landlord and the assignee (the buyer). Thus the buyer becomes automatically liable on the original covenants for as long as he or she has the lease. Accordingly, when the lease is again assigned, the seller's liability ceases (except as to indemnity or covenants breached while he or she was in possession) and passes on to the new buyer.

Similarly, when the original landlord parts with the freehold, the successor is responsible for complying with the landlord's covenants. Usually, this liability persists only while he or she remains the freeholder. However, as mentioned above, the original landlord is still bound by contract to the original tenant. It is the new landlord who stands in privity of estate with the current tenant.

Sub-letting

If the original tenant does not wish to dispose of the flat outright and, as an alternative, sub-lets the property, the sub-tenant has no relationship with the freeholder. There is privity neither of estate nor of contract between them. The contractual tie is between the sub-tenant and the tenant, and privity of estate exists between them. The tenant will, therefore, take care to ensure that the sub-lease contains exactly the same covenants as the head-lease from which it was carved. Although the landlord cannot sue the sub-tenant for breach of a leasehold covenant, in limited circumstances Parliament has allowed the sub-tenant to sue the original head landlord even though there is no contract between them.

Indemnity

It is necessary in a sub-lease to include an express **indemnity** covenant under which the sub-tenant will compensate the tenant for any breaches of covenant committed by the former.

In the case of pre-1996 leases, on assignment the original tenant will seek protection against being sued for a breach of covenant committed by an assignee. It is usual practice for an express indemnity covenant to be inserted into the assignment whereby the assignee will indemnify the original tenant against such claims. This should be clearly worded and could read: 'to pay the future rent and observe the covenants on the part of the lessee contained in the lease....'

Leasehold Property (Repairs) Act 1938

The landlord's ability to recover damages for breach of a covenant to repair is restricted by the above Act. The Act applies to all properties where the lease, as initially granted, was for over seven years and when there are at least three years remaining unexpired. The Act prevents the landlord from enforcing a breach of a covenant to repair (whether by damages or forfeiture of the lease: see pages 105-10) unless, at least one month before commencing proceedings, he or she has served a notice on the tenant which identifies the breach. The tenant is given the right to serve a counternotice which, if served, requires the landlord to obtain the permission of the court before proceeding with the legal action.

Examples

● In 1954, Joan was granted a 99-year lease of a flat. The lease imposed extensive and onerous repair covenants on the tenant. In 1965, she assigned the lease to Betty who, in 1990, sold the lease to Doris. Doris has allowed the property to fall into severe disrepair.

The landlord has a choice whether to sue Doris (privity of estate) or Joan (privity of contract), but cannot sue Betty because neither type of privity exists between them. Generally, the landlord would prefer to sue Doris.

Doris is, however, bankrupt. There is no point suing her trustee in bankruptcy because there are insufficient assets to meet the claim. The landlord will, therefore, sue Joan for compensation. Some 30 years after selling the flat, Joan is faced with liability for something which she has not done and over which she has no control.

Fortunately for Joan, she has a right of indemnity (whether expressed or implied into the assignment) against Betty. She will join Betty as a co-defendant to the landlord's action. Accordingly, Joan will pass on responsibility to Betty and it will be Betty who carries ultimate responsibility. Betty's right of indemnity against Doris is worthless because of the latter's bankruptcy. There is nothing that Betty can do.

- Landlord Brian grants a lease to Tony who, in turn, sub-lets the flat to Ray. Ray is in breach of a covenant contained in the head-lease. Brian cannot sue Ray, but he can claim against Tony. Tony can recover compensation from Ray only if the sub-lease contained both the covenant which has been breached and an express indemnity covenant. Otherwise, Tony will have to foot the bill.
- Brian sells the freehold to Liz. Liz is in breach of one of the land-lord's covenants. Tony can sue either Brian (contract) or Liz (estate). If there is an explicit indemnity covenant in the sale of the reversion, Brian (if sued) could claim indemnity from Liz. Even without such a covenant, Brian would still be able to sue Liz at common law under an ancient rule of general application that allows a party to recover from the assignee money paid under legal compulsion (e.g. the enforcement of a debt).

Post-1996 leases

The major purpose of the Landlord and Tenant (Covenants) Act 1995 is to overcome the above problems associated with the original tenant remaining liable for breach of covenant by a subsequent tenant. The new law is much simpler to state and understand.

The Act also offers the landlord the opportunity to escape from future liability following an assignment of the reversion. It achieves this by abolishing the privity of contract relationship, subsequent to assign-ment, between the original parties. However, this operates only if the assignment is not in breach of a covenant restricting such transactions.

As regards the tenant, this release occurs automatically, but for the landlord to be released an application must be made and agreed by the tenant or approved by the court. Clearly, once the tenant or landlord is released, neither can sue nor be sued on the covenants. As this marks the end of original tenant liability, the indemnity covenants implied by statute are of no application.

Although these changes affect only leases granted after 1 January 1996, the Act does contain several provisions which apply equally to new or old leases. Consult your legal adviser if you need to know how it affects your liability.

Examples reworked

If the leases in the above examples were granted after 1 January 1996, the change in the law produces the following effects. In connection with the lease granted to Joan:

- on a future assignment to Betty, Joan will no longer have any liability;
- on Betty later assigning the lease, the landlord will have to sue Doris;
- on Doris becoming bankrupt, the landlord will have to bear the loss

In relation to Brian:

- when the freehold is sold to Liz, Brian can apply to the court to be released from liability on the covenants he entered into with Tony. If he is released, then he can no longer sue or be sued on those covenants. If release is refused, then the old rules apply as stated above.

Sub-letting

The Act focuses on assignments and leaves largely untouched the rules which apply to sub-tenants. The only exception to this relates to covenants to do with how the premises are used, where the Act allows the covenant to be enforced directly against any owner or occupier of the leased premises (i.e. including a sub-tenant). Accordingly, the landlord will not (with the exception of the user covenant) be able to enforce tenants' covenants directly against the sub-tenant. The tenant will remain liable for the sub-tenant's breaches.

Remedies for breach

The normal remedies for breach of contract are available to both the landlord and the tenant for breaches of covenant. Under the old rules (i.e. before the Landlord and Tenant (Covenants) Act 1995 came into effect), assignees of the lease or of the reversion enjoy the same rights. In relation to leases granted after 1 January 1996, an assignee will automatically be bound by, and be able to enforce, all covenants which relate to the premises leased or the reversion sold.

Not surprisingly, both parties have a number of ways of dealing with a breach of any express or implied covenant within the lease. Some of the remedies benefit the landlord alone, while others are open to both parties. The general remedies open to both are an action for damages, specific performance and injunction.

Remedies for both landlord and tenant

Damages

When there is a breach of covenant (e.g. if the tenant sub-lets when he or she is not allowed to), the aggrieved party (i.e. the landlord) can sue for compensation. It can, however, be years before the case is resolved by the courts. The case will go before either the county court or the High Court, depending on the amount claimed in damages. It is possible to represent oneself, but usually a solicitor will be employed both to pursue and to defend a claim. Damages are an attractive remedy where the breach is substantial and where monetary compensation is what the person suing wants. The amount of damages awarded is based on the position the aggrieved party would have been in had the covenant been observed. This means that the court must estimate the amount of loss that the injured party has suffered. As regards a claim by the landlord for disrepair, however, the compensation awarded cannot exceed the amount by which the value of the reversion has diminished. There is no such limit in the case of other breaches and it does not affect the tenant's claim for disrepair.

Specific performance

The party who seeks to enforce a covenant can apply to the court for the discretionary remedy of specific performance. This means asking the court to order the other party to perform the agreed contractual terms. The other party is then told to perform the bargain and, if the order is not complied with, it becomes a contempt of court. The court can then act on behalf of the defaulting party and carry out the contract.

As the remedy is discretionary, it is not always available and will usually be declined if compensation would be adequate. If declined, the court will award damages to the claimant. In practice, it is unlikely that the landlord would be granted specific performance against the tenant; the latter does not face the same difficulty. It would be granted where the judge feels that it is fair and just to do so (e.g. where the landlord has failed to maintain common parts).

Injunction

It is necessary to go to court for an injunction, but (unlike the length of time involved in getting compensation) a temporary injunction can be obtained within days and will operate until the matter is heard formally by the court. An injunction can be positive (i.e. ordering someone to do something) or negative (restraining someone from doing something). This remedy is particularly useful with respect to the landlord's covenant of quiet enjoyment and tenant's covenants relating to use of the premises and preventing assignment, for example. It is, however, a discretionary remedy and is not available as of right. There is no injunction to compel the landlord or tenant to carry out repairs. Such a breach is better dealt with by damages or specific performance. In basic terms, whereas specific performance makes a party honour (i.e. perform) the contract, an injunction is designed to stop breaches of the contract occurring or continuing.

Remedies for tenants

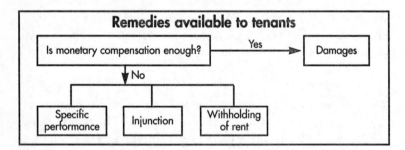

Withholding of ground rent

A self-help remedy which the tenant may use where, for example, the landlord has failed to comply with a repairing covenant, is for the tenant to carry out the works and deduct the cost from future payments of ground rent. The right has been extended to allowing the tenant to deduct the costs from rent arrears (i.e. rent already owed to the landlord). It does not, however, apply to the withholding of service charges; it allows the tenant to withhold ground rent so as to accumulate the capital sum to carry out necessary repairs which the landlord refuses to undertake.

Several conditions must be met for the withholding of rent (in order for the repair work to be carried out) to be lawful:

- the landlord must be in breach of a repairing covenant. There is no room for errors here and the tenant has to be absolutely sure that this is the case;
- the tenant must have given the landlord written notice of the need for repair and warned him or her (in writing) of the possible action to be taken;
- the tenant's expenditure must be reasonable and proper. It is advisable to obtain at least two estimates regarding the work proposed and, obviously, to choose the lower.

The tenant's right to withhold ground rent is not lost if there is a change of landlord.

An alternative strategy is to withhold rent and, rather than carry out the repairs, wait for the landlord to sue for the rent arrears. By making a cross-claim, the tenant might be able to obtain compensation for breach of the landlord's covenant to repair. The tenant would thus recover for loss arising from the disrepair and not be limited merely to the cost of effecting reasonable repairs.

The advantage of these forms of self-help is that the tenant does not have to initiate court proceedings and can sit back and wait for the landlord to decide what action to take. The disadvantage is that it all takes a great deal of time during which the repairs remain outstanding. Moreover, the landlord might attempt to forfeit the lease for non-payment of rent, but the court would grant the tenant relief and the landlord would be unsuccessful.

Statutory help

Where the landlord is in breach of a covenant to repair, the Landlord and Tenant Act 1987 allows the tenant(s) to apply to the court for an order appointing a manager of the building to take over responsibility from the landlord and for a compulsory purchase order so that the tenant(s) can buy out the landlord's freehold. These remedies are discussed further in Chapter 14.

Remedies for landlords

The covenant to pay ground rent is treated differently from all other covenants given by the tenant. In long residential leases, it is common for there to be a nominal ground rent payable. Rent becomes due on the day stipulated for payment and is in arrears from the following day. Several sanctions can be employed by the landlord against a tenant in arrears.

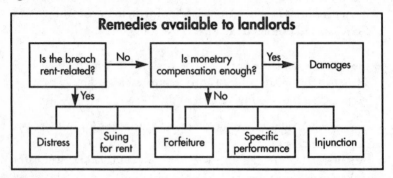

Remedies available to landlords

Suing for rent

Rent is a debt, and arrears are recoverable for up to six years by way of an action for breach of contract. Once judgment has been given in favour of the landlord, then, if the tenant either cannot or will not pay, it will need to be enforced. There are two methods of enforcement: obtaining an attachment of earnings order and sending out the court bailiffs under a warrant of execution.

Distress

Distress for rent is a simple remedy of self-help which the landlord can employ against a tenant without, generally, going to court. This ancient (and some would say outmoded) remedy allows the landlord, subject to certain restrictions, to enter the tenant's flat (but not by force) and seize and later sell goods found there. Because a long lease involves only a small ground rent, it is unlikely that the amount of arrears will justify the use of distress. Nevertheless, distress is sometimes used as a means of intimidating tenants (i.e. by sending in the bailiffs and seizing the tenant's goods) to quit the premises at the end of the lease. Distress does not terminate the lease.

The remedy is hedged with restrictions:

- distress applies only to rent arrears (or payments expressly reserved as rent in the lease; for example, service charges). It is not suitable when the amount of rent is in dispute;
- there has to be a lease. The remedy does not cover any relationship other than that between landlord and tenant;

- the remedy is not available where the landlord has sued the tenant for the debt (i.e. rent arrears) or set in motion proceedings to forfeit the lease (see pages 105-10);
- the remedy cannot be exercised between sunset and sunrise and never on a Sunday;
- entry to the flat must not be made by breaking an outer door, but it can be through an open (but not closed) window. Once inside, however, internal doors can be forced;
- certain goods are immune from seizure: clothes and bedding (up to £100 in value); tools of the trade (up to £150); perishable foods; tenant's fixtures; and things in actual use when the distress is levied.

The landlord may exercise this remedy in person, but normally a bailiff certified by the county court as being qualified to do the job is used. If distress occurs, the landlord or bailiff must give or leave for the tenant a notice which states the reason for the distress and the place of intended sale of the goods seized. No sooner than five days later, the goods can be sold and the landlord can discharge the rent arrears (and recover expenses) from the proceeds. Any balance must be paid to the tenant.

A danger for the landlord is that wrongful distress gives the tenant the right to seek substantial damages for consequential loss. Two final points about distress: first, the landlord does not need to physically remove the goods from the flat. There is a concept known as 'walking possession', which allows the goods to stay on the premises, but which entails that legally they are impounded and cannot be removed or used by the tenant. Second, the landlord can remove and sell the goods of a third party found on the premises if it is reasonably believed that they belong to the tenant. Once they have been sold, there is nothing that the third party can do.

Forfeiture

Forfeiture for breach of covenant is the most powerful weapon in the armoury of the landlord. It allows the landlord to 're-enter' the tenant's flat and put a premature end to the lease (see Chapter 16). The landlord can, if forfeiture is successful, then sell a new lease of the flat to a new buyer. It is of particular relevance to a long lease, which, unlike other types of tenancy, cannot be ended by a notice to quit. The rules governing forfeiture differ according to whether the breach complained of concerns the covenant to pay rent or some other type of covenant.

All well-drafted long leases will contain a forfeiture clause, and expressly give to the landlord the right to re-take possession. Forfeiture is not usually available unless there is such a clause; exceptions to this are where the premises are used as a brothel or when the tenant denies the landlord's title (e.g. by claiming to be the freeholder). It is the landlord who has the option whether to terminate or to continue with the lease. There is no equivalent of forfeiture which allows the tenant to end the lease. Accordingly, even if the landlord is in flagrant breach of the covenants, the tenant is still bound to the lease and cannot escape it.

A forfeiture clause should be drafted so as to cover two basic issues. First, it should be made clear whether the clause is to cover breaches of both negative (i.e. 'do not') and positive (i.e. 'do') covenants. This can be done either expressly or by inserting the words 'breach' and 'non-observance' into the clause which will then cover both aspects and allow forfeiture to be used for breach of any covenant.

Second, the clause should allow forfeiture for rent arrears whether or not the arrears have been formally demanded from the tenant.

Example of a forfeiture clause A typical forfeiture clause would read as follows. Note the reference to 'performed' and 'observed' covers both positive and negative covenants.

'If the rent hereby reserved or any part thereof shall be unpaid for 21 days after becoming payable (whether formally demanded or not) or if any covenant on the tenant's part herein contained shall not be performed or observed then and in any of the said cases it shall be lawful for the landlord at any time thereafter to re-enter upon the demised premises or any part thereof in the name of the whole and thereupon the demise shall absolutely determine but without prejudice to any right of action of the landlord in respect of any breach of the tenant's covenants herein contained.'

Methods of forfeiture There are two basic ways in which the landlord may forfeit and re-enter. The first is by actual, physical, re-entry; the second is by commencing court proceedings for possession.

Taking physical possession for the non-payment of rent is a risky tactic unless the premises are unoccupied. The Criminal Law Act 1977 prohibits the threat or use of violence in order to enter when any person is present on the premises. The Protection from Eviction Act 1977 provides that an eviction is lawful only with the support of a court order for possession. Accordingly, physical re-entry will often be unlawful and is not common as regards residential property. The formal means of effecting re-entry is by the service of a writ or summons on the tenant which contains an unambiguous demand for possession. This demand should not be coupled with any other claim from the landlord. The procedure for forfeiture is both awkward and complex. Due to its far-reaching effects, the remedy is the subject of major safeguards.

Protection for the tenant In the county court, the tenant can get relief – i.e. has the statutory right to halt forfeiture proceedings in the case of a breach of the covenant to pay rent – by paying in to the court all arrears and costs not later than five days before the return date specified on the landlord's summons. In the High Court, the proceedings are automatically halted where at least six months' rent is in arrears and the arrears are paid (with costs) at any time prior to the trial. In other cases, relief can also be granted by the court to the tenant on such terms (normally to make good the breach of covenant) as the court thinks appropriate. If relief is granted, the lease will continue in existence. The scope for relief depends upon which court the proceedings are brought before.

In the county court, forfeiture will be averted if the tenant pays all arrears and costs within four weeks of the possession order or within such period as the court deems fit. If the tenant fails to do this, the possession order is likely to be enforced and further relief will not normally be available. It is, however, possible for the tenant to apply for an extension at any time before the landlord recovers possession. Once the landlord has taken possession, the tenant can still apply to the court for relief within six months of that recovery of possession. This, however, is unlikely to succeed.

In the High Court, there is a general discretion to grant relief against forfeiture, and it is likely to be granted unless the tenant's conduct has been extreme or the breach unlikely to be remedied. The tenant can make an application at any time before trial which will, provided that all arrears and costs are discharged, normally be granted. Alternatively, the application can be made within six months of possession being granted to the landlord, but relief will not be granted if it would cause hardship to a third party (e.g. a new tenant) or the landlord.

If forfeiture is allowed, third parties, for example, a sub-tenant and the tenant's mortgage lender, may be disadvantaged. Such persons also have a right to apply to the court for relief. The court usually favours the request of such third parties. Accordingly, the forfeiture becomes final only once the court order has been issued and all claims for relief denied.

Forfeiture is rare when the breach of covenant can be remedied (e.g. if the arrears and costs are paid by the tenant, sub-tenant or mortgage lender). Because of this, forfeiture is not commonly achieved for breach of a rental covenant in a residential lease. Nevertheless, the threat of forfeiture can be exploited to the landlord's advantage: for example, writing to the tenant's mortgage lender may persuade the lender to perform the tenant's covenants and to add the cost on to the mortgage debt. The lender will be allowed to do this under the mortgage agreement and will normally prefer this route to applying for relief before the court.

Forfeiture for non-rent-related breaches Forfeiture for breach of a covenant other than non-payment of rent is governed by different procedures. Before forfeiture can take place, a special notice has to be served on the tenant. This has to be done regardless of whether physical re-entry or court action is the method of forfeiture adopted by the landlord. The notice is a device whereby the tenant is given a last chance to make amends and perform the covenant. The notice must specify:

● the breach of covenant complained of;
● where appropriate, how the breach can be remedied (e.g. by repair);
● if relevant, that compensation be paid to the landlord as a result of the breach.

Any notice that does not comply with these requirements is void, and forfeiture cannot lawfully take place. Where the notice is valid and the breach is capable of remedy, the landlord cannot proceed until the tenant fails to remedy or to pay compensation within a reasonable time. If the breach is not capable of remedy (e.g. where a stigma is attached to the premises because of illegal or immoral use), the landlord may proceed with the forfeiture after a reasonable interval (e.g. four weeks). Sometimes it is uncertain whether or not the court will regard a particular breach as being capable of remedy. To avoid doubt and invalidity, the landlord should require the tenant to remedy the breach 'so far as the same is capable of remedy'.

The tenant may be able to claim relief against forfeiture by making a counterclaim or by separate summons before the landlord recovers possession. After possession has been taken, and unlike in the case of a breach of rental covenant (as discussed above), no relief can be granted. Relief is regulated by a flexible discretion, but is unlikely to be granted if the tenant's breach was wilful or if the breach is incapable of remedy.

Forfeiture for disrepair This merits special attention because further limitations are imposed by the Leasehold Property (Repairs) Act 1938. This Act applies to leases granted initially for longer than seven years and which still have at least three years remaining unexpired. In certain circumstances, the Act makes it necessary for the landlord to obtain the approval of the court before pursuing the remedy of forfeiture or damages. The landlord must inform the tenant of the right to claim the protection of the 1938 Act and to serve a counternotice. If such counternotice is served within 28 days, the leave of the court allowing the landlord to proceed can be given only if the landlord can show that:

- the value of the reversion has been substantially diminished;
- the breach needs to be remedied immediately to prevent substantial diminution; to comply with statute; to protect the interests of other occupiers; or to avoid heavier repair costs in the future;
- there exist special circumstances which make it just and equitable for permission to be given.

Losing the right to forfeit The landlord can lose the right to forfeit the lease by waiving the particular breach complained of. This can arise from any act (see below) on the landlord's part which is inconsistent with the intention to end the lease. Once waiver of a breach has occurred, it is irrevocable.

Waiver is decided by the courts and not by what the parties actually intended. It is the act (not the motives) of the landlord which the court will examine. Waiver can arise from ignorance, clerical error or by a careless expression in correspondence. Acts which could amount to waiver include, for example, the landlord's acceptance of, or demand for, rent for periods after the breach of covenant; and negotiations to grant a new lease at the end of the current one. The breach of covenant may be a 'once and for all' breach (e.g. of covenant against sub-letting) or it may be a continuous breach (e.g. of repair or user covenant or increasing arrears of rent). However, even if the landlord waives a continuing breach on one occasion, the lease can be forfeited on the recurrence of the breach.

Effect of forfeiture There are a number of consequences arising from the forfeiture of a lease. First, once re-entry has lawfully occurred, the former tenant becomes a trespasser. Reasonable force can be used to evict him or her and to remove his or her goods. The lease is at an end and the former tenant no longer has to observe the covenants (e.g. is no longer liable to pay ground rent).

Second, the forfeiture of the head-lease automatically destroys any sub-lease granted by the former tenant. As mentioned, the sub-tenant has the right to apply to the court for relief.

Third, a mortgage lender who holds the lease as security can seek relief against the forfeiture of that lease.

CHAPTER 10

CO-OWNERSHIP

IT IS common for a person to buy a flat (or a house) jointly with a spouse, friend or relative. The number of people who can co-own a single flat is not, however, limited to two. Unfortunately, English law is not renowned for its simplicity, and the recognition and enforcement of the property rights of individuals living together are complicated matters. The same rules apply irrespective of whether it is a flat or a house.

Joint tenancy and tenancy in common

There are two recognised and distinct types of co-ownership: the joint tenancy and the tenancy in common.

Where there is a **joint tenancy**, the co-owners own the whole of the property together and on the death of one, the other(s) acquire the property automatically regardless of the terms of any will or the rules that apply on dying intestate (i.e. without a will). This continues until there is only one owner remaining, and is known as the right of survivorship. It is advisable to declare on the lease whether the owners are to hold as joint tenants or not.

Conversely, if the co-owners are **tenants in common**, each owns a share in the property which they can deal with as they wish. On death, the share of the co-owner can be left by will to someone or passed to next of kin by virtue of intestacy. The shares of tenants in common do not have to be equal. If, for example, one party provides 75 per cent of the purchase price and the other contributes 25 per cent, it would be sensible to have a three-quarters and one-quarter share respectively. It is best to have this expressly declared on the lease, but it is likely to be presumed by the courts if dispute arises.

It is up to the buyers to decide what type of arrangement suits them. The nature of the relationship between them and the amount of the financial contributions each has made to the purchase will be the key factors.

Examples

- Jan and John are married and buy a flat together, with Jan financing one-third of the purchase price, John the other two-thirds. The couple are not overly concerned about the commercial aspect of the transaction. They both make sure that their names are on the lease and expressly declare themselves to be joint tenants. If one of them dies, the other will own the entire flat absolutely and automatically. There is no need to process a will. If Jan and John at some stage go their separate ways, each will be entitled to a 50 per cent interest in the flat, even though they paid different amounts when they bought the flat.

- Sally and Kenneth, who are not married, buy a flat to live in together. Although they love each other, it is not their intention that, on the death of Kenneth, Sally will acquire his share and *vice versa*. Kenneth has children by a previous relationship and wants to ensure that they are provided for. This security is offered by the lease expressly stating that they are tenants in common.

  If Kenneth had provided only one-third of the purchase price, Sally might feel justified in making sure that he has only a one-third interest in the flat (and, thus, one-third share in the proceeds of any subsequent sale). Provided their respective shares are made clear on the face of the lease or assignment, if the relationship ends, the situation is uncomplicated. If Sally and Kenneth had jointly taken out a mortgage together to buy the flat, then, despite the difference in their shares, they are still equally liable to repay the mortgage. This remains so even if they split up and Kenneth lives elsewhere.

Ingredients of a joint tenancy

If the title to the flat is taken in joint names then the co-owners must be joint tenants of the legal estate (i.e. the paper title). The important issue is what happens to the real ownership (i.e. the entitlement to any proceeds of sale if the flat is sold). This is grandly called 'a beneficial interest under a trust for sale'. This will become clearer in meaning as the chapter progresses.

This is why a declaration on the lease, as to whether the parties' real ownership is as joint tenants or as tenants in common, is crucial. If the solicitor or conveyancer omits to state how the parties are to hold the lease, assignment or sub-lease, then he or she has been negligent and can be sued for any loss.

The four unities

Under a joint tenancy the co-owners have a single ownership of the flat (i.e. they together own the whole and do not own distinct shares). For a joint tenancy to exist, all of the so-called four unities must be present. These are:

- **The unity of possession** This means that each joint tenant is as much entitled to possession of any part of the property as the others.
- **The unity of interest** The interest of all the joint tenants must be identical; that is, for example, they must all have the same leasehold estate.
- **The unity of title** Each joint tenant must claim title from the same conveyance.
- **The unity of time** The title to the flat must be conveyed in the joint tenants at the same time.

For a tenancy in common to exist there need only be the unity of possession (interest, time and title being irrelevant). Without unity of possession, there would be no co-ownership at all.

Telling the two types of tenancies apart

Many co-owners are unaware of what type of tenancy was created when they bought their flats. If a dispute arises or one of the co-owners dies or wants to move out, however, they will need to know what the legal situation is. The first document to check is the lease. If this expressly declares the co-owners to be joint tenants or to be tenants in common, then the declaration is decisive. If the lease is silent on the issue, the court will be left to determine what

113

relationship has been created. In order to do so, the court will adopt the following approach.

- First, it will look to see if the four unities are present. If they are, a joint tenancy could exist; if not, it must be a tenancy in common. This means that the four unities are a necessary, but not sufficient, condition for the existence of a joint tenancy.
- If the unities are present, the court will look for words of severance that indicate a tenancy in common. Such words include 'equally', 'share', 'between' and 'to be divided amongst'. If such words are present, a tenancy in common of the equitable estate will be created.
- If the unities are present and no words of severance exist, the court will have to consider certain presumptions that apply. A joint tenancy, except where the purchase money was provided in unequal shares or the property is part of a business partnership, will be favoured.

Converting a joint tenancy

It is possible to sever a joint tenancy of the equitable estate and create a tenancy in common. There are a variety of ways in which this can be achieved. The simplest method is by serving a written notice on the other joint tenant making clear that severance has occurred. In addition, any serious attempt by one joint tenant to sell, lease or mortgage part of the property would also sever the joint tenancy (even if without the knowledge or agreement of the other joint tenants). On the other hand, oral statements, commencement of divorce proceedings and the leaving of a will do not have any effect.

If there are more than two joint tenants, the party who severs affects only his or her share. The other co-owners remain joint tenants among themselves.

Example reworked

Jan and John are considering divorce. The joint tenancy does not now suit either partner, if only because neither wishes to benefit the other on death. Jan seeks to remain in the property until the flat is sold. They will now seek to sever (or end) their joint tenancy and convert it into a tenancy in common. Following severance, the property would be held as tenants in common and the right of survivorship ended. When Jan dies, her 50 per cent interest in the flat could be left by will to whomever she pleases. (She has a 50 per cent share because she and John were previously joint tenants; the fact that she paid less of the original purchase price than John is immaterial.) The same rule applies in the case of John.

Converting a tenancy in common

Just as it is possible to change a joint tenancy into a tenancy in common, the reverse can be achieved. This will require a written agreement converting the tenancy in common (preferably formally drafted in a deed).

Example reworked

Sally and Kenneth have a child together and wish to convert their tenancy in common into a joint tenancy and activate the right of survivorship. This can be done by creating a 'trust' in writing. There is no formula or special way of doing so and a deed is not required. Their names already appear on the lease or assignment as legal owners. Once the tenancy has been converted, Kenneth would no longer be regarded as having only a one-third share in the flat and both he and Sally would now together own the flat in its entirety.

Trust for sale

In every case of co-ownership, the law employs a device known as a 'trust for sale'. This artificial and somewhat confusing notion requires that the co-owners hold the legal ownership (the paper title) of the flat on trust for themselves as beneficiaries. The legal estate is always considered to be held as joint tenants. Behind this paper title, what really counts is the ownership in equity (i.e. who benefits and in what proportions if the flat is sold) and this is where the distinction between a joint tenancy and a tenancy in common bites.

The purpose of using a trust is to make the procedure for selling the flat easier and to ensure that the co-owners obtain their proper share of the proceeds of sale.

When the flat is conveyed into more than one name, the trust for sale will arise automatically. Nevertheless, it is preferable for the conveyance to make express reference to the trust.

The lease may, for example, expressly state that Bill and Ben hold the legal estate on trust for sale for themselves beneficially. If they are to be tenants in common, the lease might read:

'The purchasers agree that they are in equity tenants in common in the following shares: Bill two-thirds and Ben one-third.'

If the lease fails to mention the trust, it is implied by law.

Subject to any exclusion order made by a court (for domestic violence), Bill and Ben have an equal right to occupation of the flat and, when it is sold, have rights to the proceeds of sale of the property in proportion to their shares in it.

A duty to sell?

Under the trust for sale, the law regards Bill and Ben as being under a duty to sell the flat. This is, of course, not what the couple will actually wish to do because they will be interested, for some time, in retaining the flat as a home. So this duty to sell (hence the description 'trust for sale') is yet another legal pretence, because Bill and Ben have the power to postpone sale indefinitely and, therefore, the flat will generally be retained until they decide to sell and move elsewhere. As discussed below, if a dispute arises where one co-owner seeks to sell against the wishes of the other, the court has the discretion to order sale.

Buying from co-owners

The 'trust for sale' ensures that when the flat is sold, at whatever distant date, the process of transfer to the new buyer is simplified. The buyer will be able to obtain an absolute title without worrying about the beneficial interests of, say, Bill and Ben. To be sure that the transaction proceeds smoothly, the buyer should:

- take the lease, assignment or sub-lease from the legal owners (the trustees) as stated on the lease or assignment;
- pay the purchase monies collectively to at least two trustees (i.e. make the cheque or banker's draft payable to both of them).

The buyer is then not liable for any misappropriation of the purchase monies. If, for example, Bill absconds, having withdrawn the funds from a joint bank account, then Ben cannot look to the buyer for satisfaction.

Co-owners' decision to sell

If all the co-owners of a flat consent to its sale, there is no problem. The difficulties arise when there is a dispute between the co-owners, for example during the breakdown of a relationship. The general rule is that the sale of the flat cannot proceed unless all the co-owners agree.

In circumstances where one co-owner refuses, the other(s) may apply to the court for an order compelling the reluctant party to join in the conveyance. Due to the nature of the 'trust for sale', the court will usually grant the order. Nevertheless, the court enjoys a wide discretion to make such orders as it thinks fit and sometimes orders that the sale should not take place. There are two main situations where the sale may not be enforced:

● when a formal agreement has been made by the co-owners not to sell the flat without the consent of all;
● when the co-owners bought the property in order to provide a family home. The court will be unwilling to allow the property to be sold against the wishes of one co-owner while there are dependent children in the property. In such a case, the court is likely to postpone sale until the children are of school-leaving age. If this involves the other spouse or partner moving out of the co-owned property, the court might stipulate that the person remaining in the flat pays a rent for the continued occupation. If the parties are married, then such matters will normally be resolved under the wide-ranging matrimonial jurisdiction of the court.

If creditors are involved

If a co-owner becomes bankrupt and the debtor's trustee in bankruptcy (appointed by the court on bankruptcy to take charge of the bankrupt's affairs) seeks an order for sale, other considerations are brought into play. The court retains its discretion as to whether or not to order the sale, but it now has different conflicting issues to balance. Here, however, the tug of money will generally prevail over the interests of the family, and an order of sale will usually be granted. The Insolvency Act 1986 provides that, unless the circumstances of the case are exceptional, the interests of the creditors outweigh those of anyone else. The Act does, however, show some temporary compassion to the family and offers a limited opportunity to preserve – essentially for one year – the family home.

There are two ways in which the Act can delay, but not cancel, the rights of creditors and postpone the prospect of the family being made homeless:

- the bankrupt is offered limited rights of occupation, but only when the flat is also occupied by a person under the age of 18 years. The bankrupt cannot be evicted from the flat without the authorisation of the bankruptcy court. In reaching a decision the court must take on board all the circumstances of the case and, if it does order a stay of possession, this is unlikely to keep the bankrupt in occupation for longer than one year following bankruptcy;
- the bankrupt's spouse (but not cohabitant) is given certain rights of occupation. Such rights will also indirectly benefit the bankrupt. The spouse's right of occupation can be terminated only by order of the bankruptcy court. The court must take into account all the circumstances, but, even if the spouse's right is upheld, the protection is effective only for one year following bankruptcy. It should be noted that the spouse's statutory right of occupation given under the Matrimonial Homes Act 1983 (see page 122) does not bind a trustee in bankruptcy.

Co-ownership by implication

It is possible that the name on the title deeds or registered at the Land Registry is that of one party only. As a general rule, the law presumes that the person whose name appears thus is the only owner of the flat. Nevertheless, as regards married couples and cohabitants it is possible that, for example, by contributions to the purchase price or the mortgage repayments, the non-named party has acquired some ownership of the flat in equity. This will not be reflected in the lease and such contributions can be made on the purchase of the lease or subsequently. The married person is in a stronger position than the unmarried counterpart because, on divorce, the court has a wide discretion to redistribute ownership between the couple.

There are two broad ways in which a person not named on the title deeds or entered as registered proprietor can acquire what is termed 'beneficial ownership' and become, through implication, a co-owner.

The first is where there has been a non-written agreement or understanding between the parties as to beneficial ownership. This will normally be evidenced by an express discussion (for example, 'this flat is as much yours as mine'). This agreement shows the intention to give the party a share in the property, but it is arbitrary because it hinges upon something that is not in writing. The problem with this is that it might be a phantom intention which the person making it never really intends to implement.

The second means by which implied co-ownership can arise is by an inferred agreement. Here the court looks to the conduct of the parties and from that may infer a common intention to share ownership. If it finds that the non-owning partner has made monetary payments (e.g. financial contributions to the deposit, mortgage repayments or substantial property improvements) the court will readily imply the intention to share ownership.

It should be noted that certain contributions, like looking after the home and family (e.g. rearing children, decorating, and doing house-work) are not, in themselves, sufficient. The situation changes, however, if non-owning partner looks after the children and thus frees the legal owner to go to work and earn the money that pays for the mortgage. This will be viewed as an indirect contribution and can generate a co-ownership of the flat.

A co-owner who obtains an interest by the inference of a common intention will, invariably, be a tenant in common. The share will be calculated with reference either to the value of the contributions made or to what the court assumes the intention of the parties had been.

Example

Grant has owned a flat for the last 20 years. He has paid off the mortgage and the title is registered solely in his name. He meets Eve and falls in love. Eve moves into the flat and lives with Grant.

After two years, Eve feels insecure and asks Grant about their long-term future. She says that she will move out unless the title to the flat is registered in her name too. Grant does not want the relationship to end, but most certainly does not want Eve to have co-ownership of the flat that he had spent many years acquiring. He decides to blur the issue and says: 'Don't worry. It's your flat as much as mine.' Eve stays.

What Grant fails to appreciate is that (if the discussion can be proved) he has, contrary to his intention, given Eve half-ownership of the flat. If Eve had not enquired, then she would have had nothing.

Avoiding unwanted co-ownership by implication

Regarding the rule concerning agreements and understandings – which do not have to be put in writing to be binding – the easiest means of avoiding a phantom intention being relied upon is not to have any such discussion in the first place. If the discussion is unavoidable, then it is wise to tell the truth and not make up any palatable excuses.

In the context of an inferred agreement arising from conduct, the trust is dependent upon there being a financial contribution towards the initial or on-going purchase of the flat or improvements, rather than the use of the flat. So to prevent a co-ownership by implication, avoid getting direct contributions to the purchase price and mortgage repayments. Any monetary payments should be classified as 'rent'. If money belonging to a third party is to be spent in the acquisition of the flat or its improvement, then the safest course is to have a signed agreement between the parties that the money is merely a loan or gift and is not designed to give that party a share in the ownership of the property. Any form of words will suffice provided that the intention not to give an interest in the flat is clearly spelled out. An example might be:

> 'The parties agree that the legal and beneficial title to the property is vested solely in Jim and that Jules does not acquire any interest whatsoever in the property by reason of his contributions.'

Subject to any express discussion to the contrary, this should prevent a co-ownership situation arising.

Advancement

Sometimes the presumption of a trust is displaced by an outmoded concept known as 'advancement'. This presumption arises where there is a special relationship between the parties under which it is natural for one party to provide for the other. Curiously, the rule applies only to 'gifts' by husbands or fathers (not cohabitants) to wives or children, respectively. It does not apply to wives advancing money to their husbands. Any payments made by a husband to the purchase price, for example, might be regarded as a gift and, if so, would not give the husband a beneficial ownership of the flat. Not surprisingly, the courts do not like the presumption of advancement and try to avoid its application. It can readily be rebutted by some clear understanding to the contrary between the parties.

Married couples

Although as yet no legislation governs the property rights of cohabitants, the situation of married couples is different. Acts of Parliament, such as the Matrimonial Causes Act 1973, are in force which protect the property rights of married couples. The issue of implied ownership (see pages 118-20) is not relevant because, on divorce, the courts have the flexible jurisdiction to redistribute property rights. Issues of property law and ownership yield to the higher demands of relating the means of both parties to the needs of each. The court, therefore, adopts a forward-looking perspective, unlike with cohabitants where it analyses events in detailed hindsight. Prior to divorce, the wife can apply for a declaration of property rights under the Married Women's Property Act 1882. This may result, for example, in the court ordering the conveyance of the property into joint names.

Improvements

The Matrimonial Proceedings and Property Act 1970 provides that if a husband or wife makes a substantial contribution to improvements to property, the contributing spouse will receive a share (or, if already a co-owning tenant in common, an increased share) in the improved property. This does not apply, however, if there is agreement to the contrary.

Right to occupy

The Matrimonial Homes Act 1983 offers a spouse who has no legal ownership in the flat a statutory right to occupy the matrimonial home. The right extends to the flat and any garage, garden, yard or outhouse forming part of the lease. The spouse has no right to move into any premises which have never been the matrimonial home (e.g. a post-separation flat). This right allows him or her protection from eviction if the flat is in occupation or, if not, the right to re-enter and occupy. It gives the spouse a status of irremovability until divorce, but it does not extend beyond divorce. Either party may apply to the court, while the right is on-going, for an order declaring, enforcing, restricting or terminating the right. The court can make such order as it considers fair.

The statutory right of occupation will bind a buyer of the flat only if it is protected on the land charges register (unregistered land) or the Land Register (registered land). In the former system, this will involve the entry of a Class F land charge; in the latter the entry of a notice on the charges register.

Domestic violence

There also exists domestic violence legislation under which an ouster order (removing one partner from the home) can be obtained. At the time of writing, there is no power under such statutes to adjust ownership rights. Nevertheless, an Act of Parliament is being proposed so as to allow a court hearing a case of domestic violence to re-adjust the parties' property rights.

Property re-adjustment

On divorce, the court has the power to order the transfer of specific property from one spouse to the other. Any such order will take effect on the decree absolute being made. In deciding how to exercise its power, the court must take account of the welfare of any children; both spouses' financial resources (e.g. income, earning capacity and personal property); the loss to each that will arise on divorce (this also takes into account the standard of living, needs, obligations and responsibilities of each spouse); the age and health of the parties; the duration of the marriage; the conduct of the parties; and any contributions made by looking after children and the home.

The matrimonial home is often the key asset of the family. It is the task of the court to ensure that both spouses and their children are suitably housed. Unfortunately, it is usually the case that there will not be enough funds to maintain two distinct homes without a drastic drop in the standard of living of one or both parties. If there are children involved, the court will normally prefer the option of keeping them in the family home.

The court can make the following orders:

- the sale of the matrimonial home, but not until the children of the marriage reach a certain age (e.g. 16 years). The court may order that the proceeds of the eventual sale be distributed in equal shares between the parties. Meanwhile, the parent with custody is allowed to live in the flat and is obliged to meet all the outgoings;
- an outright transfer whereby the entire ownership of the flat is transferred to one spouse. This could be in lieu of a maintenance order or on condition that the other spouse receives a lump-sum payment or a financial charge on the property;
- immediate sale or permission for a spouse to occupy the flat for life or for a defined period. If the latter type of order is adopted, it is common for the resident spouse to pay an occupational rent.

Problems for buyers of co-owned flats

The major difficulty facing a buyer is discovering whether or not the flat is impliedly co-owned. The trust for sale will not be disclosed by the conveyancing documentation and will not appear on any register. Therefore, the buyer will often be unaware that there is anyone other than the seller with an interest in the property under a trust and will be paying the purchase money only to the sole seller. The danger exists that the buyer could be bound by such an undisclosed interest.

The issue of whether the beneficial interest of a non-legal owner of the flat will bind the buyer depends largely upon whether the land is unregistered or registered. If unregistered, a buyer will be bound by that equitable interest if he or she has actual, constructive or imputed notice of the co-owner's rights. This means that the right will bind if the buyer or the buyer's agent (e.g. solicitor) either knew or should have known of the co-owner's interest. If so, the buyer will be bound; if not, then he or she will take the flat free of the interest. There is no land charge that can be registered here. The concept of 'overreaching' considered below applies equally to unregistered land as it does to registered land.

In the case of registered land, the general rule is that a buyer will be bound only by an interest which is protected by an entry on the Land Register. A massive exception to this rule applies, however, to the rights of a person in actual, physical, occupation of the property. Any rights that such person has over the land will bind the buyer because they are protected as an overriding interest. This means that a co-owner through implication has only to maintain occupation of the flat for his or her rights to bind a buyer. It does not matter that the buyer took all reasonable steps to discover the presence of other occupants or asked the seller whether anyone else resided in the flat. The overriding interest will still be binding. The only defence is if the buyer had asked the occupier claiming the right whether anyone other than the seller resided in the flat and the occupier had failed to disclose it.

Solutions for buyers

To avoid being bound by an undisclosed co-owner's interest in the flat, the buyer should inspect the property to see if anyone else is living there and, if suspicious, search the electoral role and make enquiries of neighbours. If the presence of someone other than the seller is detected, the buyer should obtain (before completion) that person's signature on a release form. This will be effective to defeat that occupier's interest. If no one else lives there, then the buyer will not be bound by the interests of the co-owner.

A final solution for the buyer is via the legal mechanism known as 'overreaching'. This means that, even if someone is in actual occupation and has an overriding interest, on the purchase money being paid to two trustees (or a trust corporation, e.g. a bank) the interest of the co-owner will be overreached and will not bind the buyer. It does not matter that the buyer knew of the co-owner's rights. Overreaching would be relevant where there are two legal owners (e.g. husband and wife), but a third party (e.g. a parent) has a beneficial interest in the flat. Thus the buyer will be forced to pay the purchase monies to the two spouses/trustees (as legal owners) and, on doing so, will overreach the parent's interest. The parent, in this example, will have to follow the proceeds of sale and make a claim against the sellers.

Implications for lenders

Where mortgage money is used to purchase the flat, the mortgage will normally take priority over the co-owner's rights in the property. Although technically the conveyance takes place moments before the creation of the mortgage, the co-owner will not have the opportunity to move into occupation before the lender's interest has been created. Therefore, in registered land there will be no scope usually for a claim by someone in actual occupation, because the flat would need to be occupied when the mortgage was created.

In addition, it is presumed that any other co-owner is impliedly consenting to the mortgage and to the relegation of his or her interest behind that of the lender. Accordingly, with first mortgages the lender will be protected from the claims of a co-owner.

The situation is more difficult with second mortgages (which may be raised to finance a business project, buy a car or extend or improve the flat, for example). The major difference here is that the co-owner will now be in occupation of the flat and the lender might be stuck with notice of the rights of the co-owner (unregistered land) or be bound by an overriding interest (registered land). The lender is, therefore, more vulnerable than with first-mortgage transactions. There are, however, two ways in which the lender can protect itself.

● First, if there are two legal owners and the mortgage money is advanced to them, the interest of any other co-owner will be overreached. The interest ceases from that point to be an interest in the land and does not bind the lender.
● Second, where the lender discovers that there is an adult other than the legal owner living on the premises, it will make it a condition of the advance that the adult sign a release or a disclaimer of rights document. This generally will give the lender priority, but it is not watertight.

CHAPTER **11**

INSURANCE

BUYING and owning a flat are major commitments and it is wise to take precautions in case things go horribly wrong. Different types of insurance are bound to crop up during the process of buying a flat: you may be asked to insure your life, your ability to make mortgage repayments, the contents of your flat and the flat (and the building it is in) itself. The last of these – insuring the premises of the flat – is something the lender of a mortgage will absolutely insist on, because the flat is the only security the lender has if the borrower defaults and therefore needs to be maintained in good condition throughout the term of the mortgage. Moreover, insurance of the premises is the subject of one of the main covenants between a landlord and a tenant (see Chapter 8). The bulk of this chapter will, therefore, concentrate on this kind of insurance.

Life assurance

All investment-linked mortgages and some repayment mortgages may require you to take out life assurance such that if you should die during the term of the mortgage the amount of the loan outstanding will be repaid by the insurance company to the lender (see Chapter 3 for details). If you are buying a flat with someone else, both (or all) of you may be asked by the lender to take out life assurance.

Home loan protection

It is normally recommended and advisable practice for the borrower to take out an insurance policy to cover mortgage repayments if he or she becomes unemployed or falls ill. This cover is obviously an attractive proposition for many borrowers, but it adds to the monthly cost of the mortgage. Moreover, it has become clear that many claims by borrowers have been defeated because of the small print and hidden clauses within insurance agreements. Recently, to make matters worse for the insured, the government announced the possibility of taxing payments made by the insurance company under such policies.

The policies are not cheap. Premiums are worked out per £100 of cover. The largest building societies currently charge between £6 and £8 per £100. The premiums may also reflect changes in interest rates. The benefits of such policies are also limited. For example, some policies cover the person insured for a period of 12 months following unemployment, whereas others extend protection for two years. Following ill-health, the cover might extend for three years, but all policies exclude pre-existing medical conditions from protection. Another problem is that it might take months before any insurance payments are received by the borrower. Clearly, such policies need to be read and understood thoroughly before any cover is bought.

Normally, your mortgage lender will offer you this type of insurance cover, but you can arrange it privately through any insurance broker.

Home contents insurance

Home contents insurance is a must for all home-owners. Lenders, however, will not insist upon this type of cover (unlike premises insurance: see pages 128-31), but in this age of rising burglaries and with the risk of flooding through burst pipes etc. it would be tempting fate not to take out such insurance. The cost of the premiums reflects the amount of cover that you desire and also the area in which your flat is situated. If the area is noted for a high number of burglaries, the premiums will tend to be higher than in a 'safe' area. Some insurance companies will refuse to issue a policy if the flat has no window locks and does not have a good security lock on the outside doors. Reductions on premiums may be obtained if the flat is within a neighbourhood watch scheme and/or if a burglar alarm is fitted, or if a combined contents and premises (see below) policy is bought from the same insurer. Contents insurance should be taken out from the time your goods are moved into the flat. As with all policies, you should check carefully the conditions and exclusions set out by the insurance company.

Premises insurance

It is usual for the lease to make provisions for the insurance of the premises, by either the landlord or the tenant, against damage or destruction. Such insurance will cover the fabric of the building, including walls, roof, windows and garage. Often the covenants in the lease will state who is responsible for the insurance, ensure that there is adequate coverage and deal with what will happen if catastrophe strikes. Perils to be covered should include fire, explosion, storm, flooding, earthquake and lightning. Some policies will also cover accidental damage (e.g. breaking a window with a step-ladder). Subsidence coverage will normally carry a large excess (e.g. £1,000) which the insured will have to meet personally and which will not be paid for by the insurance company. If the property has already been underpinned, it may be difficult to find an insurance company willing to issue a premises policy.

The burden of showing that damage arose from an insured peril rests on the flat-owner. In disputed claims, much depends upon the view of the loss adjuster hired by the insurance company. A recognised arbitration system is run by the Insurance Ombudsman*.

Who should do the insuring?

The lease may contain a covenant obliging the landlord to do the insuring and may allow him or her to recover this expenditure from the tenant by way of what is called 'insurance rent' or, as is more common, under the service charge provision (see page 131 and Chapter 12). Occasionally, the tenant may be responsible for insuring the premises.

The decision as to who will insure will be governed largely by the structure of the building. If the building is a block of flats in multiple occupation with common parts and facilities, the landlord will normally insure the whole property under a single policy. It is easier for the landlord to assess the amount of cover required. The tenant may have some say over the risks against which the landlord insures but, as is emphasised below, none at all as far as the choice of company and cost of insurance (and hence the premiums) go (see pages 129-30). If the policy is in the sole name of the landlord, the tenant and the lender should insist on their interests being noted on the policy so that they can themselves make a claim against the insurance company if necessary.

As regards a building divided into two self-contained flats, the burden may fall on each flat-owner. The landlord may, however, exert some control by specifying the risks to be covered by the policy. The tenant's mortgage lender will also influence the policy taken out by the tenant.

Proof of insurance

Where one party is to insure the premises, the other will need to know that an adequate policy has been taken out and, moreover, is still in existence. There are several ways in which this can be ensured:

- the lease could insist that the policy is taken out in the joint names of the landlord and the tenant;
- a covenant can be inserted into the lease which requires the party who is supposed to take out insurance cover to produce the policy, and the last receipt for payment of the premium, either on request, on specified events (e.g. when the lease is being assigned) or at stated intervals;
- as the landlord who insures a whole building may not wish a tenant to see the policy in its entirety because it deals with all the other flats in the building, a covenant can be inserted whereby the landlord will produce evidence (e.g. extracts from the policy) to confirm that insurance has been taken out. If the premiums are passed on to the tenant by way of the service charge, the Landlord and Tenant Act 1987 gives the tenant the right to inspect the policy.

A specified insurer?

Both parties will try to ensure that the policy taken out is with a reputable insurance company. The landlord might seek to use a company that pays monetary commission for putting the business its

way, whereas the tenant may want the cheapest quote to be accepted.
The lease may guide the parties:

● if the tenant is to insure, the covenant may specify a named
company or one to be nominated by the landlord. This can be
financially disadvantageous for the tenant, but the expense can be
minimised by a provision allowing insurance by 'any company
approved in writing by the landlord, such approval not to be
unreasonably withheld';

● where the landlord is to insure, the lease often limits the choice to
a reputable company. The tenant, however, has no control over
the choice or the cost of insurance. Although for most people this
is not problematic, tenants at the mercy of unscrupulous landlords
could find that they are being exploited over this issue. One
common scam is for the landlord to insure the premises – often
based on higher-than-warranted valuations – through companies
owned by his or her family or friends. Then he or she can charge
high premiums for the insurance, and the tenants have to either pay
up or go to court to have the lease varied (see Chapter 14).

Amount of cover and risks

Under-insurance (i.e. where deliberately or not the premises are
under-valued so that a lower premium is paid) can constitute a major
problem for both parties. If a claim is made, the insurance company
will simply scale down the amount to be paid out. It is also possible
to over-insure, which will entail higher premium costs than is
necessary. Therefore, the lease will attempt to specify the degree of
cover sought by using one of several expressions. 'Adequate'
coverage means that the extent of cover is as recommended by the
insurance company. 'Full value' cover means that the policy covers
the full market value of the premises, but might be considerably less
than the cost of actually reinstating (i.e. re-building) the flat.
Coverage 'for the full cost of reinstatement' requires extensive cover
to include the actual cost to repair or to re-build the premises from
scratch. The landlord will prefer this last form of insurance cover.
The Association of British Insurers★ has produced a guide to
calculating re-building costs.

The lease may specify, either in a definitions section or in the
covenant itself, certain risks against which the premises must be

insured. It is impractical to spell out each and every potential risk and, accordingly, the clause will be comprehensive and flexible. For the tenant, it is important that the insurance cover at least matches the extent of his or her obligations to repair the flat if it is damaged. The amount for which the flat is insured should be reviewed periodically and especially when improvements to the flat have been carried out.

The service charge

Where the service charge (see Chapter 12) includes a payment for insurance, the tenant can require the landlord to supply written details of the insurance cover. This is governed by the Landlord and Tenant Act 1987. These details must reveal the amount of the cover, the name of the insurer and the risks insured against. The landlord may meet this request by letting the tenant have a copy of the appropriate policy. The tenant is also given the right to inspect the original policy, and the premium receipts, and to take a copy of them. If the tenant is unhappy about the policy (e.g. the premiums are excessive or the coverage inadequate), an application can be made to the court for it to order the landlord to change insurers and/or the policy.

In practice, a major difficulty is to assess the value of a block of flats for the purposes of insurance cover. The insurers themselves, and also surveyors, are sometimes unable to suggest a figure. The danger, of course, is that the block will be under-insured. This may encourage individual flat-owners to take out further insurance. This might, moreover, be required by a mortgage lender who will be keen to ensure that the total insurance coverage is sufficient to protect its security for the loan. In the event of a claim, however, the tenant cannot claim for the same loss twice.

CHAPTER **12**

SERVICE CHARGES

IN ADDITION to having to pay ground rent, a tenant may be obliged by a covenant in the lease to pay an annual service charge to the landlord, his or her agent or a management company (see Chapter 13). It is clearly in the landlord's interests to place the financial burden for repair and maintenance of the structure and common parts of the building upon the shoulders of the tenants. Although, if the building is let to a small number of tenants (e.g. a small conversion let out to four tenants), this can be done by imposing a comprehensive repair covenant upon each tenant, when parts of the building are leased to many tenants a different method must be adopted – so the landlord inserts into the leases a service charge provision. Such schemes are particularly common with blocks of flats. The amount of the service charge will reflect the cost to the landlord of performing his or her obligations under the lease. The principle behind a service charge provision is that the landlord retains responsibility for repair, maintenance and general running costs of the building, but passes on the costs to the tenants. By doing this he or she achieves what is known as a 'clear lease', and this makes the freehold reversion more marketable.

Service charges and the lease

What is a service charge?

A service charge is the amount payable, directly or indirectly, for services (porterage and cleaning, upkeep of garden and lifts, for example), repairs, maintenance, insurance and other overheads incurred in the management of the property. Some leases do not contain a list of services which can be billed for in the service charge, but instead contain a general and wide-ranging clause.

The key issues which should be clearly defined in the lease include:

- what services are to be provided by the landlord and for what he or she can charge;
- the method of payment and collection of the service charge;
- the apportionment of the charge as between the tenants;
- the procedure for certifying the expenditure;
- the provision of a reserve or sinking fund.

A specimen clause

The service charge provision might be drafted along the following lines:

i) The tenant hereby covenants with the landlord to contribute and pay parts [a formula or percentage will be stated] of the costs, expenses, outgoings and matters mentioned in the schedule hereto

ii) the contribution under paragraph (i) of this clause for each year shall be estimated by the managing agents for the time being of the landlord (hereinafter referred to as 'the managing agents') or if none the landlord (whose decision shall be final) as soon as practicable after the beginning of the year and the tenant shall pay the estimated contribution by two equal instalments on 25 March and 29 September in that year.

The landlord hereby covenants with the tenant to supply to the tenant not less frequently than once every year a summary of the costs expenses outgoings and matters mentioned in the schedule hereto for the previous calendar year which summary shall also incorporate statements of the amount (if any) standing to the credit of the tenant.

The nuts and bolts of the charge will then follow in a schedule to the lease which gives the details of what the tenant is liable to contribute to. Although the precise catalogue of the services to be provided by the landlord and to be paid for by the tenant will depend upon the particular building, the schedule might mention:

- the cost of the landlord insuring the premises;
- the expenses of the landlord in carrying out the obligations under the lease regarding repairs, cleaning, painting and lighting of common parts, for example. There might be provision to cater for any future, additional running costs arising from the development or extension of the building. It is in the tenant's interests that the clause does not cover 'improvements' and 'rebuilding'. Repairs could be limited to 'necessary' repairs and the landlord might seek the flexibility of carrying out repairs and maintenance 'as often as in the opinion of the landlord is reasonably necessary'. The tenant, if possible, should avoid remedial work done on the building owing to a defect in design, workmanship or materials from falling within the clause;
- the costs incurred by the landlord for the repair and maintenance of a lift;
- the expense of decorating the exterior and the interior common parts of the building;
- the fees and costs paid to any managing agent appointed. The tenant should ensure that management costs are reasonable. Where the landlord acts as the management agent, the fees should be limited to services actually performed by him or her. A provision which allows him or her remuneration equivalent to a percentage of the general administrative overheads should be avoided;
- the fees and costs paid to any accountant, solicitor or other professional in relation to the audit and the certification of accounts. The clause might also allow for the payment of wages and salaries of employees;
- all other expenses (if any) incurred by the landlord in relation to any arbitration or court action concerning the charges;
- that the landlord can employ contractors to carry out his or her obligations under the lease or, if he or she carries them out personally, claim the normal charges (including profit) for the work;
- that provisional assessments and demands may be made;
- that a sinking fund be set up to cover the future replacement of major items such as lifts and boilers or the undertaking of major repairs and maintenance (e.g. decorating the exterior of the building). This will help spread the expenditure for these costs over a few years;
- that the landlord may charge interest on money borrowed from the bank to carry out the repair and maintenance obligations.

Qualifications

The landlord may seek to qualify the obligation to perform services. This can be done in several ways. First, the covenant might require him or her only to use 'reasonable' or 'best' efforts to provide the services or to provide them 'only so far as is practicable'. Liability might also be excluded for such things as, for example, shortages of fuel and workers, mechanical breakdown and the replacement of equipment.

Second, the lease may reserve for the landlord the right to change, add or withdraw services. The tenant should be wary of such provisions and argue that the lease should allow variation only on the grounds of good estate management (i.e. only if a reasonable landlord would make the changes).

Third, the covenant might prescribe the standard of services as being 'such standard as the landlord considers adequate'. This is not in the interests of the tenant because, apart from the right to a management audit (see below), there is no effective way of challenging the adequacy of the services provided. Nevertheless, some assistance is afforded by the Supply of Goods and Services Act 1982, which implies that the services are to be performed with reasonable care and skill and (subject to the lease) within a reasonable time. It is better practice for the lease to expressly require the services to be provided to a reasonable standard, but in relation to certain items more detail should be required. The provision of heating, for example, might be connected to specific dates and times when it is turned on; service periods might be set; and minimum temperature levels might be established.

Management audits

The Leasehold Reform, Housing and Urban Development Act 1993 allows for a quality-control check on the services actually provided by the landlord. This will help to quell fears that the tenants are not getting value for money and will provide proof in any court action which arises from an alleged breach of service covenant.

Residents of flats can serve a notice requiring an audit of the landlord's management of the premises. The entitlement extends only to tenants who hold under a long lease and pay a service charge to the landlord. Such a tenant is known as a 'qualifying tenant' and, although a tenant can own and qualify in relation to more than one flat, there can only be one qualifying tenant for each flat. If the flat is co-owned, only one of the co-owners can serve the notice. Further conditions are attached according to the number of dwellings included in the premises:

- if there is only one dwelling let to a qualifying tenant, the right can be exercised by that tenant alone;
- where there are two dwellings in the premises let to qualifying tenants, either or both may exercise the right;
- as regards three or more dwellings, it is necessary that at least two-thirds of the qualifying tenants jointly seek the audit.

The audit is of the management functions which the landlord is obliged to carry out under the lease(s). Its purpose is to check whether those obligations are discharged, and the sums paid by the tenants applied, in an efficient and effective fashion. The measure of quality control is in a code of practice, intended to promote desirable practices in the management of premises, published by the government.

The audit will be carried out by a professional, appointed by the tenant(s); he or she is given rights to inspect the premises and accounts. The notice served by the tenant(s) on the landlord must:

- identify the tenant(s);
- identify the auditor;
- specify any documents which are to be inspected;
- specify a date, between one and two months hence, when the premises will be inspected.

The landlord then has one month from the notice to make available any requested documentation. If he or she fails to comply, the auditor can (within two months of the notice) apply to court for an order compelling his or her co-operation.

A fair share?

The landlord will seek to be fully reimbursed for the services provided. The lease should, therefore, ensure that his or her obligations to perform and the tenant's obligation to pay correspond. Once more, everything hinges upon the wording of the lease. Few tenants would object to the landlord being properly refunded for the cost of providing the service obligations.

Each flat-owner has a covenant to pay as the service charge a proportion of the expenses incurred by the landlord in the provision of the services (the total of the proportions paid by all the tenants should add up to 100 per cent). Sometimes certain items of expenditure are shared among only some of the flat-owners (e.g. some flats may have a garage while others do not; and a ground-floor tenant may not have to pay for the upkeep of a lift). In other cases the apportionment may be calculated in a broad sense, that is, each flat-owner may have to pay the same proportion regardless of the size and position of the flat. Some schemes may calculate the contribution according to former rateable values of the flats; others might make the calculation according to floor space of an individual flat. Whichever method is used, there will be tenants who feel that they are unfavourably disadvantaged.

Prospective buyers should be aware that when there is an un-scrupulous or inefficient landlord or management company, the apportionments may add up to more than 100 per cent of the expenses or they might be based upon incorrect data (e.g. old rateable values or floor space). In such cases, the tenant must challenge the figures and, as a last resort, the matter may have to go to court.

Method of payment

The lease will normally describe the service charge as additional rent. This enables the landlord to exercise the remedy of distress and to forfeit the lease (see Chapter 9) without the necessity of serving a formal notice on the tenant.

The landlord will wish to have funds available to meet expenditure as it falls due, so the lease will require some form of advance payment. The common method by which this is achieved is for the lease to require quarterly (or half-yearly) payments from the tenant based upon certified estimates of expenditure. When the accounts are certified at the end of the financial year, adjustments to cover under-payments and over-payments can be made. Any refund to the tenant should be made as soon as is practicable or discounted from the next payment. These matters will often be dealt with in the lease.

Statutory limitations

There is some limitation on the amounts that can be legitimately charged. This is laid down by the Landlord and Tenant Act 1985, which imposes duties upon landlords with respect to service charge costs and estimates. As a general yardstick, service charges should be limited to costs reasonably incurred during the past year. In addition, the works and services concerned have to be provided to a reasonable standard.

The tenant is free to request written details of the costs and how they have been calculated, and the landlord must respond. Such information must also disclose what bills have been paid and those that remain outstanding. The landlord must give the tenant reasonable access to any supporting accounts if he or she wants to inspect or even copy them. Where a written summary of the costs is provided following a request by a tenant, it must be certified by an accountant who is neither a partner nor an employee of the landlord. The accountant's certificate is no guarantee of reasonableness or arithmetical accuracy.

The problem of tenants being billed for unjustifiably high service charges by unscrupulous landlords is discussed in Chapter 17.

Tenants' associations

A tenants' association is one which is representative of the tenants and recognised as such by the landlord, a tribunal known as the Rent Assessment Committee (a specialised body dealing with landlord and tenant disputes – consult the telephone directory to find the one nearest you) and the court. The Landlord and Tenant Act 1985 allows an association of residents who pay service charges (as long leaseholders in blocks of flats generally do) to apply to the landlord to be 'recognised'. Such an application should be made in writing and state how many flats are represented by the association. This should be more than 60 per cent of the flats in the block. The letter should be sent by recorded or registered delivery. If the landlord does not respond by sending a notice of recognition, the association can apply to the Rent Assessment Committee for a certificate of recognition.

The officials of the association act as agents for the members as a whole, and the members are liable personally in respect of any obligation incurred by the association. The association will, usually, have no substantial assets.

The importance of a recognised association lies in the collective bargaining power the members have in relation to the landlord. In addition, under the Landlord and Tenant Act 1985 the association has the right to be heard on the question of major repairs before estimates are asked for. A tenants' association can act as a watchdog to ensure that its members and the landlord abide by the covenants contained in the lease. If legal action against the landlord is appropriate, the association can initiate the action on behalf of all its members (not an individual member). Whether recognised or not, however, the association does not have a legal personality and cannot itself go to court. Instead, one member can take representative action on behalf of all the flat-owners even if some are non-members of the association.

The association can negotiate with the landlord over a variety of matters including the quality of the services provided, their cost, the contractors to be used and the consideration of estimates, for example. Even where the landlord takes no notice of a complaint, the fact that the association has made it may be considered a preliminary to taking legal action.

The acts of the association may bind only its members (and not non-associate tenants) and, moreover, individual members can disengage themselves from the acts of the association if not in agreement. Unless such tenants notify the landlord to the contrary, however, the latter can assume that the association has the authority to bind all its members.

The Federation of Private Residents' Associations★ will provide an information pack on how to set up a tenants' association.

The rights of tenants' associations

When the landlord employs a managing agent, the rights of a recognised tenants' association are strengthened by the Landlord and Tenant Act 1987. If, when a tenants' association serves the notice asking for recognition, there is no managing agent, the landlord must serve a notice on the association before appointing an agent in the future. This notice must inform the tenants of the name of the agent; identify those responsibilities of the landlord which the agent is to take over; and allow one month for the association to make comments.

Where a managing agent has been employed at the time the association seeks recognition, the association must be informed of the identity and functions of the agent and allowed to make comments as to the effectiveness of the particular agent.

A landlord who has recognised an association must, every five years, serve a further notice on the association informing them of any changes in the duties of the managing agent. If the landlord proposes to change the agent, the above procedures as to notification must be followed.

Consultation

Where the landlord wishes to carry out works on the premises (repairs, construction or maintenance, for example) further restrictions imposed by the Landlord and Tenant Act 1985 apply. If the cost of such works is more than the greater of £50 multiplied by the number of dwellings or £1,000 (these figures change from time to time), the excess is recoverable by the landlord only with the approval of the court or when certain specified conditions are satisfied. These requirements are to do with estimates and consultation, unless the work is carried out in an emergency, and differ according to whether the tenants are represented by a recognised tenants' association or not.

The rules are that when a landlord wishes to carry out work above the maximum figure and no recognised tenants' association exists, the landlord must take the following steps:

● obtain a minimum of two estimates for the proposed work of which one, at least, must be from a person wholly unconnected with the landlord;
● provide for each tenant (or display where it is likely to come to the attention of all tenants) a notice which describes the intended works, contains a copy of the estimates and invites comments;
● give, as a general rule, at least one calendar month's notice of the proposed works (except in emergencies);
● have regard to any observations received. This does not mean, however, that the landlord must act on the comments provided by the tenants.

If there is a recognised tenants' association, the landlord must:

- give the secretary of the association a detailed specification of the proposed works and allow a reasonable period within which the association may suggest to the landlord the names of firms from whom estimates should be obtained;
- obtain a minimum of two estimates, at least one from a person wholly independent of the landlord;
- provide a copy of the estimates to the secretary of the association;
- give each tenant a notice describing the works, summarising the estimates, offering (free of charge) the right and opportunity to inspect and (at the tenant's expense) to take copies of the detailed specifications of the intended works and estimates, and invite observations;
- have regard to the comments made by the tenants;
- unless there are urgent safety reasons, not start the works earlier than the date specified in the notice (at least one month's advance notice).

Arrears and assignment of the lease

The Landlord and Tenant (Covenants) Act 1995 restricts the ability of the landlord to recover unpaid service charges from a previous tenant, following assignment of the lease. The Act requires the landlord to notify the former tenant of the debt within six months of it falling due; the notice fixes the former tenant's liability. This liability can be increased only if the notice forewarned the tenant that the debt may be greater when the landlord serves a further notice (within three months of the final calculation) which provides details of the increased amount claimed.

Certification of the charge

Every service charge provision should allow for certification of the charge, provide the machinery by which it is to occur, and stipulate that the cost involved can be recovered as part of the charge. The most common means adopted is for the lease to require the landlord to produce certified or audited accounts as soon as practicable following the end of each financial year. The certificate should be drawn up by an expert (auditor or surveyor). Until the accounts are fully certified, the tenant will normally not be liable to pay the charge. Any time limits specified will not be strict, unless the lease makes them so.

Trust funds

The Landlord and Tenant Act 1987 imposes a trust (the landlord, managing agents or management company being the trustees) on all money paid as service charges and on any income from investments of those payments. The purpose of the trust fund is to defray the costs for which the charges were raised and, over and above this, is for the benefit of the existing tenants. The major advantage of the trust is that the money belongs to the tenants and cannot be taken by the creditors of, for example, an insolvent landlord.

The lease may contain a clause setting up the trust and this might require that any money paid by way of a service charge shall be held:

> ...in trust for the tenant until applied towards the tenant's contribution towards the costs expenses outgoings and matters mentioned...Any interest or income of funds for the time being held by managing agents or if none the landlord pending application as aforesaid shall be added to the funds.

Unless there are any express terms in the lease about the distribution of the trust fund, the entitlement of each tenant is proportional to his or her contribution to the service charge. When a lease is assigned, the outgoing tenant will not be entitled to a refund of his or her share of the fund; this will be acquired by the incoming tenant. However, the former should find out how much his or her credit in the fund is worth and, when the contract is being negotiated, ask the latter for a payment equivalent to this sum.

Reserve and sinking funds

It is wise for the lease to provide for reserve and sinking funds to cover irregular and major expenditure (e.g. the replacement of lifts, roof and heating system and refurbishment). This should ensure that flat-owners will not be faced with too large a bill at any one given time because sums will have been put aside to spread the cost over a number of years.

There are various matters that should be clarified in the lease:

- the end to which the funds can be put. The circumstances when the landlord may have recourse to the funds should be spelled out;
- where and how the money is to be kept. The landlord or management company must invest such money and the funds are held on trust for the current tenants. This ensures that the money is preserved for the tenants and accrues interest to be added to the fund;
- the accounts should be audited each year and the amount of the contribution to the fund should be assessed annually by a qualified third party. The tenant should ensure that the landlord can claim contributions only as are reasonable;
- if the landlord sells the reversion, because the money belongs to the tenants, the lease should require the trust fund to be transferred to the new buyer, who then will become the trustee;
- the expenditure predicted must be limited to the duration of the lease so as to prevent the landlord from amassing a sum for use after the lease has ended.

CHAPTER 13

MANAGEMENT AND MANAGEMENT COMPANIES

MUCH responsibility may fall on the landlord in connection with the maintenance and repair of the common parts and the provision of services. The expenditure will be recovered from the tenants' service charges. Unless the building consists of no more than two flats, normally there will need to be some system of management of the premises. While everything is going well and the building is maintained, a tenant might not be concerned about who provides the services. If the landlord, the managing agent or the management company is neglectful and the building is falling into disrepair, it becomes a serious problem and an urgent issue for the tenants. It might, under such circumstances, be better for the tenants to buy out the landlord's freehold interest and set up their own management company. There are statutory rights which entitle tenants to purchase their landlord's interest in the building (see Chapters 14 and 17).

Management might take various forms, and the more common ones are considered below.

Direct management

In this form of management, the landlord manages the building directly or through agents, carries out the obligations of maintenance and is reimbursed by the revenue from ground rents and service charges. The flat-owners have no say in the management of the building. Usually, the landlord employs a managing agent and the fees for such professional assistance are passed on to the tenants.

In relation to a block of flats, the landlord may be keen to be free of what is an onerous and unenviable responsibility and may look to one of the other forms of management.

Concurrent lease

Here the landlord grants to managing agents a concurrent lease, interposed between the landlord and the flat-owners, so that the agents acquire the rights and obligations of the landlord for the duration of the lease. The agents should be a reputable business (perhaps of surveyors) with sufficient assets to carry out their obligations. They will be responsible for collecting the ground rents and the service charges (which will include their fee). The flat-owners should, in theory, not have to worry about the shift in responsibility. The landlord remains liable on the covenants to the tenants.

Tenants' management company

In its basic form a tenants' management company draws its membership exclusively from the flat-owners and owns the freehold to the building. The original landlord, having disposed of the freehold (and, if the lease was created after 1 January 1996, having the opportunity to be released from covenants), essentially drops out of the picture. It is likely that this type of management scheme will be employed extensively under the tenants' right to buy the freehold (collective enfranchisement) given by the Leasehold Reform, Housing and Urban Development Act 1993 (see Chapter 17).

The tenants can buy an 'off the shelf' company from a firm which specialises in creating companies; they are thereby free of the administrative work involved in compiling the documentation and registering the company. It is up to the tenants what type of company to operate: a company limited by shares or by guarantee, or one of unlimited liability. As the issue of share capital and the concept of unlimited liability are out of place in a management company, it is likely that it will be a company limited by guarantee. At a later stage, if the tenants wish, they can wind up the existing company and create another one which better suits their needs.

Powers and purpose

The company will need to set out its purpose and powers in the documents which create the company: the memorandum and the articles of association.

The memorandum will disclose the following:

- the name of the company, which will usually be the name of the block or the street where the flats are situated;
- the objectives underlying the company's formation. Normally these will be to acquire the freehold, to manage, to borrow money if necessary, and to enhance the value and beneficial features of the building;
- the limitation of each member's liability to a nominal sum (e.g. £1) in case of debt or legal action being brought against the company;
- the restriction of membership to flat-owners.

The articles of association will contain further fine-tuning and will usually deal with the following:

- the recognition of the purposes as set out in the memorandum of association;
- the cessation of membership on the sale of the flat;
- the provision of voting rights for each member;
- the procedure for calling annual general meetings and extraordinary general meetings and the regulation of proceedings at such meetings;
- the election procedure for directors and the power to appoint a secretary;
- the necessity to produce annual audited accounts and the place where those accounts are to be kept.

By virtue of forming a management company, the tenants can in theory do as they please with the building. In practice, however, to avoid disputes and to achieve unanimity, much turns on strong and effective leadership within the company.

Who runs the shop?

The company must be run by someone and it must have directors and a secretary. Often the board of directors is elected by and from the flat-owners, the secretary (usually a solicitor) being appointed by the board. An auditor will also have to be employed annually. The fees for such professionals will be taken from the ground rents and service charges.

Normally it is desirable for the actual management of the building to be placed in the hands of a professional (such as an estate agent or surveyor). The manager is appointed by the board to see to repairs, maintenance and provision of services, and the collection of ground rents and service charges. If there were no manager, obviously there would be some financial savings, but the burden would be likely to fall on a few conscientious flat-owners and the risk is that the building might fall into neglect.

Once the freehold is vested in the company, the position of a flat-owner is not really affected. The value of any individual lease is untouched. The management company will become the new landlord and the covenants will continue to exist between it and the flat-owners.

It is better for all flat-owners to become members: indeed, pressure may be brought to bear on a buyer when an existing lease is assigned, in the form of a covenant in the assignment which compels him or her to become a member of the company. The disadvantage of non-membership is that the tenant has no say in the running of the company and the management of the building.

Tenants who set up such a freehold-owning management company should ensure that there is only one share/vote per flat and that, where there remain some tenants who do not wish to participate in the purchase of the freehold, their votes are left in abeyance.

The financial liabilities of the individual flat-owner will, in practice, be the same whether a member or not because all tenants will still have to pay the appropriate service charge.

Interposed management company

It is possible for a tenants' management company to exist while the landlord retains the freehold title: the company could take a lease of the whole building and covenant to carry out the landlord's obligations, and collect the service charges and ground rents. A covenant will be given which allows the landlord to terminate the company's lease if the management is not good enough. This is the same as a concurrent lease considered above, except that it is the tenants' management company which becomes the managing agent. This does not affect the individual flat-owners' leases. The landlord remains liable on the covenants in the original leases.

The flat-owners, as members of the company, have to ensure that the company can finance the day-to-day running of the block. A deposit may be required from each tenant to establish a float to finance initial repairs if the service charges previously received by the landlord are insufficient. It is usually desirable that a 'profit rental' be agreed with the landlord. This simply means that the company receives more in ground rents from the tenants than it pays out to the landlord (who would normally agree to this because the work and responsibility of managing the building have been passed on to the company). This helps to top up the company's sinking or reserve fund.

CHAPTER 14

Repair: express covenants

THE state of repair of houses and flats is a crucial issue. First, it affects the comfort and enjoyment of people living in the property. Second, it dictates the value and marketability of the house or flat. Third, it affects whether a mortgage will be granted to a prospective buyer. As regards leases of flats, disrepair brings with it other concerns for the flat-owner. The lease will place obligations on the tenant or the landlord to put and keep the property in repair. If these obligations are not met, the defaulting party can be sued for compensation by the other or be ordered by a court to carry out the repairs. The tenant, moreover, could be faced with an attempt by the landlord to put an end to (i.e. to forfeit) the lease. The landlord's costs of repairing the property will also be passed on, via the service charge, to the tenants. A prospective tenant of a flat in a rundown building might well be dissuaded from buying the lease if the service charge is likely to be high over the next few years.

Express covenants

The covenants to repair are, therefore, central to any lease of a flat. These covenants will often be explicitly stated within the lease, but in certain situations, and where the lease is silent, covenants can be read into it (i.e. they are implied).

Most repair-related obligations are expressly set out in the lease (for those that are implied, see Chapter 15). The clauses relating to repair must be carefully drafted and a variety of important matters should be addressed. These are:

● whether the burden is to be carried by the landlord or tenant;
● the nature of the covenants to be given;

- the type of disrepair to be covered;
- the subject matter of the covenants;
- the standard of repair work required.

Burden

Not surprisingly, landlords will seek to place the responsibility of repair, as far as is possible, upon the tenant. However, when the lease is of only part of a building – as is the case with a flat – it is often unrealistic to place major repair obligations on each tenant. The landlord will need to assume repair responsibilities in relation to those parts of the structure which it would be impractical for any (or all) of the tenants to maintain (for example the roof or the lift). Otherwise, difficulties and potential unfairness would arise when working out the obligations of each tenant and whether contributions are to be made by other tenants. It is likely, therefore, with multi-occupancies that the landlord will take on board major repairs and recoup the costs through the levy of a service charge. In such cases, the tenant will normally remain liable for internal repairs.

Content of the covenants

Although the wording and detail of repair covenants can vary greatly, under a typical long lease the repair covenants entered into by the tenant are:

- to keep the premises in good repair. As has been pointed out, this will normally refer only to internal repairs, with the landlord usually liable for structural and external matters. In a small block, however, the covenant may stipulate good repair both internally and externally;
- to do specified works of repair or maintenance at stated intervals, for example, to paint the outside once every three years and the inside once every five years;
- to deliver up the premises in good repair at the end of the lease or to pay a required sum if they are not.

If the premises are in disrepair at the start of the lease, a covenant by the tenant either 'to put' or 'to keep' them in repair imposes the obligation on the tenant to remedy existing defects.

The landlord may enter a covenant to repair (e.g. when the building is let to various tenants in separate flats). Again there are many ways in which this covenant could be drafted. Commonly found examples mention 'the structure and exterior' of the building, but it is necessary to appreciate that the exact wording used determines the extent of the landlord's responsibility. A straightforward example of a landlord's covenant would be:

> 'To maintain and repair and keep in good order and condition the roof foundations gutters and main structure of the building.'

Where the landlord enters a covenant to repair and a defect arises on the premises leased to the tenant, the covenant is breached when, having notice of the disrepair, the landlord fails to repair within a reasonable time. As regards defects arising on other parts of the building, the landlord's breach arises as soon as the defect appears. These rules are implied and may be altered, if both parties agree, by express wording in the covenant.

Limiting responsibility

The landlord's responsibility can be limited within the lease. This can be resisted by the prospective tenant during the initial negotiations before the lease is granted. Once the lease is granted, however, the covenants will automatically bind the next buyer of the lease and there will be little or no scope for renegotiation with the landlord. This limitation of the landlord's responsibility can be done in several ways:

- damage caused by the tenant or by unauthorised alterations may be excluded;
- the covenant may not cover all areas of the building and deliberately be insufficiently comprehensive;
- the repair obligations may be reduced by expressions such as, for example, 'the landlord's best endeavours' to keep the property in repair.

Meaning of 'repair'

The meaning of 'repair' itself is not clear cut. Repair may be defined as restoration by renewal or replacement of a part of the building, but does not include a reconstruction or renewal of the whole (or a substantial part) of the building or what can be described as an 'improvement'. Accordingly, disrepair relates to the physical state of the property and not merely a lack of amenities or inefficiency. Whether work is classified as 'repair' is, therefore, a matter of common sense and degree. The approach adopted by the courts to this question is to examine the terms of the lease in the context of the particular building, its state of repair at the commencement of the lease and the work required as a whole. Generally speaking, it makes little difference whether the tenant's covenant is expressed to keep the premises 'in repair', 'good repair', 'tenantable repair' or any other similar phrase. All that is necessary is that the covenant states the premises to be repaired, that they are to be maintained in that condition and, as regards tenant's covenants, are to be left in a state of repair at the end of the lease.

What repair covenants cover

Subject to contrary provision in the lease, a covenant to repair obliges the person making the promise to:

● put the premises into repair, even if the building is old and dilapidated. This is another reason why the tenant should commission a detailed survey before taking the lease;

● repair each part as and when it needs repair. This carries with it the making good of the decorative state of the premises;

● carry the risk of accidental damage or destruction. Hence the need for a comprehensive policy of insurance;

● within limits, correct defects in the building arising from design or construction faults. This will often form an express part of the covenant. If it does, and in order to protect the tenant, a compulsory litigation clause might be included within the lease requiring the landlord first to sue the builder and architect, as appropriate.

Subject to the wording of the covenant, the person making the promise will not normally be required to rebuild premises which are beyond repair; to replace a badly designed or constructed part of the building, unless it has fallen into disrepair; to put the property into perfect repair; or to clean drains and pipes, etc. It may also be the case that a tenant's covenant will expressly exclude liability for 'fair wear and tear' (i.e. disrepair caused by ordinary, natural causes). This does not mean, however, that the tenant can idly stand by and watch the ravages of time take their course. He or she would still be required to take reasonable action to preserve the building (e.g. treating external woodwork) and to repair consequential damage to the property following 'fair wear and tear'.

Potential problems

Both parties should pay close attention to which parts of the building are covered by the covenants to repair. There should be a clear demarcation between the responsibilities of the landlord and those of the tenant(s). The landlord might be obliged to repair the exterior, the structure or the foundations, timbers, load-bearing walls and roof, for example. Despite the common use of these expressions, some uncertainty can still arise.

First, the term 'exterior' is somewhat unclear. The covenant must make clear what it refers to. For example, is it the exterior of the whole building or the exterior of the tenant's part of the building? Does it include access ways or staircases? Does it refer only to the finish of the building or extend to what lies beneath the finish?

Second, the lease should expressly state whether 'structure' includes internal walls, partitions and windows in addition to the roofs, external walls and foundations.

Third, the listing of different parts of the building may add precision, but there is a danger that an important part may be accidentally omitted and the conclusion might then be that the omitted part has been deliberately excluded from the scope of the covenant.

A modern drafting technique is to define clearly the tenant's property within the premises section of the lease and to tie in the repairing obligations with that description. Accordingly, the lease may define the tenant's premises as being the space within the surrounding walls, floors and ceilings. It may also make specific reference to internal walls, wall finishes, windows and landlord's fixtures (e.g. sanitary fittings). If so, what is not mentioned is considered to be within the ambit of the landlord's repair covenant.

Standard of repair

Regardless of the wording of the covenant, the standard of repair is in all cases geared to the age, character and locality of the premises. The aim is to achieve a level which would make the premises reasonably fit for the occupation of a reasonably minded tenant likely to take the lease. The landlord can, however, exert a tighter control over the quality of repair. A simple method would be to insert into the covenant a clause which requires the tenant to repair 'to the satisfaction' of the landlord or the landlord's surveyor or to repair under the 'supervision' of the latter.

Decoration

As part of the repair obligations, the tenant will usually be obliged to decorate and redecorate. Sometimes the work required is set out in detail, but often the tenant's obligation is general. The timing of the work is also normally spelled out. Where the tenant is made responsible for external decoration, it will normally be required every three years; internal decoration usually to be at five-yearly intervals. Often there is the extra requirement that decoration will take place in the last year of the lease. The timing, however, can be left more open-ended. The covenant may require decoration 'as often as is reasonably necessary' or 'as often as in the opinion of the landlord is reasonably necessary but not more than once every three years'.

The landlord may give a covenant to decorate, but will then recover the cost from the tenants via the service charge. The landlord will often avoid specifying times and will reserve flexibility. A landlord's covenant could read:

'To decorate in good and workmanlike manner and with appropriate materials the exterior and common parts of the building as often as in the opinion of the landlord is reasonably necessary.'

Alterations and improvements

It is not uncommon for a tenant to seek to alter and improve the premises leased. If the lease is silent on the matter, the tenant is restricted only by planning controls, any express covenant to leave the property in repair at the end of the lease and the general law which prevents the tenant damaging the value of the landlord's freehold interest. The landlord can, generally speaking, prevent the carrying out of such works only if they seem likely to damage the property, reduce its value or adversely affect its character. It is not unusual, therefore, for the landlord to impose restrictions expressly in the lease. The tenant needs to be aware of any hidden obligations to improve, and the statutory provisions by which any restrictions imposed by the landlord can be modified.

Landlord's restrictions

It is the usual practice for the lease to include express covenants (to be made by the tenant) designed to ensure that the soundness, nature and value of the property are maintained. These covenants can vary in wording and detail, but most tend to be comprehensive in coverage. An example of this type of covenant would be:

> 'Not without the landlord's previous written consent at any time during the said term to cut maim or remove any of the main walls beams columns timbers floors or any structural parts of the demised premises or commit or permit any waste or damage to the demised premises or to the floors or timbers thereof or to make or permit to be made any alteration in or addition to the main structure or in any external decoration thereof (except as aforesaid).'

Although the reference to 'cutting and maiming' in the above covenant is somewhat old-fashioned, it is still commonly used in leases. When used, the phrase can prohibit even minor jobs such as the drilling of holes and the fixing of wall lights. The term 'alteration' embraces also 'improvement' and is directed at works which will affect the construction or the appearance of the building. This would not, however, cover small jobs such as attaching shelves, mirrors and mantelpieces, for example. The use in the covenant of the word 'additions' gives the landlord further protection because it extends to works that would normally fall outside the meaning of 'alteration'. The prevention of alterations to the external appearance would not prohibit major preservation work on the premises.

The covenant might also oblige the tenant, at the end of the lease, to restore the premises to the same condition as they were in prior to the alteration or improvement. Other restrictions could be attached, for example, to obtain the landlord's consent before applying for planning permission; to submit for approval by the landlord all plans and specifications; and to pay the landlord an indemnity for any damage and liability incurred.

Absolute or qualified?

A covenant against alterations may be absolute (i.e. all alterations are prohibited) or qualified (i.e. prohibited except with the consent of the landlord). An absolute covenant does not require that the landlord refuse consent to the proposed works only on reasonable grounds; therefore his or her reasons for refusal cannot be challenged.

A qualified covenant will expressly refer to the need for the landlord's consent and this consent cannot (despite whatever may be said in the lease) unreasonably be withheld. However, there is nothing to stop the landlord from attaching reasonable conditions to the consent. These may, for example, require the tenant to pay compensation to the landlord for any loss and the reinstatement of the premises at the end of the lease.

Hidden obligations

Although there is no implied obligation to improve the premises, it is possible that such an obligation might be concealed within a tenant's covenant. This could occur in the following situations:

- a covenant to comply with statute law might carry with it the obligation to carry out improvements required under a particular Act of Parliament or Regulation (e.g. to put the property into a habitable condition or to have a gas vent installed);
- the performance of a covenant to repair could involve the tenant in carrying out improvements as dictated by modern building techniques and prevailing building regulations.

A buyer will have to trust in the skills of the conveyancer in order to discover such hidden pitfalls.

Statutory help

During the tenant's ownership of the flat, the covenants and their enforcement are only as effective as their wording in the lease is accurate and certain. There may be disagreement between the tenants and the landlord as to the need to repair, and the repair covenant itself may be unclear. There may also be complications as to who is to pay for any works and to what extent. If the situation cannot be resolved, the Landlord and Tenant Act 1987 offers some help. The Act gives the tenant certain limited rights:

● to have a manager appointed to take control of the building;
● to make a compulsory purchase of the landlord's freehold;
● to have the court vary the terms of a problematic or defective lease.

The Act goes some way towards helping tenants who experience problems with their landlord. The rights given to the tenants by this Act are intended to be used when a tenant faces serious disrepair problems and nightmare landlords. However, exercising these rights involves going to court, which can be an expensive and lengthy process. It will also further aggravate a tenant's relations with the landlord. It is likely that the law will be changed to toughen sanctions on rogue landlords and to simplify the process of enforcing tenants' rights.

Appointment of a manager

The 1987 Act introduced a new and relatively simple procedure whereby two or more tenants can apply to the county court for an order appointing a manager to take over control of the premises from the landlord and/or to act as a receiver of ground rents and service charges. The basic idea is that, when a landlord is in default, a manager can assume responsibility for the building and rectify the default.

There must be two or more flats in the block for the right to arise, and the landlord must not be a resident in the building, nor a housing association, trust or a local authority. Before the application for an order can be made, the tenants must, generally, serve a notice on the landlord specifying in detail the nature of the complaint and notifying the intention to apply for a manager order. The court can, however, dispense with the need to serve a tenants' notice when it is not reasonably practicable to do so (e.g. where the landlord cannot be traced).

When the breach is capable of remedy (e.g. the necessary work can be carried out), a reasonable time must be offered within which the situation can be rectified. The notice must make clear that, if the breach is remedied, no further action will be taken. Once any period specified in the notice has expired, the court can be asked to issue a management order.

An order is made where the court is satisfied that the landlord is in breach of a repair or maintenance covenant in the lease, the breach is likely to continue and it is just and convenient to make the order.

Once issued, the order may be permanent, of limited duration or suspended in effect. It may, however, be revoked or varied subsequently at the request of either the landlord or the tenants. The order will not only appoint a named manager, but also provide for the manager's remuneration and state the general functions which are to be carried out. The payment to the manager might be jointly shared by the landlord and the tenants. The manager's function will include repair, maintenance and insurance. The tenants can register the order under the Land Charges Act 1972 or the Land Registration Act 1925, as appropriate, in order to protect it against any new buyer of the freehold.

The cost of obtaining a management order is prohibitive and offers little assistance where the landlord has insufficient funds to finance the repairs, etc. The order, however, still has value because it can be followed by an acquisition order allowing the tenants to make a compulsory purchase of the freehold.

Acquisition orders

The 1987 Act allows long leaseholders to purchase (without the landlord's consent) the freehold, but generally only when there is an exceptional case of neglect and abuse, and when the building is in a severe state of disrepair. This, however, often makes the acquisition a singularly unattractive bargain to enter into.

The court may make an acquisition order only if it is satisfied that it is appropriate and either:

• the landlord is in breach of the obligations concerning repair, maintenance, insurance or management of the premises; that the breach is likely to continue; and the appointment of a manager would not be an adequate remedy; or,

● for the three years preceding the application a manager order was in force.

To apply to the court, the tenants must be long leaseholders in a block which contains at least two flats and in which the landlord is not resident. In addition, at least 50 per cent of the internal floor space of the building (excluding common parts) must be used for residential purposes. The qualifying tenants must, moreover, constitute a two-thirds majority of the flat-owners in the building. Usually, a notice needs to be served on the landlord declaring the proposed application. The court, however, enjoys a discretion to make a compulsory purchase order even if no notice was given or the notice given was in some way defective. The order can be made even if the landlord cannot be found.

The tenants must nominate a person(s) or company to whom the property is to be conveyed, and the terms of the purchase should be agreed between the landlord and tenants. If the parties cannot agree the terms, a body known as the Leasehold Valuation Tribunal (consult the telephone directory to find the one nearest you) works out the terms for them. The basis for this must be what is fair and reasonable. If they cannot agree a price, it will be set by the court according to the open market value of the premises in its current condition (reduced to take account of there being no vacant possession because the flats are occupied). Once granted, the order ends any interest the landlord held in the premises.

Variation of leases

It is possible that the lease as drafted is defective in some way (e.g. it does not adequately cover repair). Unless the tenant and landlord agree to change the lease, it is necessary to go to court for the defect to be corrected. Before the 1987 Act, any variation of a lease proved to be a costly adventure because, unless the landlord consented, it had to be done via the High Court. Moreover, there was no method which readily catered for the variation of more than one lease at one time.

The Act introduced a fundamental change by allowing the county court to amend a defective lease on the request of either the tenant or the landlord without the consent of the other party. The right to apply for a variation extends to both tenants and landlords. The grounds on which an application may be based are that the defective lease fails to make satisfactory provision on one or more of the following matters:

- the repair and maintenance of the flat or the building;
- the insurance of the premises;
- the repair and maintenance of any installations and/or the provision of any services reasonably necessary to ensure that the occupiers have a reasonable standard of accommodation;
- the recovery of expenditure incurred for the benefit of the other party (e.g. insurance, service charges and legal expenses);
- the computation of the service charge payable under the lease.

Tenants should be aware that any variation which increases the obligation of the landlord is likely to result in a higher service charge levied on them.

Multiple variations are available to cover the situation where the tenants share the same landlord (even if the flats are in different buildings). This is so even if the leases are not identical.

Before the court can make a single order varying two or more leases (whether or not in the same building), the application must be supported by at least 75 per cent of the parties concerned and not opposed by more than 10 per cent. If there are fewer than nine leases involved, all or all but one of those tenants must consent.

The court can vary the lease(s) as it sees fit (but cannot terminate the landlord's choice of insurer or right to nominate one). There are, however, no guidelines to help the court's decision to vary. The general rule is that a variation order will be made unless it would be unreasonable to grant the order or would substantially prejudice the landlord or the tenant.

Any variation order binds the parties to the lease(s). A memorandum of any variation made will, usually, be endorsed on the lease(s).

CHAPTER 15

FITNESS, REPAIR AND SAFETY

IN A block of flats, the landlord usually retains possession and control of the common parts and will covenant for their repair and maintenance. The tenant will then be responsible for the maintenance and repair of the individual flat concerned. As regards those flats not in a block, the liability to maintain and repair both the building and the flat traditionally rests on the shoulders of the tenant.

In addition to those covenants which are explicitly stated in the lease, there are a variety of obligations imposed by the general law which are not. Many of these obligations will be imposed on the landlord. This chapter looks at the issues of repair and safety, and describes briefly what safeguards the law provides to a tenant.

Fitness and disrepair

The problem of unfit housing is acute in the UK. Although the problem seems to be worst in London, in most big cities properties appear to be falling into disrepair faster than existing disrepair can be remedied. The preservation of housing stock is clearly of social importance. The public interest suffers if repairs are not carried out because buildings then decay and become dilapidated. The courts and Parliament have, therefore, gradually introduced laws which place some obligations on the landlord to maintain and repair.

Although the general rule of *caveat emptor* ('let the buyer beware') applies to flats – i.e. a person buying a flat is offered no guarantee about its state, and has to perform his or her own tests to check that it is satisfactory – it does give way in certain and limited circumstances recognised by the courts and Parliament. Irrespective of what is said in the lease, certain obligations are imposed on the landlord by law. The only obligation imposed by law upon the tenant is to use the premises in 'a tenant-like manner' and not to commit 'waste'. This could make the tenant liable for causing wilful or negligent damage and, moreover, places the responsibility for minor flat maintenance upon the tenant.

The somewhat hesitant progress made by the courts towards establishing a basic standard of habitation under a residential lease has been achieved by applying the laws of negligence and nuisance and also by reading into residential leases certain contractual obligations on the part of the landlord.

The Landlord and Tenant Act 1985

This Act offers some protection for tenants who pay a ground rent which does not exceed £80 per year in London and £52 per year elsewhere. It implies a condition on the landlord's part that the property is fit for human habitation at the start of the lease and that it will be kept in such condition throughout the lease. The protection is, however, severely limited because it does not apply to leases of three years or longer, or where the tenant is obliged by covenant to put the property into a condition reasonably fit for human habitation.

The 1985 Act imposes further obligations on the landlord as regards leases for fewer than seven years. Provided that the landlord has been notified of the disrepair, he or she is then subject to an implied covenant:

- to keep in repair the structure and exterior (including drains, gutters and external pipes) of the whole building;
- to keep in repair and proper working order the installations for the supply of water, gas, electricity, sanitation and heating.

The obligation of the landlord extends not only to the flats let but also to the common parts. The landlord cannot contract out of or otherwise sidestep this duty. However, the duty does not extend to repairs attributable to the tenant's fault or which arise because of fire, flood or inevitable accident. The standard of repair required varies according to the age, locality and character of a particular property. The landlord has the right to inspect the premises on giving 24 hours' written notice. Local authorities have wide powers under the Housing Act 1985 to require a landlord to carry out repairs (see pages 169-72).

Defective Premises Act 1972

This Act imposes on a builder, architect and others involved a duty to build or extend premises properly. The requirement is that the work is done in a workmanlike or professional manner with proper materials. If the property is not fit for habitation when completed, the tenant may recover damages. This duty does not apply (and is not necessary) if the premises are covered by a National House Building Council (NHBC)* guarantee (see Chapter 7).

Control of Pollution Act 1974

This Act regulates noise pollution and gives the local authority the power, if a tenant makes a complaint to the environmental health officer, to issue an 'abatement notice' in respect of any noise amounting to a nuisance. The notice will be served on the person responsible for the nuisance and will require the nuisance to be terminated. Failure to comply with the notice is a criminal offence. If the local authority declines to act, the individual can apply to the magistrates' court for an abatement notice.

In the context of landlord-tenant relations, the landlord of a building in which the lifts make an excessive noise and disturb the tenants would be within the scope of the Act. Moreover, the Act may be used by one tenant against another to stop noise and disturbance. It would be a case of informing the environmental health officer and hoping that the complaint was acted upon. In addition, there might be local by-laws which control noise emanating from, for example, stereo systems, car alarms and animals (e.g. barking dogs). The environmental health officer should be able to provide details of such local laws.

Quiet enjoyment

The covenant of quiet enjoyment, which is implied into every lease, may also help in maintaining the quality of the premises. A landlord who, for example, undertakes to maintain the roof of a building, but fails to keep it watertight, will be in breach of the covenant for repair and also that for quiet enjoyment if the tenant's flat is affected. It would be similar if, in winter, the landlord failed to lag a water-pipe which was within his or her control, and the pipe burst causing damage to the tenant's premises.

There would be a clear breach of the covenant (and possibly it would constitute the criminal offence of harassment of tenants) if the landlord intentionally disconnects the tenant from mains services. The tenant may initiate civil proceedings in the county court and seek compensation or an injunction.

Safety in the home

The home is a potentially hazardous place. Countless domestic accidents occur each year and most accidents involving children arise in the confines of the family home. As a general rule, it is the tenant (and not the landlord) who is liable for any injury happening on the leased premises. There are, however, some circumstances where the landlord, or someone else, will be liable. Some of the exceptions to the general rule have been created by the courts, while others arise from Acts of Parliament.

Contractual duty of care

A duty of care is imposed on the landlord of a block of flats to preserve the amenities and the common parts of the building enjoyed by the tenant. The landlord is, therefore, under a duty to take reasonable care to keep such things as lifts, rubbish chutes and stairways safe and efficient. An aggrieved tenant can apply to the court for an order compelling the landlord to carry out whatever repairs are appropriate; if loss is suffered, the tenant can seek financial compensation.

This duty can offer redress for the tenant who suffers physical injury due to the unsafe condition of the landlord's part of the building. A tenant who is hurt, for example, by a fall on a dilapidated staircase or by tripping over a loose carpet in an unlit entrance hall is likely to recover compensation for breach of this contractual duty. The duty extends not only to hidden defects, but also to those which are obvious. A landlord could be liable, therefore, for the failure to clean a snow-covered step or an icy path. Persons other than the tenant (e.g.

family – even if living in the flat – and visitors) will not have a contract with the landlord and must rely instead on the law of negligence.

Liability in negligence

Irrespective of any contractual obligation, the law of negligence places on the landlord a duty to take care and expects him or her to act as a 'reasonable' landlord. If there is a breach of this duty, the landlord's liability will extend to all those who are reasonably foreseeable as being affected by the negligence (the tenant, the tenant's family and visitors, for example).

The law of negligence has an important function when damage arises from disrepair of parts of the building retained by the landlord. If the landlord, for example, retains responsibility for service ducts and the roof, but fails to prevent an infestation of vermin in the ducts, to clear a gutter or to repair a down-spout, the tenant could recover compensation from the landlord for any damage to property arising from such failure. In limited circumstances, the landlord might, moreover, be held liable for damage caused by a third party. An example of this is where the landlord controls a security system within the building which fails (alarms have been ineffectively installed or the porter falls asleep) and, as a result, thieves and vandals enter a flat and cause damage. In this situation the landlord might be found liable in negligence.

If the landlord is the builder, he or she might be liable under the general law of negligence for dangerous defects in the design or construction of the flat which cause injury to a tenant. This duty is designed to ensure that occupiers and visitors are reasonably safe. If the landlord is not the builder, there might still be liability under the Defective Premises Act 1972 (see page 168).

Where the landlord retains control over any part of the building (lifts, entrance hall, forecourt and other common parts), he or she will be regarded as an occupier of those parts. The tenant will be regarded as the occupier of the flat. Under the Occupiers Liability Act 1957, an occupier owes all visitors a 'common duty of care', that is, a duty to make anyone who is lawfully there safe in using the premises. The degree of safety that an occupier has to ensure is higher for children than for adults: the landlord must be prepared for children to be less careful. If the landlord has ceased to be an occupier (i.e. the whole building has been leased), the burden will fall on each individual tenant or the tenants' management company. A more limited duty is owed by an occupier to a trespasser under the Occupiers Liability Act 1984.

The landlord may attempt to avoid liability in negligence by displaying an exclusion notice (i.e. a statement that he or she accepts no responsibility for loss or injury incurred on the premises howsoever caused). Such notices are ineffective as regards death and personal injury. With respect to damage to property, they are effective only provided that they can be shown to be reasonable.

Liability in nuisance

The law of nuisance covers a multitude of sins and may enable the tenant to sue the landlord where the latter unreasonably interferes with the former's use or enjoyment of the premises.

When a landlord leases property in a state which constitutes a nuisance (e.g. a leaking pipe or a defective roof), and this results in loss or injury to the tenant or his or her property, the landlord will be liable. Where the nuisance is caused by an act of the tenant, the landlord will not usually be liable. This means that if the landlord remains liable under the lease for repair and maintenance of the part of the building which contains the source of the nuisance, he or she will be liable for that nuisance. Hence the landlord will generally be responsible for a nuisance (e.g. by noise, fumes, damp and infestation) arising from the part of the building retained by him or her. If the obligation to repair or maintain falls on the tenant and extends to the source of the nuisance, the landlord will not normally be liable. Similarly, the landlord will not usually be liable to a tenant for a nuisance caused by another tenant.

As with negligence, the tenant would need to establish fault on the part of the landlord and demonstrate loss (i.e. interference with comfort and/or physical damage or injury). Unlike negligence, only the tenant can commence legal proceedings. The tenant would, therefore, have to sue on behalf of family members or visitors.

Rylands v Fletcher

A further remedy, akin to nuisance, exists under what lawyers call the rule in *Rylands v Fletcher*, which makes a landlord liable for things brought on to the land (e.g. stored water, oil and even electricity) which then escape and cause damage. A tenant could recover under this rule even though there is no fault on the landlord's part. It is strict liability and probably (there are conflicting views) extends not only to damage to property, but also to personal injury.

Health and Safety at Work Act 1974

Although those who drafted this Act may not have intended it, aspects of this legislation have been applied to residential leases. A duty is imposed on the person who has control of the premises 'in connection with the carrying on by him of a trade, business or other undertaking'. This embraces an individual landlord (or a management company) of a block of flats. The duty is to take reasonable care to ensure that all means of access and exit on the premises, together with plant and machinery provided for use on the premises, are safe and without risk to health. Liability could arise as regards unsafe lifts and the dangerous state of common parts, for example.

If the landlord ignores the repair and maintenance of such amenities as lifts, stairways and electrical installations in the common areas, the tenant may request the local authority to serve an 'improvement notice' on the landlord which will compel the latter to discharge the obligations. Failure to comply with the notice constitutes a criminal offence.

New Health and Safety Regulations are introduced from time to time. The Management Health and Safety at Work Regulations 1992, for example, impose stringent rules (and harsh penalties) on the managers of property concerning the safety of employees (e.g. porters, cleaners and maintenance workers) and others on the premises. This could render a landlord liable to anyone injured on the premises. Similarly, the Gas Safety (Installation and Use) Regulations 1994 are designed to protect tenants from carbon monoxide poisoning from the faulty installation and use of gas appliances. This makes landlords responsible for making sure that gas appliances are maintained in good order and checked for safety (by a registered CORGI fitter) at least every 12 months. This responsibility extends only to appliances and pipe-work 'owned' by the landlord. This entails that if the landlord provides gas heating as part of the services of the flat or common parts, the Regulations will apply. The legal position is more uncertain where there is no block of flats and each tenant is responsible for his or her own gas appliances. It would be necessary to show that the landlord owned the appliance. Although it could be argued that a gas fire and boiler were landlord's fixtures (but not a gas cooker and refrigerator), it is doubtful whether the courts would extend the landlord's liability to tenants with long leases.

The Defective Premises Act 1972

The Act places an obligation on the landlord to take reasonable care to prevent personal injury or damage to property which might be caused by defects (which exist at the commencement of the lease or which emerge subsequently) in the premises leased. This obligation, however, is limited to where the landlord:

- has entered a repairing covenant or has reserved the right to enter and carry out repairs;
- knew or ought to have known (e.g. by inspection) of the disrepair;
- has failed to take reasonable care in respect of repair and maintenance.

Where a tenant is injured by tripping over an uneven paving stone or when a communal garden wall collapses, for example, the landlord will be liable under the Act. This is so even if the danger had been caused by the faulty repair work of a previous landlord or tenant. The liability of the landlord, moreover, cannot be excluded by any 'exclusion' notice or term in the contract.

The Environmental Protection Act 1990

This Act, under which a local authority may intervene in cases of alleged housing disrepair, offers a further avenue of redress to the tenant. Any premises that are in such a condition as to be prejudicial to health (for example, defective wiring, ill-fitting windows, blocked drains, extensive damp and mould) or to constitute a nuisance (an unreasonable interference with the tenant's enjoyment and use of the flat) fall within the definition of a statutory nuisance within the Act.

This Act deals with the consequences of the defect rather than with the defect itself: there has to be a health hazard arising from the defect complained of. Take, for example, a defective roof. The disrepair is not itself the statutory nuisance, but if the roof leaks, and the water damages the tenant's flat, this would become the nuisance. The Act, therefore, assumes importance where the landlord retains control or possession of some part of the building and the damage emanates from that part.

The tenant has two possible ways of getting redress. First, he or she can go direct to the magistrates' court for a 'nuisance order' (i.e. a summons) against the landlord. A hearing will then be conducted and, if the court finds in favour of the tenant, an abatement order will be issued. Legal aid is not available for this private court action, but costs can be awarded against the landlord and a compensation order can be made by the court.

Alternatively, the tenant may complain to the Environmental Health Department of the local authority and is entitled to have the complaint investigated. If it is found that the defects amount to a statutory nuisance, the local authority will serve an abatement notice on the landlord. This notice will specify the nuisance and may require the landlord to carry out specified repairs. Subject to a landlord's appeal, a failure to comply by the date set in the notice will constitute a criminal offence. The local authority has the alternative option to do the work itself and invoice the landlord for the work.

Housing Act 1985: local authority action

The Housing Act 1985 sets out to ensure that buildings (including flats) used for residential purposes meet certain basic standards. The general test is that the premises must be fit for human habitation (see below). Houses and flats which are unfit should be repaired or withdrawn from domestic use. The Act gives local authorities wide-ranging powers to deal with disrepair and poor-quality housing.

The local authority is obliged to inspect its area from time to time in order to decide whether any action under the 1985 Act is necessary. The government can compel a local authority to carry out this inspection if necessary. The authority does not have to act on the request of local residents.

When faced with unfit accommodation, the authority has a number of courses of action available. It is also given broad powers to enter premises to carry out its inspection or, where relevant, repairs.

The Act covers several other areas which are of related concern:

- the prevention of housing already in serious disrepair from deteriorating further;
- actions to remedy conditions which are physically interfering with the comfort of the tenant;
- slum-clearance projects;
- the declaration of improvement areas;
- the award of improvement grants.

Some of these provisions may involve a tenant being temporarily or permanently displaced from the flat and, accordingly, a scheme for re-housing and compensation is contained in the Act.

Unfit for habitation?

Many of the Act's provisions depend on the flat being unfit for human habitation. The Act stipulates that a flat is deemed to be unfit if, in the opinion of the local authority, it is not reasonably suitable for occupation on one or more of certain prescribed grounds. These are unsoundness; serious disrepair; damp; unsatisfactory internal arrangement; poor ventilation; inadequate water supply, drainage or sanitary provisions; and lack of cooking facilities. It should be appreciated that there is no legal requirement that the flat have a bathroom, inside toilet, hot water system or modern wiring system.

The required standards of fitness are not particularly high, but a major defect in one of the prescribed areas, or several small defects, may amount to the flat being regarded as unfit for occupation. The disrepair or defect must either prevent the flat from functioning as a residence or constitute a danger or serious inconvenience to the tenants.

Once the flat is deemed unfit, the responsibility for the next move lies with the local authority. Two ways of proceeding are open to the authority: a 'repair' notice and a 'time and place' notice.

The 'repair' notice

If the authority determines that the best way to proceed is through repair, then a 'repair' notice will be served. Such a notice is appropriate where the flat can be rendered fit for habitation at a reasonable cost. The repair notice can also be employed where, although not technically unfit, the premises are in such state of disrepair that they materially interfere with the personal comfort of the tenants (see page 172).

The notice is served on the person having 'control' of the flat. As regards a long lease, this will generally be the tenant. If the whole building is in disrepair, then the notice should be served on all long leaseholders.

In calculating whether the work can be undertaken at a reasonable cost, the local authority (and, if there is dispute, the county court) must have regard to the value of the flat in its present state, the expenditure required and the value of the premises when repaired.

The local authority's notice must specify the works necessary to render the premises fit. The authority may order the repair of the shell of the building, the treatment of rotten timbers, and the construction of a new bathroom, for example. Sufficient details must be provided so that a builder can offer an estimate of cost. A 'reasonable' period is given in which the works are to be carried out.

Depending upon the repair covenants in the lease, it may be that the tenant will have to foot the bill. Although the days of guaranteed home-improvement grants have now gone, a local authority renovation grant may be available to help with the cost. Otherwise, the tenant may have to raise a loan or take out a second mortgage.

The repair notice allows the flat-owner 21 days within which to appeal to the county court. If there is no appeal, and the notice is not complied with, the authority may itself enter the flat and carry out the works, for which it will recover the costs from the tenant or the landlord depending on their respective repair and maintenance obligations. Failure to comply is also a criminal offence.

The time and place notice

If the flat cannot be repaired at a reasonable cost, the authority must take more stringent measures. A notice must be served on all persons having an interest in the flat (landlord, tenants and mortgagees, for example) which states the time and the place where the future of the premises is to be discussed. The time must not be less than 21 days from the service of the notice. The purpose of this meeting is to induce the tenant or landlord voluntarily to undertake the necessary repairs.

If no such undertaking emerges, the authority will seek assurance that the premises will not be used as a residence; make a demolition or closure order (demolition is inappropriate when it is only one flat that is unfit); or initiate compulsory purchase proceedings of the whole building. There is a right to appeal against the authority's decision.

A tenant who is made homeless by such an order may have rights to re-housing and to compensation.

Substantial disrepair

A tenant can complain to the local authority that the flat is in a state of disrepair for which the landlord is responsible and that either substantial repairs are necessary to bring it up to a reasonable standard or its condition interferes materially with the personal comfort of the tenant. Substantial repairs could be major repairs or a number of smaller repairs. A notice alleging interference with personal comfort may be issued only at the request of a tenant with a lease of less than 21 years remaining at the time of the notice.

If the authority is satisfied on either point, it has the discretion to serve a repair notice on the landlord. This is a power, not a duty to act. The premises must be capable of being repaired at a reasonable cost; i.e. the flat or building must be worth the cost of the repairs.

Clearance areas

Slum clearance is a last-resort method of dealing with large sections of unfit housing. It is a potential threat to tenants in a rundown area. The idea of area clearances is that the local authority purchases the buildings and then demolishes them. Certain pre-conditions must be satisfied, however, before the declaration of a clearance area can be made:

- houses in the area must be unfit for human habitation or be dangerous or injurious to the health of the occupiers because of the bad arrangement of the premises;
- other buildings in the area must also be dangerous or injurious;
- the best way of dealing with the problem must be to demolish all the buildings within the area (it is policy to try and exclude fit buildings from the clearance area);

- the local authority must have the finances to carry out the programme;
- the local authority must be able to re-house any displaced occupiers.

Before the properties are subject to compulsory purchase, there will usually be a public inquiry into the proposals. Tenants and other occupiers will be entitled to re-housing and compensation.

Compulsory improvement

There are two other situations in which a local authority may require the improvement of a dwelling by a tenant, even if it is not in a state of disrepair and unfitness. These are where the premises are in a local authority 'action' or 'improvement' area and the property is lacking in standard amenities (for example, a fixed bath or shower, a wash-basin and a sink supplied with hot and cold water, and a toilet). The flat must have been built or converted since 3 October 1961 and the dwelling must be capable of being brought up to standard at reasonable cost. A local authority grant might be available to assist a tenant.

Grant aid

It is difficult to state accurately the type, extent and amount of financial assistance which is available from a local authority, because the schemes are constantly being revised and are governed by complex regulations. It is essential to check the schemes and regulations that are current at the time of the application. No work should be carried out prior to the application being considered. In order to claim a grant, the applicant must be either the landlord or a lease-holder with a fixed term which has at least another five years to run.

The grant system was changed dramatically in 1989, and the following is merely a brief introduction to the types of grant available:

- renovation grants to improve or repair a house or flat. The grant is means-tested (i.e. it depends on the financial status of the applicant) and the test varies according to whether the claimant is a landlord or tenant;

173

- common-parts grants are designed to finance the improvement or repair of common parts in a building which contains flats. The claimant can be the landlord or any tenant in the building, and the grant is dependent upon at least three-quarters of the flats in the building being occupied;
- disabled-facilities grants are to provide assistance with the costs of making the property suitable for a disabled occupier;
- multi-occupation grants (e.g. relating to a block of flats) are available to a tenant to make possible the installation of basic amenities, fire escapes and related repairs;
- minor grants are available to cover, for example, insulation costs.

Coal-mining subsidence

The Coal Mining Subsidence Act 1991 requires the 'responsible person' (e.g. the Coal Authority) to notify owners and occupiers (i.e. landlords and tenants) of any land which may be affected by mining proposals. This notice will highlight the possibility that the property might be affected by coal-mining subsidence and alert the landlord and tenant to keep a watch for tell-tale signs (cracked plaster and sticking doors).

If damage owing to coal-mining subsidence occurs, property-owners (including holders of long leases) can apply to have the premises repaired or may be entitled to compensation.

The claim

A claim for subsidence damage should be made as soon as any damage occurs. The latest time for making a claim is six years from when it was reasonable for the damage to have been discovered. The claim should be against the mine-owner, who will then inspect the property. Generally, the mine-owner will carry out or authorise any necessary repairs according to a previously agreed itemised schedule of repairs. The repairs will, however, be carried out only once the land is stable, and what is termed a 'stop notice' can be issued to delay permanent repairs. Emergency works can be carried out prior to the claim, but the mine-owner must be informed as soon as possible what works have been carried out and the reasons for such works.

Compensation

In exceptional circumstances, the mine-owner will, instead of making repairs, pay compensation. Such circumstances include:

● where repairs are not physically possible because the building is too badly damaged;
● where the cost of repairs is significantly greater than the reduction in the value of the property;
● where the condition of the property is such that it is impossible to repair in isolation the damage attributable to subsidence.

Other liabilities

Apart from repair and compensation, the mine-owner will have to pay for the claimant's legal and surveying expenses as well as costs (postage, phone calls, etc.) associated with the claim. If the property becomes unsafe or uninhabitable because of the subsidence damage, the claimant will also be entitled to receive payment for equivalent alternative accommodation. The responsibility of looking after the house while the owner is in alternative accommodation rests with the mine-owner, so the latter will be obliged to keep the property secure and weatherproof. The mine-owner will also pay reasonable moving and storage expenses, and excess living costs (e.g. light, heat and travel costs).

If the property cannot be sold because of subsidence damage, the mine-owner might be required to purchase it at its undamaged value. The claimant must, however, demonstrate a good reason for selling the property (e.g. a new job in a different area). When the property has to be demolished, the mine-owner must either rebuild it or pay compensation based on the full market value of the property. An extra 'home loss' payment may also be provided.

Dispute resolution

While many disputes will be settled without major problems, the claimant has the right to take the case before the Lands Tribunal★. Arbitration is, however, a quicker, cheaper and less formal way of settling disputes. Two independent arbitration schemes have been set up by the Chartered Institute of Arbitrators★ to deal specifically with subsidence claims:

- the Householder's Arbitration Scheme, which, on the payment of £50 (plus VAT), will deal with uncomplicated disputes;
- the General Arbitration Scheme, which, on the payment of £75 (plus VAT), caters for more complex disputes.

CHAPTER 16

ENDING THE LEASE

WHILE the lease is in existence the tenant is, for all intents and purposes, the owner of the flat. The landlord has no right to enter the premises, unless it is to follow up a right given by the lease (e.g. to view the state of repair) and cannot sell to anyone else the right to occupy the flat. As regards leases created before 1 January 1996, moreover, the original parties remain liable to observe the covenants throughout the duration of the tenancy. As pointed out earlier (see Chapter 9), with respect to leases granted after that date, the Landlord and Tenant (Covenants) Act 1995 allows the tenant to be automatically discharged from covenants following assignment of the lease, and the landlord to apply for such release on the assignment of the reversion. It is, therefore, important to know how and when a lease is terminated.

A lease can be brought to an end in a variety of ways. A fixed-term lease (the type of lease with which this book is concerned) will normally continue until the term of years expires. It is, however, possible for the lease to be terminated prematurely either by the landlord forfeiting the lease for breach of covenant by the tenant, or by one party buying out the other's interest. When the tenant sells or gives up the lease to the landlord this is known as surrender; when the tenant buys the landlord's freehold, this is called merger. Each of these methods is described below, along with safeguards provided for the tenant by Parliament.

Expiry of time

A fixed-term lease (i.e. one that runs for a specified number of years) must, at some stage, expire. The lease comes to an automatic end on the expiry of the period agreed; this is known as effluxion. There is no need for any notice to be served and, at common law, the landlord will be entitled to possession (i.e. to evict the tenant) without further ado. The exercise of this right by the landlord has, however, been modified by Parliament.

When drafted, the lease will specify the number of years it is to run for and stipulate the commencement date of the term. The exact date of expiry, if not expressly stated, can easily be calculated. So, for example, a lease granted for 38 years from 4 January 1960 will not automatically expire until the first moments of 5 January 1998. Although the landlord may wish the tenant to vacate the property after midnight on 4–5 January, the tenant will, thanks to the provisions of the Landlord and Tenant Act 1954 (see below), normally be allowed to remain in lawful occupation. This is known as security of tenure.

Parliamentary safeguards for the tenant

There are various measures that Parliament has taken to protect the tenant from eviction at the end of the term of the lease.

The Landlord and Tenant Act 1954

This Act protects long leaseholders after their lease has expired. Most long leases will fall within the protection of the Act.

Scope A lease will fall within the protection of this Act, which is valid until 15 January 1999, provided that it was granted before 1 April 1990; it is a long lease (i.e. granted originally for over 21 years) and is at a low ground rent (i.e. one less than two-thirds of the former rateable value of the flat). For these purposes rent does not include service charges and insurance premiums. In addition, the tenant must occupy the premises wholly or in part as a residence. Moreover, the lease must not contain a clause prohibiting protection under the 1954 Act.

One important exception to this protection is where the flat is in a non-purpose-built block and the landlord has a flat in the same building. In such a case, the tenant would have no security of tenure under the Act.

The protection The importance of the 1954 Act is that it allows a tenant to stay in possession of the flat after the lease has expired, so the landlord can get a court order for possession only on one or more of the following grounds, namely where:

- the tenant has failed to pay rent or observe the terms of the lease concerning insurance;
- the tenant has caused a nuisance or an annoyance, or has been convicted of using the premises (or allowing them to be used) for an illegal or immoral purpose (e.g. as a brothel);
- the landlord, the landlord's adult children, parents or parents-in-law reasonably require the flat for their own occupation;
- there is suitable alternative accommodation available for the tenant;
- the landlord proposes, for the purpose of re-development after the expiry of the lease, to demolish or reconstruct the whole or a substantial part of the premises.

If the landlord fails to establish any of the prescribed grounds for possession, the tenant is entitled to remain in possession (i.e. to continue living in the flat). By a leap of legal logic, the result is that the tenant will have a status of irremovability and pay a periodic rent as agreed or as determined by a person known as the rent officer. A new periodic tenancy will automatically arise unless and until the landlord can obtain a possession order from the court.

Strategies for the landlord In order to prevent the protection under the 1954 Act arising at the end of a long lease, the landlord must take certain steps. A notice of termination must be served on the tenant at least 6 months, but less than 12 months, in advance. This notice must state the ground for possession upon which the landlord intends to rely. If the tenant continues to live in the flat beyond the expiry of the lease, or serves a counternotice resisting the landlord's claim, the landlord has to apply to the court for a possession order. If the landlord is successful, the tenancy will be deemed to have ended on the contractual expiry date and the tenant evicted. Where the landlord fails to establish a sufficient reason, the lease will continue after its expiry date on new terms either as agreed or ordered by the court.

For the tenant, this is not as good as having a fixed-term lease, but it is better than being made homeless. A shrewd tenant may be able to negotiate a capital sum in return for leaving the premises. This might be the only way the landlord can regain possession. Alternatively, the tenant might be able to negotiate a new lease from this vantage point.

Where the landlord does not wish to recover possession, it may be agreed that the tenant should have a new tenancy. For this there is, generally, no need to go to court. The landlord will serve a notice on the tenant which contains proposals for the terms of the new periodic tenancy. If terms cannot be agreed, then application will need to be made to the court, which will then work out the contractual provisions and attempt to strike a reasonable balance between the interests of both parties.

It may be that the tenant wishes to quit the flat at the end of the long lease. In this case, the Act requires that one month's notice be given to the landlord. This notice can be timed so as to expire on the exact date on which the long lease expires.

The Local Government and Housing Act 1989

The Local Government and Housing Act replaces the 1954 Act in relation to leases entered into after 1 April 1990. Moreover, from 15 January 1999, even those tenancies created before 1 April 1990 will be automatically brought within the 1989 Act. The 1954 Act will, therefore, have no role to play from the beginning of 1999.

To fall within the 1989 Act, the lease must be long and must be at a low ground rent. The same rules apply as under the 1954 Act, except that as regards tenancies entered after 1 April 1990, the maximum rent is £1,000 per year (Greater London) or £250 per year (elsewhere). The scheme of the new provisions is similar to that under the Landlord and Tenant Act 1954. The potential responses of the landlord and the tenant are also, essentially, the same.

The Protection from Eviction Act 1977

This Act protects all tenants of residential premises by making the unlawful eviction or harassment of the tenant a criminal offence and a civil wrong. To prove harassment, the tenant must satisfy the court (usually the magistrates' court as regards criminal cases and the county court in the context of civil proceedings) that the landlord or any other person committed acts which were likely to interfere with the peace or comfort of the occupier or withheld services reasonably required for occupation, and that these acts were intended to cause or be likely to cause the occupier to leave the premises. Examples of harassment would include threats, nuisance, intimidation, deliberate failure to do necessary repairs and changing the locks.

To lawfully evict a residential occupier the landlord must obtain an order from the court authorising his or her re-taking of possession of the flat. This is unless the landlord reasonably believes that the tenant no longer lives in the flat.

The police have the powers to prosecute for either offence, but often the task falls on the shoulders of the local authority. Many local authorities have Tenancy Relations Officers, whose function includes dealing with harassment and eviction matters. A private prosecution is also a possibility. Nevertheless, few offenders are ever prosecuted. This is because very few eviction and harassment incidents are reported, and because local authorities tend to deal with the matter without recourse to the criminal court. In addition, although the penalties potentially include imprisonment and a hefty fine, the court has a habit of imposing a low penalty on a convicted offender.

Premature ending of the lease

Forfeiture

Forfeiture, a means by which the landlord can bring the lease to a premature end when the tenant is in breach of a leasehold covenant, is considered in detail in relation to remedies for breach of covenant (see Chapter 9). Tenants cannot forfeit if the landlord is in breach. Most leases contain a forfeiture or re-entry clause which allows the landlord to put an end to the lease. Forfeiture, however, is hedged with complex and technical rules and, moreover, is not often granted by the courts. The tendency of the courts is, as far as is possible, to assist the tenant and not to allow forfeiture. Although it is a means of early termination, forfeiture is an unpopular, unpredictable and often unsuccessful avenue for the landlord to pursue.

Surrender

Surrender involves the tenant giving up or selling the lease to the immediate landlord. The lease then becomes part of the landlord's reversion and is at an end. At first glance, it might be difficult to envisage why a tenant would willingly give up the lease to the landlord. It might, however, benefit the tenant in the following situations:

- where the landlord offers the tenant money;
- when the surrender of the old lease is conditional upon the landlord granting to the tenant a new and longer tenancy;
- towards the end of a long lease and when the property is in disrepair – the tenant might prefer to give up the flat voluntarily rather than defend forfeiture proceedings for breach of repair covenant.

Surrender usually occurs by negotiation. It can be express or implied:

- an express surrender must be contained in a formal deed, but no special wording is required, provided that the intention to give up the lease is made clear. There must be agreement of both parties and there must be delivery up of the premises to the landlord;
- an implied surrender can arise without a deed. There must be an act by the tenant which shows the intention to give up the lease (e.g. moving out of possession or returning keys) and the act must be accepted by the landlord.

Subject to contrary agreement, on surrender the landlord is entitled to sue the former tenant for breaches of covenant which occurred before the date of surrender. Any obligations that would arise at the end of the lease (e.g. to repair or to redecorate) do not survive surrender. The landlord might seek self-protection by inserting a condition into the contract or deed of surrender that such obligations are performed prior to surrender.

As regards sub-leases, the surrender of the head-lease will not affect their validity. The landlord will remain bound by the rights of sub-tenants. Therefore, the landlord should ensure that he or she knows of all sub-tenants and that any sub-leases are terminated (by the tenant) before accepting the surrender.

Merger

Merger is the mirror image of surrender and occurs when the tenant buys out the landlord's freehold (e.g. by exercising an option to purchase, see Chapter 17). This is not the same as collective enfranchisement (see Chapter 17) because here it is an individual and not a group of tenants buying the freehold. The general rule is that when the respective estates of landlord and tenant merge, the lease comes to an end and the landlord's reversion is said to 'drop down' and 'drown' the tenant's lease. Merger can arise only at the tenant's instigation because the landlord can never force the tenant to purchase the freehold. As with surrender, merger does not affect any existing sub-leases. A merger clause will usually be incorporated into the conveyance of the freehold (for a specimen merger clause see Chapter 8). If a merger occurs, other tenants in the building will have a new landlord (i.e. the former tenant who buys the freehold).

Disclaimer

Under the Insolvency Act 1986, the trustee in bankruptcy (i.e. the person appointed by the court to represent the debtor's interests) of a tenant may 'disclaim' the lease if it constitutes property that is not readily saleable or gives rise to a liability to pay money or perform some other onerous act. All leases will, therefore, be within the power of the trustee to disclaim. On disclaimer, the lease is ended and the bankrupt is discharged from all further liability in respect of it.

As regards leases granted before 1 January 1996, if the bankrupt is someone who had bought an existing lease of the flat from a previous owner, disclaimer will not absolve the original tenant (i.e. the previous owner) from liability under the covenants. Of course, if the bankrupt is the original tenant, then he or she will be freed from the covenants. All outstanding claims will be made against the bankrupt's assets.

In relation to leases created after 1 January 1996, the original tenant will be liable for a subsequent tenant's breaches only if the former has agreed to become a guarantor for the latter. In such a situation, on the bankruptcy of the latter and the disclaimer of the lease, the former will be discharged from further liability.

CHAPTER 17

THE RIGHT TO BUY A FREEHOLD AND RENEW A LEASE

THE Leasehold Reform, Housing and Urban Development Act 1993 (the 1993 Act) contains complex reforms which strike at the heart of the relationship between landlord and tenant. Aimed to overcome the difficulties associated with the ownership of a wasting asset – primarily the depreciation in the value of the flat and the inability to sell towards the end of the lease – these reforms allow certain tenants of flats to join together and buy the freehold reversion of the whole building (**collective enfranchisement**), and the individual tenant to obtain, on the payment of a capital sum and a nominal (peppercorn) rent, a new 90-year lease of an individual flat (**lease renewal**).

Ways of buying the freehold

Collective enfranchisement is not the only way of buying the freehold to a flat. Other methods, some of which have been discussed in earlier chapters, are listed below.

- The Landlord and Tenant Act 1987 granted statutory rights to tenants to buy the freehold where the landlord allowed the premises to fall into severe disrepair (see Chapter 14).
- Tenants can form a management company and buy the freehold from the landlord (see Chapter 13), but only when the landlord consents. It is likely that this type of management scheme will be used by groups of tenants when they participate in collective enfranchisement.
- A tenant can buy out the landlord's freehold by merger, i.e. by exercising an option to purchase (see page 204 and Chapter 16).

The idea that tenants can purchase the freehold to their premises is not new (see box on page 184). Nevertheless, it is only since 1 November 1993 that tenants of flats have had a general entitlement to buy out their landlord's interest. In addition, the right of a tenant of a private-sector flat to renew the lease represents another major development, although it has been a right enjoyed by business tenants for over 40 years and available to tenants of houses since 1967. This chapter deals first with the 1993 Act and its implications, and then with measures that tenants who do not qualify under the Act can take to buy the freehold or renew the lease.

Collective enfranchisement and lease renewal

Words of warning

The 1993 Act is complex and highly technical in language and procedure, and even solicitors are finding it difficult. The bulk and detail of the legislation are intimidating, and the process involved may prove both time-consuming and expensive. The eligibility criteria for enfranchisement are extremely tight, and many tenants will find that they do not qualify. The set procedures must be followed within the specified time limits; if they are not, the tenants can be landed with increased costs and long delays or even suffer from the application being deemed withdrawn in certain circumstances (see below). The Leasehold Enfranchisement Advisory Service*, a government-funded organisation, will advise tenants interested in either buying the freehold or renewing their lease.

The potential expense, aggravation and long-term responsibilities associated with enfranchisement can be off-putting (especially with large blocks of flats) and it is anticipated that many tenants will be content with the renewal of their leases. This is attractive in the long term, particularly if the tenant is happy with the landlord's management of the premises; moreover, further renewals may later be obtained.

The processes for both collective enfranchisement and lease renewal involve a daunting chain of notices and counternotices, and it is advisable to engage the services of a legal adviser. For enfranchisement a qualified valuer must also be used.

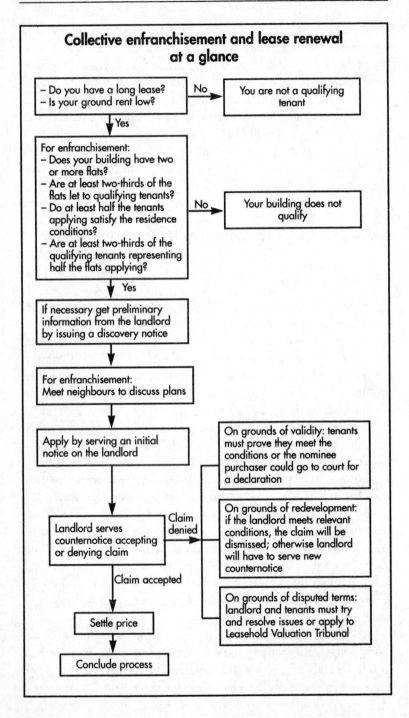

Collective enfranchisement and lease renewal
at a glance

- Do you have a long lease?
- Is your ground rent low?

No → You are not a qualifying tenant

Yes

For enfranchisement:
- Does your building have two or more flats?
- Are at least two-thirds of the flats let to qualifying tenants?
- Do at least half the tenants applying satisfy the residence conditions?
- Are at least two-thirds of the qualifying tenants representing half the flats applying?

No → Your building does not qualify

Yes

If necessary get preliminary information from the landlord by issuing a discovery notice

For enfranchisement:
Meet neighbours to discuss plans

Apply by serving an initial notice on the landlord

Landlord serves counternotice accepting or denying claim

Claim denied →

On grounds of validity: tenants must prove they meet the conditions or the nominee purchaser could go to court for a declaration

On grounds of redevelopment: if the landlord meets relevant conditions, the claim will be dismissed; otherwise landlord will have to serve new counternotice

On grounds of disputed terms: landlord and tenants must try and resolve issues or apply to Leasehold Valuation Tribunal

Claim accepted ↓

Settle price

Conclude process

Collective enfranchisement: criteria at a glance

Tenants can buy the freehold if the following conditions are satisfied (see pages 188-91 for detailed explanations):

- they have long leases (originally for more than 21 years) at a low rent;
- at least two-thirds of the flats are let to qualifying tenants;
- there are at least two flats in the building;
- no more than 10 per cent of the building is occupied for non-residential purposes (e.g. as offices);
- two-thirds of the qualifying tenants, who between them own at least half of the total number of flats in the block (see example on page 191), join in the purchase;
- at least half of the qualifying tenants have lived in their flats either for the last 12 months or for 3 out of the last 10 years.

Attractions of enfranchisement or renewal

There are a variety of reasons why long leaseholders might be tempted either to buy collectively the landlord's freehold or to take a new lease. As regards enfranchisement, the motives of the tenants could include:

- **Control** On purchasing the freehold the tenants will, for most intents and purposes, own the building in which their flats are situated, albeit normally through a nominee company. This means that through their voting rights within the company they can exert control over repairs and maintenance of the property as well as the cost and quality of services provided to the tenants.
- **Security** On enfranchisement, the tenants' company will control the grant of any new leases in the block and will be able to renew the leases of the existing tenants at a reduced price. Once a renewed lease is next sold on, the individual tenant may make a substantial gain.

As regards the right to renew, the principal benefits for an individual tenant include:

- **Independence** Unlike enfranchisement, there is no need to obtain the co-operation of other tenants. If, however, a notice is later served for enfranchisement, the pre-existing lease renewal application is suspended.
- **Security** Taking a new lease avoids the problems associated with

the old lease being a wasting asset (i.e. that it runs out). Further renewals can be obtained.

- **Management** The landlord (or where relevant the management company) will still continue to manage the building and there is no need for the tenant's involvement.
- **Cost** The price paid for renewal will tend to be similar to that payable for enfranchisement, but might be lower than the new lease will be worth in the longer term.
- **Procedure** The procedure is easier for renewal than for enfranchisement in that it is an individual making the running rather than a group. Moreover, the landlord is less likely to be opposed to renewal than to enfranchisement.

Conditions for qualification

Do the premises qualify?

Although both rights apply only to residential premises, as regards collective enfranchisement the 1993 Act sets out more elaborate conditions to be satisfied. With renewal, the straightforward rule is that, if the premises contain a 'flat', the right will apply to that flat. For these purposes, a 'flat' is defined as a separate and horizontally divided part within a building which is constructed or adapted for use as a dwelling (i.e. a home).

As regards the enfranchisement of blocks of flats, however, there are a number of further conditions to be met:

- the premises must be, in whole or in part, a self-contained building;
- the building must contain at least two flats;
- at least two-thirds of the flats must be held by qualifying tenants;
- those applying must represent at least two-thirds of the qualifying tenants and half of the flats in the building;
- the freehold to the building (or part to be purchased) must be owned by one person.

Exceptions Tenants cannot buy the freehold or renew the lease if the building is within the precinct boundary of a cathedral or on certain land owned by the National Trust.

In addition, tenants cannot buy the freehold (but can renew their leases) if:

- there are no more than four flats in a converted property and the freeholder (or an adult member of his or her family) has lived in one of the flats as his or her only or main home for the last 12 months;
- more than 10 per cent of the internal floor area of the premises, excluding common parts, is used for non-residential purposes. Therefore, many tenants who have flats above business premises will be outside the enfranchisement scheme.

Is enfranchisement voluntary?

It is important to realise that no tenant can be forced – by either the landlord or other tenants – to participate in collective enfranchisement.

- A notice to start off the process for enfranchisement must come from the tenants – i.e. the landlord cannot force them to buy the freehold.
- If a qualifying tenant decides he or she does not want to be a part of the process to buy the freehold, and the other tenants are successful in buying it, they will then become his or her new landlord, and he or she will continue to be a tenant.
- A tenant can join in the process later, but if he or she is not an assignee of a participating tenant, the agreement of all the existing participating tenants is required. The nominee purchaser must be notified. If the tenant is the assignee of a participating tenant, he or she has the right to join in the process, but the nominee purchaser must be notified within 14 days of the assignment of the desire to join in.

Who qualifies?

Not all tenants have the right to join in and buy the freehold or to obtain a new lease. Tenants of a charitable housing trust, tenants of business premises and sub-tenants whose sub-leases were created in breach of a covenant in the head-lease fall outside the 1993 Act. Such tenants are disentitled and can claim neither right. Those who own qualifying leases on more than two flats in the building cannot be qualifying tenants for collective enfranchisement, but may be for lease renewal.

For both enfranchisement and renewal, a **qualifying tenant** is one who has a long lease of a flat at a low ground rent (see page 190-1).

There can be only one qualifying tenant per flat. The 1993 Act states that joint tenants of a flat are to be regarded as one legal unit and that, when a long sub-lease has been granted, it is the sub-tenant who qualifies. In that case, the interest of the person sub-letting (i.e. the sub-lessor) will be bought out.

Residence conditions For collective enfranchisement, at least half of those applying to buy the freehold must at the time of the application have occupied their flats (as their main or only home) for:

● the last 12 months; or
● periods (not necessarily consecutive) amounting to 3 of the last 10 years.

In order to renew a lease, a tenant should have occupied his or her flat (again, as the main or only home) for:

● the last three years; or
● periods (not necessarily consecutive) amounting to 3 of the last 10 years.

A company cannot pass the residence test. Where a flat is owned jointly, only one tenant needs to satisfy the residence criteria.

Long lease Generally speaking, a long lease is one which was originally granted for a period exceeding 21 years. It does not matter if the lease has now less than 21 years to run or the tenant claiming the right is not the original tenant.

Low rent The definition of 'low rent' is somewhat complicated. The rent (that is, ground rent) is low when either no rent was payable during the first year of the lease (or any later renewal) or where (excluding any service charge, penalties or additional rent for insurance, repairs and the like) the rent payable during that year did not exceed specified amounts (see below). The rule does not take into account what happened to the rent after that first year. The limits on ground rent vary according to when the lease (or the last renewal) was granted.

● If it was before 1 April 1963, the rent must not have exceeded two-thirds of the letting value (i.e. the market rental value) of the flat at the start of that year. A chartered surveyor or valuer will know the letting value of a lease.

- If the lease was granted on or between 1 April 1963 and 31 March 1990, the rent must not have been more than two–thirds of the rateable value of the flat at the start of that year. Local authorities will have lists of the former rateable values of properties within their areas.

- In any other case, a low rent is one less than £1,000 per year (in Greater London) or £250 (elsewhere).

Example

Rivermead Court consists of six flats, all held on long leases for 99 years granted in 1980 at nominal ground rents. Four of the flats are occupied by their owners who have lived there (as their main residences) for over 12 months. The other two flats are sub-let on short-term tenancies.

Of the four owner-occupiers only three are interested in buying the freehold (the fourth is an elderly tenant who has no desire to get involved). In such a case, the qualifying conditions appear to be met:

- the three who wish to buy have long leases at low rents;
- two-thirds of the flats (i.e. four) are let to qualifying tenants;
- the block contains more than two flats, and no part of it is non-residential;
- two-thirds of the qualifying tenants own, between them, at least half the flats in the block (i.e. the three who want to buy own half the block);
- at least half of the qualifying tenants (in this case, two) have lived in the flats for more than 12 months.

Therefore, the three tenants who want to buy can, if they wish, proceed. If they are successful in their bid, the fourth qualifying tenant (who did not participate) will lease his or her flat from them.

Other key characters

Apart from qualifying tenants, there are others who are heavily involved in the processes of collective enfranchisement and lease renewal.

Nominee purchaser

For practical reasons, when tenants group together and buy the freehold, they normally cannot hold the legal title to the newly acquired freehold themselves. Only up to four people can be joint legal owners of the freehold. When embarking upon collective enfranchisement, and when there are more than four participating tenants, they must nominate someone to act on their behalf throughout the process. This person, called the 'nominee purchaser', holds the land upon trust on their behalf.

The nominee can be an individual, group of individuals (not exceeding four) or, as is more likely, a company set up by the tenants. The company is not usually a trustee but will have both legal and equitable ownership of the building. The tenants will hold the shares of the company and thereby own the freehold. To decide on who to appoint or, if needed, to find out how to terminate the services of a nominee and appoint a replacement, it is best to talk to a solicitor.

Reversioner

The other party to the enfranchisement claim is the 'reversioner' – usually the freeholder of the premises. When the tenants apply to buy the freehold, it is the reversioner who must respond to the claim. If the freeholder cannot be found, the court can nominate any other intervening landlord (i.e. a sub-lessor) to act in that capacity.

Although the reversioner represents the interests of any sub-lessors involved in the claim, those landlords can ask for a replacement to be appointed if the reversioner is unwilling to act, incapable or absent. They or the nominee purchaser can also seek a replacement when it is believed that there is or is likely to be delay or default by the reversioner. In any event, any landlord may elect to deal directly with the nominee purchaser and to be separately represented in proceedings.

Competent landlord

The claim for lease renewal is made against the tenant's immediate landlord provided that, if that landlord is also a tenant, he or she holds a sufficiently long lease from which the proposed new lease can be carved. For example, if a long sub-lease has been granted, the sub-tenant applies to the sub-lessor only if the latter has over 90 years of his or her own lease left to run. If not, the competent landlord will be the next landlord in the chain who does satisfy that condition or, if none, the freeholder. Once more there is a facility which deals with situations when the competent landlord cannot be found. The competent landlord has the ability to bind all other landlords, but they can elect for separate representation in the proceedings.

What is purchased?

Owing to the differences between buying the freehold and obtaining a new lease, the physical extent of the property bought and the nature of the interest acquired will vary.

On enfranchisement the purchase covers not only those flats let to the tenants, but also includes the freehold of the building and any ancillary property which is either 'appurtenant' to the leased areas (e.g. garage, outhouse, garden or yard) or which constitutes common parts (e.g. lifts, stairways, corridors and shared storage rooms).

Where sub-leases have been created, the interest of any intervening (that is, superior) leaseholder will, at additional cost, also be bought out.

Although the general rule is that the tenants decide what premises they want to buy, they can be required by the freeholder to purchase other parts which otherwise would be either of no practical use or benefit to the freeholder (or intervening landlord) or would be incapable of reasonable management or maintenance by that person.

With lease renewal, the position is more straightforward. The tenant will obtain a new lease of the flat together with, for example, any garage, outbuildings, garden and yard belonging to, or usually enjoyed with, the flat and which are let to the tenant under the terms of the existing lease. The landlord retains the freehold estate.

The procedure

A major feature of the enfranchisement and renewal processes is the service of written notices and counternotices. Before proceedings are commenced, it is imperative that the qualifying tenants can identify the freeholder, any intervening landlords and, in the case of enfranchisement, other tenants and licensees of the premises or common parts.

Discovery notice

A tenant can request preliminary information from the landlord even before he or she gets any formal process under way. This is done by means of a **discovery notice**, which the landlord must reply to within 28 days. Such a notice could help a tenant to find out if his or her building fulfils the criteria for collective enfranchisement; whether there are other parties with an interest in parts of the premises, and if so their names and addresses; and whether there are any ongoing enfranchisement claims. The last of these is important for those who wish to renew their leases too. If the tenant seeks renewal and an enfranchisement claim has been issued, or is subsequently made before the new lease claim is settled, the new lease proceedings will, as mentioned earlier, be suspended until the freehold claim has been dealt with.

Dealing with neighbours

For collective enfranchisement, it is necessary that other tenants join in the claim to buy the freehold. Therefore, it is necessary to arrange a meeting between the tenants. The meeting should decide:

- whether the building satisfies the qualifying conditions;
- how many tenants will participate in the claim (i.e. at least two-thirds of all qualifying tenants representing at least half the flats in the building);
- whether at least half of the participating tenants satisfy the residence condition;
- whom to employ as a surveyor or valuer;
- how the finance is to be raised;
- who is going to represent legally the tenants.

Initial notice

The claim for a new lease or enfranchisement must be commenced by the tenant(s). This is done by the service on the competent landlord (new lease) or the reversioner (enfranchisement) of an additional notice. As regards enfranchisement, the notice must:

- fully identify the qualifying tenants and their leases;
- contain particulars identifying the participating tenants as having long leases at low rents;
- name the nominee purchaser;
- give details of the property to be purchased and include a plan of the premises;
- specify any leasehold interest which is to be purchased;
- after a surveyor's valuation, suggest a purchase price for the entire transaction;

- in the case of council tenants, provide particulars of the flats to be the subject of 'leaseback' (see below) to the council.

In the case of a new lease, the notice must:

- identify the tenant making the claim;
- identify the flat concerned;
- provide details of the tenant's lease;
- specify the capital premium to be paid;
- suggest the terms of the new lease.

In both cases, the notice of claim must demonstrate also that the premises and the tenant(s) are within the scope of the 1993 Act and state a date, at least two months hence, by which time the recipient of the notice must respond by the service of a counternotice.

Counternotice

The Act obliges the reversioner (enfranchisement) or the competent landlord (new lease) to give a counternotice in response to the initial notice, which must be served by the date specified in it. This counternotice must either:

- accept the claim if appropriate, and suggest counter-proposals as to terms. Unless there is misrepresentation or concealment of a material fact, any acceptance of the claim is binding upon the reversioner/competent landlord; or
- state that the tenant(s) is (are) not qualified under the 1993 Act or that the claim will be opposed in court on the basis that the premises are intended for redevelopment (see pages 197-8).

Leaseback

As regards enfranchisement, the reversioner can obtain a 999-year leaseback (at a nominal ground rent) of those flats that are not occupied by the qualifying tenants. In some circumstances (e.g. where the landlord is a local authority) this leaseback is mandatory, while in others it hinges upon the choice of the reversioner. Details of this must be included in the reversioner's counternotice.

Non-service of counternotice

If the counternotice is not served within the time specified in the notice of claim, the nominee purchaser (enfranchisement) or tenant (new lease) has a further six months to apply to the court for the terms of the transaction to be decided. Before this can occur, however, the court must be satisfied that the tenant(s) can make a valid claim under the 1993 Act and that the other party has been served with the appropriate notices. The court can then, after the expiry of a further two months, make an order either vest-ing the freehold in the purchaser or granting a new lease, as appropriate.

Concluding the process

The nominee purchaser and the freeholder are allowed a period of time to agree the terms for buying the freehold. If agreement is not forthcoming, either party is free to refer the matter to the Leasehold Valuation Tribunal. Applications to the tribunal (consult the telephone directory to find the one nearest you) must be made within six months of the freeholder's counternotice, otherwise the application for enfranchisement is deemed to be withdrawn. The tenants do not have to pay the landlord's costs incurred on an application to the tribunal (see page 201). If terms are agreed, the parties must enter into a written contract within two months.

When the freehold has been purchased by a group of tenants, and assuming they buy through a company, a share in the company will pass to any tenant. The company should be set up such that it allows only tenants to be shareholders.

Change of tenant

While the claim is ongoing, it is possible that a tenant may sell the lease, become bankrupt or die. The 1993 Act covers such situations in that it permits the new tenant, trustee in bankruptcy or personal representative to stand in the shoes of the previous tenant. Although this occurs automatically when the claim is for a new lease, as regards enfranchisement different rules operate: the new tenant or the trustee must notify the nominee purchaser of the change within 14 days following the assignment of the lease. If the tenant dies during the process, the deceased's personal representative automatically becomes the participating tenant unless he or she chooses otherwise and, moreover, notifies the nominee purchaser within 56 days.

When the freehold has been purchased by a group of tenants, and assuming they buy through a company, a share in the company will pass to any new tenant. The company should be set up such that it allows only tenants to be shareholders.

Change of heart

Once the process for either collective enfranchisement or lease renewal is initiated, the tenant(s) can withdraw and put an end to the proceedings at any time. The means of achieving this, however, varies according to which right was claimed. In the case of a new lease, the tenant can serve a notice of withdrawal on the landlord(s) at any time before a new lease is granted. As regards enfranchisement, the participating tenants may withdraw their claim by the service of a withdrawal notice on the nominee purchaser, the reversioner and any other relevant landlord involved in the proceedings. This notice must be served before a binding contract has been entered into (or a vesting order – see page 199 – has been made). In enfranchisement, if one tenant refuses to proceed, with the result that the other tenants together fall short of the qualifying number required, the whole process will fail. The other tenants may have to content themselves with applying for a renewal of their individual leases.

In both situations (and until withdrawal) the claimant(s) remain jointly and individually liable for the costs incurred by the other side (see page 201). It should also be appreciated that a claim can be deemed withdrawn when the claimant(s) fail to adhere to the time limits and procedures set out in the 1993 Act. If withdrawal occurs, no new claim can be entertained for 12 months.

In relation to enfranchisement, it may be that a qualifying tenant who had chosen originally not to join in the proceedings has subsequently sought to become a party to the claim. This is permissible with the consent of all the participating tenants and provided the nominee purchaser is notified immediately. Within 28 days of such notification, the nominee purchaser must inform the reversioner and any other landlord of the change. If the tenant is not allowed to join in, when the freehold is bought he or she will be in the same position as before, but with a different landlord.

Reasons for refusal of a claim

Although it is not possible to contract out of the Act, there are several ways in which a reversioner or landlord can attempt to prevent the enfranchisement or renewal claim proceeding either at all or, at the least, on the terms proposed.

Questioning status

The reversioner or competent landlord could wish to challenge the status of the tenant(s). In the context of enfranchisement, this is helped by the right of the reversioner, exercisable within 21 days of the tenants' claim, to serve a counternotice on the nominee purchaser requesting that the leasehold title of certain named tenant(s) be proved. The nominee has a further 21 days to respond and, on a failure to do so, if the named tenant(s) are crucial to the qualifying number count, the initial claim is deemed to be withdrawn. This right and potential trap does not apply to the claim for a new lease.

If a challenge to status is made, the nominee purchaser (enfranchisement) or the competent landlord (new lease) is entitled to apply to the court, within two months of the counternotice, for a declaration as to the validity or otherwise of the claim. If the court is satisfied as to the qualifying status of the tenants, it must confirm the validity of the initial notice and will usually require the reversioner or the competent landlord to issue a further counternotice admitting the right and containing the landlord's proposals. Where the claim is held to be invalid, the claim simply ceases to have effect.

Redevelopment

Another means by which the claim for enfranchisement or renewal can be defeated arises when the landlord shows a definite intention to redevelop the whole or a substantial part of the premises. There are, however, conditions attached to this method of opposition:

- where enfranchisement is sought, at least two-thirds of all long leases of flats in the premises must be due to terminate within five years of the initial enfranchisement notice;
- in the context of renewal, it is necessary that the tenant's existing lease will terminate within five years of the initial notice for a new lease. If this time element is not satisfied, the landlord can make an application to court which, although not preventing renewal, can operate to terminate the new lease once it is granted. The landlord can make this latter application within 12 months of the time the former lease would have ended or within five years of the end date of the new lease. The tenant will be able to obtain compensation for the loss of the flat;
- the reversioner or competent landlord must intend to demolish,

reconstruct or carry out substantial works of construction on the premises which are intended to be bought (enfranchisement) or in which the tenant's flat is contained (new lease);

- the reversioner or competent landlord must demonstrate that the works could not reasonably be carried out without obtaining possession of the flats (enfranchisement) or flat (new lease).

If these conditions are satisfied, the reversioner or competent landlord can apply to the court, within two months of the service of the counternotice, for the claim of the tenant(s) to be dismissed. Where it is stated in the counternotice that there was an intention to develop but the intention cannot be proved, the original counternotice is invalid and a replacement will need to be served by a date specified by the court. Similarly, a new counternotice is required if the reversioner or competent landlord either fails to make an application to the court or withdraws such an application.

Disputing the terms

The third approach is to allow the claim, but to challenge the terms of the proposed bargain. Within two and six months from the service of an effective counternotice, and where the terms of the transaction have not been settled, either party may apply to the Leasehold Valuation Tribunal for any outstanding matters to be decided. The tribunal has the power to make an order which binds both parties. When the terms are agreed or determined by the tribunal, and either a binding contract is not entered (enfranchisement) or a new lease is not granted, within two months of that agreement or order the tribunal has the power to make a 'vesting order' (equivalent to a binding contract). This order then enables the purchaser to pay the appropriate purchase price to the court in return for the court executing the conveyance of the freehold or a new lease.

Valuation and costs

Following service of the initial notice, the reversioner, competent landlord and any other affected landlord are given a statutory right of access to the flats in order to obtain an independent valuation. The nominee purchaser is also awarded the right to enter the premises (including appurtenant property, common parts and the flats of nonparticipating tenants) for valuation purposes provided that it is reasonable and relates to the proceedings. These rights are exercisable at any reasonable time provided at least three days' notice is given to the occupier.

Ascertaining the price

It is preferable that the parties involved agree on the price of the freehold or the new lease (and any intervening leases). However, if agreement is not achieved, the price will be calculated by the Leasehold Valuation Tribunal according to elaborate formulae prescribed in the 1993 Act. Enfranchisement, in particular, will not come cheaply. Unlike the Leasehold Reform Act 1967 which governs leases of houses, there is no discount for the purchasing tenants. In essence, the calculated price will represent the market value of the freehold, disregarding the effect that the ongoing enfranchisement proceedings will have on it or the value of the new lease to a willing purchaser.

Marriage value

In addition, the claimant(s) will have to pay at least 50 per cent of what is termed 'marriage value' and this can add substantially to the purchase price.

Marriage value is a difficult concept which, as regards enfranchisement, reflects the net increase in value to the buying tenants of 'marrying' the leasehold and freehold estates. This necessitates a valuation of the leaseholders' interest (ever-diminishing as time passes) and balancing that against the increased value of the freehold. Clearly, the freehold and leasehold estates will be worth more as one entity than when owned by different persons (because, for example, the flat-owners could now grant themselves new leases on more favourable terms than before without the payment of a capital premium or any restriction on the length of the term). If property values are high and the leases in the block are down to their last 60 years or so, this marriage value may run into thousands of pounds. Conversely, if the leases have longer terms left to run, the marriage value will be depressed.

In the context of a new lease, marriage value is the difference in value between the interests of the parties under the current lease and what they will be when a new lease is granted.

Other sums

In addition, if the value of other property near the premises and belonging to the reversioner/competent landlord is diminished, the tenant(s) will be obliged to pay 'reasonable' compensation to that person. Compensation for any unrealised development value is limited to any other property of the landlord, not the premises which are the subject of collective enfranchisement.

As regards any intermediate leasehold interests (held by sub-lessors) which are acquired, a separate price will be paid for each. Generally, the calculation will be based on the same footing as the freehold. Nevertheless, a complicated mathematical formula is specified as regards 'minor' intermediate leases which have no real market value.

Costs

In relation to costs, it is the nominee purchaser (enfranchisement) or the tenant (new lease) who must discharge the reversioner's/ landlord's legal and valuation expenses, reasonably incurred in connection with the claim. This does not, however, extend to costs associated with proceedings before a Leasehold Valuation Tribunal. Until the purchase price is paid and costs discharged, the seller retains a charge over the property for those amounts.

Management schemes

Generally, on enfranchisement, the flat-owners will themselves take over responsibility for the management of the block. In certain circumstances, however, the 1993 Act allows for the creation of estate-management schemes whereby, following an application by the former landlord and the approval of the Leasehold Valuation Tribunal, the former landlord can retain management control over the premises later acquired by the tenants. This facility is to meet the former landlord's fears that enfranchisement might make good management of the building difficult. It can also apply to the upkeep of communal gardens. The scheme will be relevant, for example, where the landlord has more than one property in the area which is leased.

The tenants will pay a service charge to the manager much the same as before. Such applications can be made only after the tenants have been notified and, if made after 1 November 1995, can be entertained only with the consent of the government. If consent is granted, the former landlord has six months in which to apply to the tribunal. The scheme may allow the landlord to:

- control the development, use and appearance of the property;
- carry out works on the premises;
- levy a service charge.

The scheme must, however, be in the 'general interest' and be required in order to maintain standards of appearance and amenity and to regulate development. In deciding whether to approve the scheme, the tribunal must take on board such matters as fairness, reasonableness, architectural and historical values, neighbouring areas and general circumstances. Often it will be in the tenants' interests for the former landlord to continue to apply organisational ability and experience in maintaining the quality of such property. If the tenants object they can make representations to the Leasehold Valuation Tribunal.

Early days?

It has become clear that some landlords are attempting either to avoid or to dissuade their tenants from exercising the right to buy the freehold. Some of the tactics used by them are discussed below.

First, landlords may routinely deny the validity of the claim by, for example, alleging that the premises or the tenants do not qualify. This prolongs the procedure and brings with it added costs.

Second, landlords may decline to negotiate and threaten a drawn-out and expensive hearing before a Leasehold Valuation Tribunal.

Third, landlords anticipating an imminent claim may engage in major works on the premises which drain any sinking funds and are claimable under the service charges from the tenants. This could ensure that the tenants have depleted funds and reduced incentives to proceed.

Fourth, as the freehold of the building must be undivided, landlords may transfer the freehold of a single flat to an associated company. This simple technique could undermine the workings of the Act and render the landlord safe from an enfranchisement claim.

Another tactic used by landlords – selling the freehold to a third party often without informing the tenants – is leading in many cases to tenants being forced to pay extremely high service charges, thereby again reducing their chances of having enough funds to participate in enfranchisement (see pages 206-7).

Options and pre-emptions

A tenant who wishes to renew his or her lease or buy the freehold, but who does not qualify under the 1993 Act, may have an alternative: the lease to his or her flat may contain a clause which allows an option to renew a long lease at the end of its term or to buy the landlord's freehold. Such options are not subject to the rigorous requirements and restrictions of the 1993 Act. The tenant might be given the right of first refusal (pre-emption) if the freehold is subsequently put on the market. As will be shown, there exists, in some situations, a statutory right of first refusal under the Landlord and Tenant Act 1987.

If not expressly contained in the lease, the option or right may be agreed separately between the parties in a distinct written contract.

Options to renew a lease

The presence of such an option can offer the tenant a valuable right in circumstances where he or she does not qualify under the 1993 Act. The option, as with all other aspects of the lease, should be drafted carefully by a buyer's solicitor; the buyer should check that the following matters are made clear:

- the time at which it may be exercised. Normally, the option would be made exercisable within a few months before the original lease is to end. It is possible that a specific date might be used as an alternative. Any time limits imposed must be strictly adhered to unless the lease provides otherwise. An option may be lost once the time stipulated for its exercise has passed;
- the manner of its exercise. The option is usually made exercisable by notice in writing served on the landlord. No set form for this notice will be required;
- the conditions that the tenant must fulfil. It may be that the option requires that, at the time the notice is served, the tenant has paid all the rent and observed all the covenants. If so, a breach of any covenant (no matter how minor) will prevent the tenant from exercising the option;

● the terms of the new lease. Normally, the new lease will (except from containing an option to renew) be the same as the old one. The option will usually provide that the tenant will pay the landlord's costs connected with the granting of the new lease.

Once created, the option contractually binds the landlord. However, the problem arises when the landlord sells the freehold to a third party and the buyer refuses to acknowledge the tenant's option. While the tenant can sue the former landlord for breach of contract, this may not be the ideal remedy for a tenant who really wants a new lease of the flat. The tenant should, therefore, protect the option by the entry of a land charge (unregistered land) or a notice (registered land). Consult a solicitor for advice. If this occurs, the tenant will be able to enforce the option against the new freeholder.

Options to buy the freehold

An option to buy the landlord's freehold by merger (see Chapter 16) is regarded as a separate agreement rather than a term of the lease. The original landlord will remain under the contractual obligation to grant the option and can, if relevant, be sued for damages for breach of contract. This remains so even if the landlord has sold the freehold to a third party. The landlord can avoid this liability by inserting a clause into the lease that the option shall become void unless protected by registration within a specified period. Registration, as demonstrated above, will also ensure that a buyer of the freehold is bound by the tenant's rights.

Two issues are usually of importance in this type of option: who may exercise the option and for how long does it remain open? Much turns on the wording and expression of the clause itself and the option can be exercised only in strict accordance with its terms. Accordingly, the option should state how it is to be exercised, whether written notice has to be given by the tenant, and the time frame within which it is to be exercised. Normally, the option will also state how the purchase price is to be ascertained (e.g. a reference to market value). As with the option to renew, the option to purchase can be made conditional upon all the terms of the lease having been performed by the tenant.

Right of pre-emption

The landlord may not be prepared to grant the tenant the future right to buy the freehold, but may instead offer the tenant first refusal when the freehold is to be next sold. The initiative clearly remains with the landlord. If and when the landlord decides to sell, the tenant will have to be notified and given the opportunity to buy.

The right of pre-emption may provide that the landlord must offer the freehold at a price stated in the lease or at a sum 'to be agreed'. If the latter, the landlord has to accept a *bona fide* bid which reflects current market values. The tenant must then decide whether or not to accept the offer. The right may, however, be drafted in such a way as to make the tenant responsible for offering a price, leaving the landlord to decide whether to accept it. In either case, if a contract is not concluded, the landlord will be able to sell on the freehold to someone else.

Problems that sometimes arise focus upon when the landlord is supposed to notify the tenant and whether the right exists beyond the first occasion that the freehold is offered to the tenant. These points should be spelled out in the lease.

Once the right has been created, the issue arises as to when it will bind third-party buyers. In unregistered land, the buyer will be bound by the tenant's right only if the buyer or agent (e.g. solicitor) knew or ought to have known of its existence. In registered land, the right cannot be protected by the entry of a notice on the Land Register. Nevertheless, if the tenant is in actual occupation of the flat, or in receipt of rent from it, the right is protected as an overriding interest and any buyer will then buy the freehold subject to it.

The Landlord and Tenant Act 1987

The Act gives to the tenants a right of pre-emption when the landlord intends to sell the freehold. Under the Act the landlord has to offer the right of first refusal to all the tenants. This does not, however, take precedence over the right of pre-emption given to any one individual tenant by the lease. The essential feature of the statutory right is that the landlord cannot dispose of the premises unless a notice has previously been served on the 'qualifying tenants' offering them first refusal. The Act extends only to certain types of property, benefits a limited number of tenants and can be side-stepped easily by landlords. The conditions imposed are less stringent than those under the 1993 Act (as regards collective enfranchisement) because under the latter the sale may be against the freeholder's wishes, whereas, under the 1987 Act the sale is voluntary.

The statutory right of first refusal has not proved popular. The Act is widely recognised as being poorly drafted, complicated and confusing. Many tenants are unaware of the law and it is not always easy to raise the necessary finance and to act within the time limits. The procedure is also time-consuming and can be stressful. In addition, the provisions are easy to avoid and there is no effective remedy against a landlord who disregards the tenants' rights. In fact, many landlords tend to sell their properties at auction for speed and convenience. Often the tenants are not aware of the auction and lose the chance to buy the freehold. The tenants usually become aware of the sale when the managing company writes to them notifying the change of landlord. The tenants, however, have the right to buy the freehold back from the new landlord on the same terms as he or she acquired it.

The nightmare scenario – and solutions

When a landlord sells the freehold to a third party (i.e. not to the tenants, and usually by auction), it is often the case that the buyer wants to make as much money as possible from the property. One tactic of abuse is to carry out unnecessary and expensive repairs to the building, charge high management fees and incur legal and surveying expenses or inflated insurance premiums (see Chapter 11), and then bill the tenants for this under the service charge. The tenants may not be able to afford the payments and may be driven to taking out a loan to cover the debt.

The unscrupulous landlord may then continue in the same vein until the tenant can no longer afford to pay or even borrow the necessary sums. The landlord might then try and forfeit the lease and, if successful, can sell the flat on to a new buyer and keep the proceeds of sale. If the flat-owner had bought with the aid of a mortgage, the lender will normally avoid forfeiture (and thereby save its security for the loan) by paying the landlord what the tenant owes, and adding the sum to the mortgage debt. In such a case the tenant may not be able to pay the increased mortgage repayments and, eventually, it might be the lender who sells the flat in order to recoup its loan (see Chapter 3) and, if appropriate, claim for any loss under its own bad-debt insurance policy. The lender or the insurance company will then continue to pursue the borrower for any amounts still outstanding. Meanwhile the landlord has a much-improved building following the expensive repairs carried out and still receives ground rents.

Tenants who find themselves in this situation have some legal rights under the Landlord and Tenant Acts of 1985 and 1987 to challenge the service charge bill and apply for the appointment of a manager to run the property (see Chapter 14). This route is, however, costly and time-consuming, and will normally require the services of a solicitor. They will still be able, in theory, to buy out the landlord's freehold under the 1993 Act, but in practice are likely to be unable to get together the necessary finance.

It should be pointed out that although such a nightmare scenario could – and does – occur, not all landlords are unscrupulous. Moreover, organisations like the Campaign Against Residential Leasehold Abuse (CARLA)* and the Leasehold Enfranchisement Association* are campaigning for changes to the law in favour of leaseholders, and offer advice to tenants facing the kind of abuses described above. The government is now considering ways of increasing protection for leaseholders from the more ruthless landlords.

Tenants who wish to apply for enfranchisement or renewal may find that after the teething problems the 1993 Act could indeed benefit them. However, many of the underlying problems between tenants and landlords will remain until the eligibility criteria for enfranchisement are widened to include more flat-owners. Another measure that would help tenants is the simplification of company structures so the formation of tenants' management companies is made easier. In the long term, however, commonhold – whereby tenants buy the freehold of individual flats, thus doing away with leases and landlords (see Chapter 1) – is the most beneficial measure for flat-owners.

CHAPTER 18

THE RIGHT TO BUY AND RENT-TO-MORTGAGE

THE right to buy council houses and flats is similar to leasehold enfranchisement in the private sector (see Chapter 17), but has proved more popular. Well over 1 million council tenants have now become owner-occupiers. The idea is that the right to buy ensures the wider spread of wealth through society, encourages the desire to improve and modernise property, allows an inheritance to be passed to future generations and stimulates independence and self-reliance. Critics of the system might argue that, when assessed against the existing background of an urgent need for inexpensive, good-quality rented accommodation, the depletion of public housing stock works to the disadvantage of the most needy.

The Leasehold Reform, Housing and Urban Development Act 1993 abolished the council tenant's rights to a mortgage and to postpone completion of the conveyancing process until finance was arranged, and (while preserving existing ones) the concept of a shared-ownership lease. The latter was a scheme whereby the tenant paid a capital sum to buy a portion (at least 50 per cent) of the lease and retained the right to buy successive portions (in blocks of 12.5 per cent) until the entire lease was acquired. This 'staircasing' had not proved popular with potential buyers. Instead, there is now a new scheme and with it a new right to acquire on rent-to-mortgage terms. This will be considered later in the chapter.

The right to buy

The Housing Act 1985 confers on certain 'secure' tenants the rights to buy the freehold of their houses or to take long leases of their flats at a ground rent not exceeding £10 per year. A secure tenant is a council tenant who has the benefit of residential security offered (to renting periodic tenants) by the Act.

Normally the duration of any long lease granted will be 125 years, but in two situations the term can be shorter:

- where the local authority does not own the freehold and merely has a leasehold estate for less than 125 years, in which case it can grant to the tenant a lease which is only as long as its own, less five days;
- where there is a block of flats and one (or more) of those flats has been sold since 8 August 1980, in which case the local authority can grant a long lease, but only for as long as the period that remains unexpired under the first long lease granted after 8 August. For example, if the first flat in the block was sold in 1981 on a 125-year lease, a flat sold in 1982 would be granted a lease for 124 years. Accordingly, if a long lease was granted in 1995, it would be for a term of 111 years.

Who can buy?

The tenant must have been the secure tenant of a public-sector land-lord (generally, a local authority, but this also includes housing action trusts, new town corporations, urban development corporations and some housing associations) for at least two years, or for periods amounting to two years, before the right to buy arises. The provisions concerning what constitutes the qualifying period are complex, but it is clear that the tenant need not necessarily have lived in one property or have kept to the same public-sector landlord during the qualifying period. The two years' occupation does not have to be continuous and a number of shorter periods of occupation as a secure tenant can be added together. Hence a person who, at some stage in the past, had been a secure tenant for the necessary length of time can exercise the right to buy when next living in council property. Subject to certain conditions, a joint tenant, spouse, parent or child (over 16) of a secure tenant, having lived in the property for the two-year period, will also satisfy the criterion to qualify as a tenant.

Excluded property

The right to buy extends generally to both houses and flats. Certain types of property are, however, excluded from the Act. Among the categories of excluded property are those where the landlord is a charitable housing trust, housing association or co-operative housing association. Also outside the right-to-buy provisions are those properties which have been modified for occupation by physically disabled persons. The right, moreover, does not extend to property which is particularly suitable for occupation by pensioners and which has been let in the past to either a pensioner or physically disabled person. Similarly, the Act prohibits sale to a tenant who is bankrupt or against whom a court order for possession has been granted to the landlord. A tenant who has obtained the house or flat in consequence of employment (e.g. a caretaker of a school) also falls outside the right-to-buy scheme.

Price and discount

The tenant will pay the market value of the property, less any discount. The property is valued at the time the right is exercised. On the grant of a long lease, the valuation is of a flat with vacant possession (i.e. as if it was unoccupied) and with a ground rent of £10 per year. The valuation disregards any improvements made by the tenant and any failure to keep the flat in good internal repair. The council carries out the valuation, but the tenant has the right to appeal to the district valuer if there is any disagreement. The valuer's decision is final.

The secure tenant will buy the property with a discount which is determined by the length of the secure tenancy and whether it is a flat or a house which is being bought. A preferential discount has been introduced in relation to flats in order to encourage more purchasers. The calculation of the discount for a flat is 40 per cent of its market value and, when the purchaser has been a secure tenant for over three years, an additional 2 per cent discount for each year as a secure tenant. There is a maximum ceiling of 70 per cent discount (i.e. after 15 years' residence), and the discount can never exceed £50,000. These figures are, however, liable to change from time to time.

The clawback

A tenant who has bought a long lease is prevented from profiting from the discount by immediately re-selling the flat for its true value.

If re-sale occurs within a specified period, the tenant will have to repay the discount either in whole or in part; this is known as the clawback. The local authority will have a charge over the flat in order to enforce any repayment.

The clawback occurs when the property is disposed of within three years of the sale to the tenant. In such a case, the whole of the discount is repayable, but is reduced by one-third for each year which has elapsed between the grant of the lease and the disposal. Therefore, if the flat is sold within one year of being bought, the tenant must refund the whole of the discount. If sale occurs between one and two years of the lease being granted, the amount to be repaid is two-thirds of the discount. On a sale arising between two and three years from the initial purchase, the tenant must repay one-third of the discount. No discount is repayable on a sale occurring three years after the lease was granted.

The clawback does not operate when the property passes on death of the tenant, is re-allocated on divorce, is compulsorily purchased or is sold to the tenant's spouse (including former spouse) or a member of the tenant's family who has resided with the tenant for the previous 12 months.

Exercising the right

The tenant must serve on the landlord a written notice stating that he or she wishes to exercise the right to buy. The local authority has four weeks in which to reply. It may either accept the tenant's right or deny that the tenant or the property is eligible. If the right is denied, the tenant must prove eligibility either to the court or to a central government official. If the right is accepted, the local authority must serve a notice on the tenant stating the price, the discount, the proposed terms of the lease, the service charges that are payable and the right to appeal against valuation. The estimate of service charges (including also repair costs) will remain binding on the landlord for the first five years of the lease. The landlord also has to give quite onerous repairing covenants and an insurance covenant.

Once the necessary steps have been taken, the landlord is bound to execute the lease. On completion, the secure tenancy comes to an end and the tenant will become the registered proprietor of the flat following registration at the Land Registry.

Rent-to-mortgage

The shared-ownership lease has now been replaced by the extremely complex rent-to-mortgage scheme, which caters for those tenants who want to buy, but cannot afford to pay the entire, although discounted, purchase price in one go. The scheme allows the tenant's current rent payments to be converted to mortgage repayments for a share of the flat, along with the right to purchase the remainder of the lease at a later date. In essence, the rent currently payable on the flat is equated with the extent of a 25-year mortgage those payments would finance. This is the initial share which the tenant acquires. He or she can subsequently increase the payments and thereby increase the share in the property. If the tenant then sells the flat, the landlord's remaining share is redeemed from the purchase money. Assistance and advice can be obtained from the local authority housing department. It is predicted that this type of buying will prove very unpopular. Because of the exclusion of those on housing benefit, it is likely that those who seek to buy will be able to take out a mortgage for the full price and have no need of the scheme.

Who qualifies?

To fall within the rent-to-mortgage scheme, the tenant must satisfy all the requirements that apply to the right-to-buy scheme (see pages 209-10). In addition, the tenant must not have made a claim for housing benefit, or have been entitled to claim housing benefit, within the 12 months preceding the application for rent to mortgage. Also excluded is a tenant whose rent is more than 80 per cent of the mortgage payments on a mortgage that would buy the flat outright. Such a tenant is expected to purchase directly rather than use the new scheme. The calculations involved here are horrendously difficult.

Exercising the right

The procedure involves the tenant serving a notice on the landlord stating that he or she wishes to exercise the right and suggesting a purchase price. The landlord must then respond as soon as practicable by a notice either denying or admitting the claim. If admitted, the tenant must then, within 12 weeks, serve a further written notice on the landlord stating the intention to proceed or to withdraw. If the transaction is to go ahead, the landlord will serve another notice which will set out the landlord's share in the flat and the amount of the discount reduced in proportion to the tenant's share. If there is no response from the tenant, the landlord will serve yet another notice and, if there is still no response within 28 days, the claim is then deemed to be withdrawn.

The local authority is, therefore, really granting the tenant a mortgage, and the mortgage repayments take the form of the continued payments of rent. The lease when granted will be essentially on the same terms as under the right to buy, except that the service charges are scaled down to reflect the tenant's share in the flat. The mortgage must be paid off if the tenant sells the flat outside the family or, if the tenant dies during the term of the mortgage, after one year following death.

CHAPTER **19**

BUYING AND SELLING IN SCOTLAND

THERE are major differences between Scottish and English law in relation to the purchase and sale of houses and flats. However, the procedure for buying and selling flats in Scotland is very similar to that for houses.

One of the most important things to remember when buying a flat is that it is part of a larger building or 'tenement' and you should therefore look at the condition of the whole property, as well as of the flat itself. In particular, you should make sure that the cost of repairing the structure and common parts of the property is shared on an equitable basis among the individual flat-owners. These matters are considered in more detail later in this chapter.

Tenure

The English concept of leasehold does not apply to the purchase of flats in Scotland. Most flats, and indeed most other kinds of property, are owned on **feudal tenure** and property offered for sale is sometimes referred to in Scotland as the **feu**. For practical purposes, this means that they are owned absolutely and can be disposed of freely rather than being held on long lease as in England or Wales.

The main distinguishing feature of feudal tenure is that the original developer of the land or estate-owner, who is known as the **superior**, can impose conditions on its future use – for instance, by prohibiting commercial use, extensions or alterations without his or her consent. It is also usual for the superior to require the future maintenance of the property in good condition and reinstatement following damage or destruction. This is particularly important for flat-owners, who will have a shared interest in the upkeep and maintenance of various common parts of the building.

Once feuing conditions have been imposed, they may remain in force in perpetuity unless the superior agrees to waive or modify them. Any buyer will be bound by the feuing conditions, but it may be possible, once he or she has bought the property, to negotiate with the superior for a waiver. Normally, the superior charges a capital payment for agreeing to waive feuing conditions. If he or she refuses to vary unreasonable conditions, or if the existence of a condition impedes some reasonable use of land, such as making external alterations or building a garage, the owner (or **feuar**) can apply to the Lands Tribunal for Scotland★ for an order to vary them. A leaflet on land obligations and how they may be varied or discharged, and the fees payable, is obtainable from the tribunal. If you think that you may be justified in seeking such an order, consult your solicitor in the first instance.

In the past, the feuar paid an annual cash sum or '**feuduty**' (similar to a ground rent in England and Wales) to the superior. (The superior therefore retains a link with a flat built on his or her property or developed by him or her.) Since 1974, the creation of new feuduties has been prohibited. As far as flats are concerned, if the overall feuduty for the building has been formally divided between each individual flat, the feuar is obliged to pay off the feuduty when he or she sells the property, leaving the buyer free of any further charge. The feuing conditions, however, still apply even if the feuduty has been redeemed.

Common parts

As explained above, it is possible in Scotland to purchase each of the flats in a block outright, rather than on only a long lease, as in England and Wales. However, the law recognises that there are various 'common parts' of the whole building in which all of the owners in the block have an interest and that they should therefore be jointly responsible for repair and maintenance of those parts. Normally, the solum (the ground on which the block of flats is built), the foundations, the roof, attic, close (stairwell or hall) and stairs, and any common services are owned by the proprietors in the block equally or on some other equitable basis. Similarly, any garden ground and, in more modern blocks, landscaped gardens, car-parking areas and door-entry systems are likely to be deemed common parts. The title deeds normally set out the basis on which the costs of repairs and maintenance are shared between the various owners.

It is also likely that there will be a common insurance policy for the block, covering loss by fire, storm damage, etc. This will result in an additional cost over and above any buildings insurance required under your mortgage, but it may be possible to persuade your lender to accept the insurance or at least take it into account.

It is customary in Scotland for management of common repairs and insurance to be dealt with by a **factor**, who is a professional property manager. The factor will organise tradesmen to do common repairs and will arrange for paying their bills. Every owner in the block will receive a half-yearly account from the factor for their share of the common repairs, plus the factor's management charge. Some factors also ask for a float – normally a small deposit of £50-100, which will be refunded when you sell the flat.

Solicitors, their role and charges

As there are no licensed conveyancers in Scotland you will need to consult a solicitor if you want to buy or sell a flat. Although in theory you could do all the legal work yourself, it is not usually practicable to do so, particularly if you need a mortgage.

If you do not know a solicitor, the best recommendation may be that of a friend or colleague who has used one for this type of work and who can give you a personal introduction. English solicitors are not permitted to practise in Scotland, but if you are moving from England or Wales, your own solicitor may have a Scottish solicitor with whom he or she deals regularly. A *Directory of General Services* issued by the Law Society of Scotland★, giving the names, addresses and telephone numbers of solicitors is available at Citizens Advice Bureaux and libraries. Leaflets explaining the role of solicitors in buying and selling houses or flats can be obtained from any solicitor. You will also find a full list of solicitors in the *Yellow Pages*.

You should ask your solicitor, at the outset, to give you an estimate of the fees involved and the outlays (disbursements) he or she will have to make. The outlays are substantial and should be budgeted for. There are no set fees, so you can shop around for competitive estimates. Do remember, however, that the level of fee quoted will be an indication of the standard of service provided.

Pricing

The general practice in Scotland is that flats are offered for sale at 'offers over' a stated figure, usually referred to as the **'upset price'**. The upset may be the minimum which the seller will consider accepting, but it may have been set low in order to attract buyers and encourage competitive bidding. Buyers will generally have to pay more than the upset, but much depends on the demand, the condition of the property and market conditions.

Sometimes flats are offered for a sale at a fixed price. This may be because either a quick sale is sought or earlier attempts to sell it at an 'offers over' price have been unsuccessful. If you want to buy a flat which is offered for a sale at a fixed price, you should be ready to proceed very quickly, because the first acceptable offer at the stated price will secure the flat.

Buying a flat

The main steps involved in buying a flat are:

- finding a suitable flat;
- arranging a loan and having the flat surveyed;
- making an offer;
- obtaining a legal title to the flat.

It is advisable to see your solicitor as early on in the procedure as possible. Things can move very fast once the process gets under way, and if you have not made contact you may miss your chance to make an offer for the flat you have decided on. In Scotland, an offer is usually prepared by a solicitor, who can also give useful general advice about buying, and assist you in obtaining a loan. At your first meeting with your solicitor, he or she can give you an outline of the whole purchase procedure from start to finish and discuss various essential matters including your price range, your mortgage and likely expenses.

Finding a suitable flat

There are three main sources of information about flats for sale in Scotland: newspapers; solicitors' property centres and solicitors' offices; and estate agents.

If you are thinking about buying a brand new flat, you could contact the sales departments of building firms in the area you have chosen or go to see the various developments.

Newspapers

A wide range of properties for sale is advertised in the principal Scottish 'quality' daily newspapers, and each has its main property day – *The Scotsman* (Edinburgh and the Lothians) on Thursdays; *The Herald* (Glasgow and Strathclyde) on Wednesdays; the *Press and Journal* (Aberdeen and Grampian) on Tuesdays, *Courier and Advertiser* (Dundee, Perth and Tayside) on Thursdays. A good range of properties for sale is also advertised in the smaller local newspapers circulating in various districts.

Solicitors' property centres

Solicitors' property centres can be found in the Aberdeen, Dundee Edinburgh and Glasgow areas and in many large towns. These are run by solicitors on a co-operative basis and are situated in shopping areas. They provide details of all properties being sold by solicitors in the area. The solicitors' property centre in Berwick-upon-Tweed is unique in that it deals with properties for sale on both sides of the England-Scotland border.

Most solicitors' property centres operate only as information centres and not as selling agents – the solicitors themselves retain the selling role. The staff at a centre are not qualified solicitors, although they are generally conversant with house purchase and sale procedures. A customer who is interested in a property is directed to the solicitor actually selling it. Full estate-agency-type particulars are available for each property (most have photographs too). The biggest centres, in Aberdeen, Glasgow and Edinburgh, each have several hundred properties on display at any one time. The service is free to people looking for property to buy.

Some solicitors' property centres publish regular property lists, most of them weekly, with full listings of all properties registered at the centre in question. Copies can be mailed to prospective buyers if requested and are available from the particular centre and from all the solicitors practising in the area. A list of solicitors' property centres with addresses and telephone numbers is available from the Law Society of Scotland.

Solicitors are allowed to call themselves 'solicitors and estate agents' and often do so. Some firms of solicitors have their own property department, where details of available properties are displayed. Many firms of solicitors employ specialist sales staff who deal with the non-legal aspects of buying and selling property.

Estate agents

There are many estate agents in Scotland. Many are part of chains owned by UK insurance companies or building societies, while others are local firms. Generally, estate agents in Scotland operate in the same way as those in England and Wales.

The larger estate agencies issue regular property lists and most of them maintain mailing lists. Estate agents in Edinburgh publish a fortnightly property list (*Real Homes*), as do those in the west of Scotland (*Estate Agency Guide*). Both these publications are available through offices of the member firms.

When you have found a flat

When you have found a flat that you would like to buy, tell your solicitor immediately. You can discuss with the seller the date of entry (see page 222) and what contents, such as carpets, curtains, light fittings, etc. ('extras'), are included, although these should be in the particulars of sale. You can try to negotiate a price, but many sellers will simply ask you to put in a formal offer via your solicitor. In Scotland details of the offer are handled by solicitors rather than estate agents. An oral agreement for the sale of a flat cannot create a binding contract, and can be repudiated by either party without any consequences. You should never write letters or sign any documents relating to a sale or purchase without consulting your solicitor. Developers of new flats usually have their own documents for intending buyers to sign, and it is very difficult to negotiate different terms. Even so, you should show the document to your solicitor before signing it so that he or she can explain the terms and effect of the document to you.

When you tell your solicitor that you are interested in buying a particular property, the first thing he or she will do is to telephone the seller's solicitor or estate agent to notify him or her of your interest. The latter will give you a chance to offer, once your interest has been notified, although he or she is not legally obliged to do so.

Arranging a mortgage

If you have not already made your loan arrangements, the next thing to do is to arrange with a building society, bank or other source of finance to lend you the money you need to borrow (see page 225). If you have any difficulty in finding the loan, your solicitor will probably be able to help you.

All Scottish banks and building societies will lend on the security of Scottish properties, subject to status. Even before you have a specific flat in mind, you should establish that the amount you require will be available on the type of property which you will be seeking and that it will be available when you want it – subject always to a satisfactory survey report on the chosen flat.

Survey

Building societies and banks require the property to be surveyed before committing themselves to making you a loan. Even if you are paying for the flat without a loan, you are strongly advised to have it surveyed before making an offer. In Scotland it is customary to have a survey carried out before you make an offer for a flat. An offer made 'subject to survey' is almost certain to be rejected by the seller unless the flat requires expensive specialist surveys or market conditions are unusual.

The survey is usually instructed by your solicitor once he or she is informed that you are interested and wish to go ahead. If your offer is unsuccessful you will have wasted the survey fee and your solicitor will expect you to pay for it there and then.

The range of types of survey is similar to that in England and Wales. The cheapest type of survey, but the one with the least detail about the property, is the lender's survey, which is little more than a mortgage valuation; the home-buyer's report gives a wider range of fairly standard information; a full structural survey normally costs much more but gives very detailed information about the condition of the property.

Lenders will always require that at least a lender's survey is done so that they can be satisfied that the flat will provide suitable security for their loan to you. However, it is you who pays the surveyor's fee and you can choose to have a more detailed survey carried out. The surveyor or lender will tell your solicitor whether the property in question is suitable for the loan which you require, the valuation placed on it, and the main points about the condition of the property. Many lenders now make a practice of giving the borrower a brief written survey report or a copy of the surveyor's report.

Making an offer

If the survey report is favourable, the next thing is to make an offer to buy the flat. An offer is a formal document, usually a letter running to several pages, or sometimes a shorter letter with a schedule of conditions attached. It specifies all the conditions on which you are willing to buy the flat. You are strongly advised not to make an offer yourself. Your solicitor will prepare it and send it to the seller's solicitor or estate agent.

In making the offer, you will have to decide, with guidance from your solicitor, how much to pay. You should also be clear when you want to move in and what extras you want to buy. If you are the only person interested in the flat, your solicitor may be able to find this out from the seller's solicitor or estate agent and may be able to negotiate an acceptable price. If more than one person is interested in buying the same flat, the seller's solicitor or estate agent will normally fix a closing date, intimating to the parties interested that offers must be submitted by a stated time on a particular date. You will have to offer 'blind', without knowing how much other people will offer. There may be quite a large gap between the highest and the next highest offers. It is not possible to get round this by making a bid of, say, '£100 more than the highest offer you receive'.

Your solicitor will normally help you decide how much over the asking price you should offer (he or she probably has access to information about prices achieved for similar flats to guide you in making your decision; the solicitor's knowledge of the market locally is important and usually helpful to you). But the final decision will be yours.

Date of entry

Stating the date on which you want to take physical possession of the property is part of your formal offer. Whether this is acceptable is largely governed by when the seller wants to move out. The date of entry is a matter for negotiation between you and the seller. If there are no compelling reasons on either side for a very early or very distant date of entry, the period between making the offer and moving in is on average between six weeks and two months. However, it is important to remember that you will have to have sufficient time to sell your own house, if necessary, and to have all the legal work for that sale completed before you take possession of the new flat.

Miscellaneous conditions

You may be interested in buying extras, such as carpets, curtains, kitchen equipment, etc. Sale particulars normally specify what is, and what is not, included in the price and your offer will normally be drawn up accordingly.

If the extra items included in the price are valuable, you may want to allocate part of the price to them – for example, if the flat with the extras costs £78,000, you could say that the flat costs £75,000 and the moveable property £3,000 – as this will give you a small saving in stamp duty (see pages 65-6). The items must be moveable for stamp duty to be saved. Ownership of more permanent fittings and fixtures (fitted kitchens, built-in bedroom furniture, etc.) is transferred together with the house, under the disposition (the legal document transferring the house) granted to you by the seller.

The remaining conditions in the offer are taken up with technical legal matters such as ensuring that you will receive a good marketable title, that the property is not adversely affected by planning proposals, that structural alterations/extensions have received local authority approval and that you can withdraw from the contract if the flat and contents included in the sale are not in substantially the same condition when you move in as when you offered for them.

If there is some special use to which you want to put the flat, such as using a part of it as an office or for a business, or if you plan to make major alterations, you must tell your solicitor so that he or she can include conditions in the offer to make sure that there are no relevant prohibitions in the title. If you are planning alterations or a change of use, you may have to make the offer conditional upon obtaining planning and/or building control permission. Sellers are usually not very keen on such offers but sometimes find that they are unavoidable.

Concluding the contract

If a closing date has been fixed and there is more than one offer, the seller and his or her solicitor or estate agent will consider all the offers made and decide which one, if any, to accept. Although the highest offer is normally the one accepted, the seller can, and sometimes does, take other factors into consideration, such as the date of entry proposed and the extras to be included in the sale.

Your solicitor will usually be informed by the seller's solicitor or estate agent, by telephone, within an hour or so after the closing time, whether your offer has been successful.

As mentioned above, your offer will stipulate that the flat is not subject to any local authority proposals, notices or orders which might adversely affect it, and oblige the seller to obtain and exhibit local authority certificates (for which the seller must pay) to this effect. Should the certificates disclose anything adverse, you are permitted to withdraw from the purchase or you could renegotiate the price. You should ask your solicitor to explain the legal and practical effects of any matters disclosed, such as the building being listed as one of architectural or historic interest.

An oral acceptance is not legally binding; usually the seller's solicitor will deliver an acceptance modifying or adjusting some of the terms of your offer, such as the date of entry, or making provisions for payment of interest on the price of the house if payment of the price on the date of entry is delayed through no fault of the seller, and to what extent and for how long any conditions of the contract may remain enforceable after you take possession. For instance, if you find out soon after taking possession that the central heating is not working, you may be able to go back to the seller and ask him or her to pay for repairs. This is called a qualified acceptance and is often delivered within a day or so of your solicitor making an offer on your behalf. If the modifications are acceptable to you (your solicitor will advise you on this), your solicitor will send a letter to the seller's solicitor confirming that a binding contract is concluded.

This is usually done within a day or so of receipt of the qualified acceptance. So the contract can be concluded within a few days of making the offer.

The written offer and subsequent letters between the buyer's and seller's solicitors relating to it are known as the 'missives'. Missives constitute a binding legal contract and neither the buyer nor the seller can withdraw without liability to pay damages. Missives are concluded by the solicitors; there is nothing for the buyer or seller to sign at this stage.

Insurance

At common law in Scotland the buyer becomes responsible for insurance of the property from the date when missives are concluded. However, it is now usual for the missives to provide that the seller will remain liable for any damage to the property and for its insurance until the date of entry, and that the buyer can withdraw from the purchase without penalty if the flat and any extras included in the sale are seriously damaged or destroyed before the date of entry.

Completing the purchase

Once missives have been concluded, your solicitor will set in train examination of the title and the conveyancing procedures to ensure that the disposition in your favour is ready for delivery by the date of entry in exchange for payment of the price.

If you are buying the flat together with your husband or wife or some other persons, you will need to think about how the title is to be taken. The terms of the title will regulate the ownership, the respective shares of the co-owners and what happens to their shares on their death. You should discuss these matters with your co-owners and your solicitor before the disposition is prepared.

A title simply in the names of two people gives each of them a separate and distinct equal share in the property. If you and your co-owner are to have unequal shares (say one-third to you and two-thirds to your brother) the title must state this. During their lives each co-owner can dispose of his or her share (by sale or gift) or can demand that the whole property be sold and his or her share of the proceeds be paid over. It is possible for co-owners to agree not to demand a sale. Where the co-owners are a married couple, the Matrimonial Homes (Family Protection) (Scotland) Act 1981 requires both spouses (or the court) to agree to any sale of the whole property or any disposal by one spouse of his or her separate share.

Two co-owners, particularly spouses, often take the title in each of their names and those of their survivor. If this is done, when either of the co-owners dies, the survivor automatically becomes entitled to the whole property. Such a survivorship title cannot usually be altered without the agreement of both co-owners and it will generally prevail over any will made by either of the co-owners.

The mortgage

As soon as the missives have been concluded, you should complete your loan application if you have not already done so.

If you are borrowing from a building society, bank or other lender, your solicitor normally acts for the lender as well for you. There are various types of mortgage available – for instance, a repayment mortgage or an endowment mortgage. In the latter the lender accepts an assignation of a life policy as an additional means of providing security for repayment of the loan. Your solicitor can advise on which type of mortgage suits you best. He or she will report to the lender on the title and prepare the necessary mortgage document, called a 'standard security'. Your solicitor will arrange for the loan money to be available in time for the date of entry and will ask you to sign the standard security and other documents by the date of entry.

If you are in any doubt about the terms of the mortgage documents, ask your solicitor to explain them to you before you sign them. Almost all such documents prohibit the letting of the property without the lender's consent. They also set out detailed conditions about maintenance, insurance, and so on, and give the lender a wide range of remedies, including ultimately the right to sell the flat if you fail to maintain your payments or otherwise fail to observe the loan conditions.

The lender's cheque will be sent to your solicitor before the date of entry and he or she will ask you to pay the difference between the price and your mortgage loan. If you are selling another house or flat, whether in Scotland or England, and you are relying on the money from the sale, which will not be available by the date of entry, you will need to make bridging loan arrangements at an early stage and you should discuss this with your solicitor.

Documents

On the date of entry, a procedure known as 'settlement' takes place, when your solicitor will meet the seller's solicitor and hand over a cheque for the full price in return for the title deeds, including the disposition in your favour. The keys are usually handed over at settlement unless other arrangements have been agreed.

Your solicitor will then register the disposition and the standard security in the General Register of Sasines or, if your property is in an area where registration of titles has been introduced, in the Land Register of Scotland. Normally the documents will be returned to your solicitor after a couple of months. If you have a mortgage, the solicitor will send the documents to the lender. If you do not, your solicitor will hand the title deeds over to you once the registration process has been completed. He or she may offer to hold them in safe custody for you, usually free of charge.

Solicitors' charges

After completing the purchase (or sometimes before doing so) your solicitor will send you the account for his or her fees and outlays (disbursements). Solicitors in Scotland do not charge according to fixed scales.

In addition to the solicitors' fees for the preliminary work leading up to and including missives, the conveyancing and the mortgage (on all of which you will have to pay VAT), there will be stamp duty of 1 per cent of the price of the flat if it is over £60,000, and registration dues for recording the documents in the Register of Sasines or Land Register. These dues amount to about 0·25 per cent of the price of the house.

Outlays must be paid on the date of entry; the solicitor may agree to accept payments of fees a month later or to have payment by instalments.

Succession

If you buy a flat in Scotland intending it as your residence or principal residence, you may acquire Scottish domicile. This may affect, among other things, the way your property is inherited on your death.

If you die without a will, Scottish law will regulate the distribution of your heritable property (i.e., land and buildings) in Scotland, and moveable property (all property other than heritable) in Scotland and elsewhere.

If you die leaving a will, it regulates the distribution of your estate, but the provisions of your will are subject to Scottish rules of succession which differ in a number of important respects from English law. The most important difference is that a spouse and children cannot be cut out of the succession to moveable estate, no matter what the will may say. They are always entitled to their 'legal rights' which, depending on the circumstances, may be either one-third or one-half of the net moveable estate.

With heritable property, regardless of the domicile of the owner, succession is governed by the law of the country in which the property is situated. Therefore, even if only a holiday home is bought in Scotland, so that there is no question of the buyer thereby acquiring Scottish domicile, the succession to that flat is governed by Scottish law.

In Scotland, a will is not automatically revoked if the person making it subsequently marries, nor are provisions in favour of a spouse automatically revoked on divorce.

Selling a flat

If you are selling in Scotland, you are likely to have been a buyer already and thus familiar with the Scottish system. Many matters dealt with in the section on buying will be of interest to you as a seller.

The main steps involved in selling a flat in Scotland are:

● advertising and showing your flat;
● dealing with offers;
● transferring title to the buyer and repaying any loan.

You should alert your solicitor to the fact that you are about to sell your flat before you put it on the market. This is because a binding contract for the sale will usually be concluded within a few days of a buyer making a formal offer, and this cannot normally be done unless your solicitor has had an opportunity to:

- look over your title deeds to ensure they are in order and that you have good title to the property. He or she will borrow them from your building society or other lender if you have an outstanding loan over the property;
- check the amount of any outstanding loan;
- order local authority searches to make sure that the property is not affected by any outstanding local authority notices, orders or proposals.

Someone who has been used to the English method of sale, where the solicitor becomes involved at only a relatively late stage, should be aware of the need to bring a solicitor into the picture early in Scotland.

Consent to sale

Where a flat is owned by two or more people, all of them must consent to its sale, although a sale can be forced by the court. Try to get agreement because legal proceedings are expensive.

The Matrimonial Homes (Family Protection) (Scotland) Act 1981 makes it imperative for a married seller whose spouse is not a co-owner to obtain the spouse's consent to a sale at the earliest opportunity and certainly before missives are concluded. Failure to do so may mean that the seller finds he or she cannot give the buyer possession of the property as provided for in the missives. This is especially important where the couple are separated or estranged.

Advertising and showing your flat

The three most common ways of marketing your flat are to:

- employ a solicitor;
- employ an estate agent;
- do it yourself.

Even if you employ a solicitor or estate agent you will probably be showing prospective buyers around the flat yourself. As the owner, you will show the property to its best advantage and know the answers to all the questions people are likely to ask. Moreover, solicitors and estate agents will generally charge extra for showing prospective buyers around property.

Selling through a solicitor

If you ask your solicitor to sell your house, you should expect him or her to provide a full estate agency service. He or she will normally also register your flat in the local solicitors' property centre, for which a charge of approximately £75-100 (more in some centres) is made. This covers display of the flat in the solicitors' property centre until sold, and insertion in the property centre's regular property listing or mailing where there is one.

A solicitor who acts for you in selling your flat will charge a selling commission over and above the conveyancing fees. Although solicitors are entitled to charge a sales commission of 1·5 per cent, many charge 1 per cent or slightly less, and it is quite common for a solicitor to charge a single percentage fee to cover both the selling and the conveyancing. Ask your solicitor for an estimate of charges before instructing him or her to act for you, and if you are not satisfied with the estimate, discuss it with him or her, or seek an alternative estimate from another solicitor.

Selling through an estate agent

Generally speaking, estate agents' terms of business are similar in Scotland to those in England and Wales. Commissions are generally 1·5 per cent of the achieved selling price, although lower charges may be negotiated, and higher charges normally apply in the case of large or specialised properties. Ask the estate agent for an estimate and make sure you understand whether items like VAT are included in the charge and whether advertising costs are extra: you may be charged for the insertion of the property in the estate agent's house magazine.

Even if you instruct an estate agent to sell your flat for you, he or she will normally pass to your solicitor any formal offers which are made. It is important to realise that as well as the estate agent's commission, you will have to pay the solicitor's fee for concluding missives and the conveyancing fees.

Selling it yourself

This entails arranging to advertise the property, showing people around it, letting surveyors inspect it, answering questions about room sizes, the price and what items are and are not included in the sale. You should prepare written particulars similar to those issued by solicitors and estate agents, but stress to people viewing the flat that these are provided only as a guide and are not to form part of any contract.

If you decide to sell your flat yourself, the only costs which you need incur are those for advertising. Although it is probably not sensible to 'go it alone' the first time you sell, if you have been through the process of buying and selling before, and if you have a readily saleable flat in which a large number of people are likely to be interested, you may feel that the saving in sales commission is justified.

If you decide to sell your flat yourself, you will still need a solicitor to do the conveyancing and should tell him or her in advance, and tell prospective buyers that formal written offers are to be submitted to him or her.

The advertisement

If you are selling through a solicitor or an estate agent, he or she will prepare the advertisement for you and agree its terms with you, and will also advise you on the upset price and the price you should expect to achieve.

Arrangements for viewing are normally made with prospective buyers, who should be asked for their names and addresses. There may be fixed viewing times or viewing by appointment, or a mixture of both. Remember that the easier you make it for people to view a flat, the more people are likely to do so and the quicker you may find a buyer. Evenings and weekend afternoons are popular viewing times.

The advertisement also sometimes states an upset price and invites offers over that price. The upset is generally fixed below the actual price that a seller hopes to obtain in order to attract buyers and encourage competition. You should be able to judge what upset to put on your flat by looking at advertisements for comparable flats in the neighbourhood. A surveyor will carry out a quick pre-sale valuation for £60-80 + VAT, which will help you to fix a price.

After the advertisement

You may gain an impression of whether people are seriously interested or not in buying the flat when they come to view, particularly if they return a second time. However, this is not always the case, and the first sign that you are going to receive an offer is usually when a solicitor telephones your solicitor or estate agent to say that he or she has a client interested in your property. You should then not sell to anyone without giving everyone who has notified an interest to you or your solicitor or estate agent an opportunity of offering.

An indication of interest is usually followed by a visit from a surveyor. If the survey is favourable, it is likely to be followed by an offer. If you are doing the selling of your flat yourself, ask buyers to lodge formal offers with your solicitor. Never sign a written acceptance of an offer or exchange letters with a prospective buyer without consulting your solicitor.

Receiving offers

If several people have expressed an interest in your flat, it is usual to fix a closing date for offers – that is, a date and time at which you will consider all offers which have been lodged. All those people whose interest has been noted will be asked to submit formal written offers through their solicitor. Your solicitor or estate agent will advise you whether to fix a closing date or not, and will suggest when it should be. Where there is competition, a higher price may be achieved if you do not rush the sale, but this may be nerve-racking for you.

On the closing date, you and your solicitor or estate agent will have to decide which offer to accept. You are not under an obligation to accept the highest offer or even any offer at all. If offers are close, you may take into account other factors such as the proposed date of entry, what extras are included in the price, or even whether or not you liked the person making the highest offer. If the price is acceptable but other conditions of the offer are not, your solicitor or estate agent can negotiate them with the person making the offer or his or her solicitor. If the top offer is too low, you may have to re-advertise. It is unethical to try to get the person making the highest offer to pay more without giving the others making offers a chance to re-offer.

Concluding the missives

If you are selling through an estate agent, he or she will normally pass the offers, or at least the offer which is to be accepted, to your solicitor. Once you have received an offer which you want to accept, or identified which of any competing offers is to be accepted, your solicitor will adjust points of details with the solicitor acting for the person who made the successful offer. When these adjustments have been made, they are confirmed in writing: this exchange of letters is, as has been mentioned earlier, referred to as the 'missives'. This process normally takes only a day or two. As with buying a house, the conclusion of missives constitutes a binding contract from which neither party can withdraw. Your solicitor will accept the offer and conduct the bargain on your behalf. Make sure therefore that you understand exactly what you are agreeing to.

In theory, it would be possible for gazumping to take place between the date when an acceptable offer is received and the date when the missives are concluded, but it would be unethical for a solicitor acting for a seller to negotiate with a third party during this period. If in such circumstances you decide to withdraw from negotiations with the person who made the successful offer and to negotiate with someone else, your solicitor would have to stop acting for you and you would have to appoint another solicitor. The absence of gazumping, and the short time between offers being made and becoming binding, are advantages of the Scottish system.

Completing the sale

Once the missives have been concluded, your solicitor will send the title deeds of the flat to the buyer's solicitor so that he or she can examine them and prepare the disposition in favour of the buyer. Your solicitor will also inform your building society, bank or other lender that the missives have been concluded and obtain a redemption statement to show the amount of the loan to be repaid on completion of the sale. He or she will prepare the discharge document and have it signed by the lender before the date of entry.

Your solicitor will instruct searches in the registers to demonstrate to the buyer that there are no adverse entries such as court decrees in respect of the property or against you as a seller. He or she answers any questions raised by the buyer's solicitor, and adjusts the terms of the disposition with him or her. You have to sign the disposition before the date of entry.

Immediately prior to the date of entry, your solicitor will agree with you what arrangements are to be made about handing over the keys (often it is best to deliver these to your solicitor on the date of entry).

On the date of entry, the disposition in favour of the buyer is handed over in return for the buyer's solicitor's cheque for the full purchase price. Out of that amount, your solicitor repays your outstanding mortgage loan, and any bridging loan, in accordance with instructions received from you or your bank and will then let you have a cheque for the balance of the price payable to you, after deducting fees and outlays. He or she should provide you with a detailed statement showing all the financial details; if not, make sure you ask for one. Your solicitor will normally send you the balance of the price and his or her statement on the day on which the sale is completed, or at the latest on the following day.

GLOSSARY

Abstract of title A summary provided by the seller of the history and validity of the legal title to unregistered land; also known as an epitome of title

Action Civil proceedings before the courts

Actual notice Actually knowing of someone's rights over a flat

Advance The mortgage loan

Advancement A presumption that when a husband/father transfers property (e.g. land or money) to a wife/child it is a gift

Assignment The sale of a tenant's entire lease to another person

Beneficial ownership Having the real ownership of a property without owning its legal title (see Equitable interest)

Beneficiary The person who is entitled to property under a trust (see Beneficial ownership)

By-law Local legislation created by the local authority for its area

Caution A means of protecting an interest on the Land Register

Caveat emptor 'Let the buyer beware'

Charge Any right or interest over the land securing the repayment of money, especially a mortgage; also used to denote a debt, or a claim for payment

Charge certificate When there is a mortgage, the certificate issued by the Land Registry or Registers of Scotland for areas where land registration has been implemented to the lender on a property which has a registered title (see Land certificate)

Charges register One of the three parts which make up the register at the Land Registry or Registers of Scotland of a property with a regis-tered title; contains details of restrictive covenants, mortgages and other interests, subject to which the registered proprietor owns the property

Chattel Any moveable possession

Civil law That part of the law (e.g. contract and negligence) which confers rights and imposes duties on individuals and deals with resolving disputes between them. Most of the actions between landlord and tenants are matters of civil law

Commonhold A proposed scheme whereby tenants can own the freehold title of their flats, with the major title being owned (and regulations laid down) by the commonhold association for that block

Common law That part of the law which is derived not from statutes but from the principles and the precedents set by earlier decisions of the court

Completion The final stage of the legal transaction when buying or selling the long lease of a flat

Constructive notice Knowledge which the buyer should have had about the flat if he or she had made reasonable enquiries

Contract Any legally binding agreement; on the sale of a property it is the document, in two identical parts, one signed by the buyer and the other by the seller, which, when the parts are exchanged, commits both the buyer and the seller to complete the transaction by transferring ownership in exchange for paying the purchase money

Conveyancing The legal and administrative process of transferring the ownership of land or any buildings on it, or a part of a building (such as a flat), from one owner to another

Co-ownership Where two or more people own the flat

County court Court which deals with small civil cases, including landlord and tenant matters

Covenant An undertaking between landlord and tenant whereby each is bound to do (such as pay the rent or to repair), or refrain from doing (such as misusing property), certain things; may be expressed (that is, set out in the lease), or implied

Criminal law That part of the law which punishes behaviour harmful to the community as a whole, as against the civil law which confers rights and duties on individual people

Date of entry In Scotland, the date a buyer takes physical possession of a property

Dealings Any transaction involving property

Deed A formal legal document which is 'signed and delivered'; the transfer of the legal title to leasehold property has to be by deed

Demised premises Property which is the subject matter of a lease with certain implied covenants

Deposit Part of the purchase price, usually 5 or 10 per cent, which the buyer has to pay at the time of exchange of contracts. The seller's conveyancer will hold the deposit either as stakeholder (in which case it cannot be given to the seller until completion) or agent (in which case it can be passed to the seller at any time)

Disclaimer The right of a tenant's trustee in bankruptcy to get rid of the lease

Disposition In Scotland, the legal document transferring the property to the buyer

Distress An ancient remedy whereby the landlord can seize and sell goods of the tenant to recover rent arrears

Easement The legal right of a property owner to use the facilities of another's land (e.g. a right of way)

Encumbrances Rights held by third parties which adversely affect the use of the flat to be bought (e.g. easements and restrictive covenants)

Endowment mortgage A loan on which only the interest is paid throughout the term; the capital is paid off at the end with the proceeds of an endowment insurance policy which is assigned to or deposited with the lender as additional security for the loan

Enfranchisement Tenant with long lease buying the freehold of a house under the Leasehold Reform Act 1967; or tenants collectively buying the freehold of the building in which the flats are situated under the Leasehold Reform, Housing and Urban Development Act 1993

Engross To put into final form (e.g. to type a document in deed form)

Enquiries before contract A set of detailed questions about many aspects of a property which the seller, or his or her legal adviser, is generally asked to answer before the buyer is prepared to sign a contract; also called preliminary enquiries

Enquiries of local authority A number of questions asked of a local authority on a printed form about a particular property; the form is usually sent with, and loosely speaking forms part of, the buyer's local search which is made before contracts are exchanged

Equitable interest Rights in a property which fall short of legal title, for example where a lease is not properly created by deed it may be an equitable lease; also used to describe the interest of beneficial ownership (arising under a contract or by co-ownership) when this is not the same as the legal title

Equity Body of law which runs alongside the common law and is designed to ensure that justice and fairness is dispensed by the courts. Equity has its own rules (to do with co-ownership and mortgages, for example) and its own remedies (e.g. specific performance, injunctions and rectification)

Equity of redemption The right of the borrower under a mortgage to redeem (i.e. pay off) the mortgage at any time

Estate Person's ownership of land (may be freehold or leasehold)

Exchange of contracts The stage at which the buyer has signed one copy of the contract and sent it to the seller, and the seller has done the same in return, so that both become legally bound to go through with the transaction

Exclusive possession The right of a tenant to exclude all others (including the landlord) from the flat

Factor A professional property manager (Scotland)

Feu Property offered for sale (Scotland)

Feuar The owner of a property (Scotland)

Feuing conditions Conditions imposed on a flat- or house-owner by the land-owner (Scotland, similar to covenants in England and Wales)

Feuduty Sum paid annually by flat- or house-owner to the land-owner (Scotland, similar to ground rent in England and Wales)

Fixed-term lease A lease which is granted for a fixed duration (e.g. 99 years)

Fixtures Articles which, being attached (by screws, concrete or pipes, for instance) to the property itself, are presumed to have become legally part of the property so that they are included in a sale, unless specifically excluded by the contract

Foreclosure A mortgage lender's remedy whereby it obtains the property rather than repayment of the loan and keeps the money already repaid; needs a court order

Forfeiture The means by which a landlord can bring a lease to an early end following a breach of covenant by the tenant; needs a court order

Freehold The absolute ownership of property until the end of time. In the case of a flat, the freehold will usually be the title owned by the landlord and will relate to the whole building and the land on which the building stands

Freeholder The person who owns the freehold. When this person creates or grants a lease (i.e. sells a flat) he or she is known as the lessor, landlord or reversioner

Gazumping When a potential flat-buyer is out-bid by a rival buyer. As well as losing the desired flat, the unlucky victim of gazumping will lose the money already spent on the conveyancing process

Gazundering When a buyer refuses at the last minute to go ahead with the purchase unless the price is reduced, or because he or she has found a more suitable property or had a change of heart

Grant The formal giving or transferring of, for example, a lease or covenant. The person who transfers is called the grantor; the person to whom the lease is transferred is called the grantee

Ground rent Small sum payable periodically to the landlord by a tenant who holds leasehold property on a long lease

Habendum The part of the lease which states how long the tenancy is to run for

Head-lease A lease from which another, shorter, lease is carved out

Injunction A court order requiring a person to do something or to stop doing something

Interest in land A right to, stake in, or any form of ownership of, property such as a flat

Joint tenants Two (or more) people who hold property as co-owners; when one dies, the whole property automatically passes to the survivor(s)

Land Includes the plot of ground and all buildings on it

Land certificate The certificate issued to the registered proprietor of a property which has a registered title, showing what is entered on the register of that property at the Land Registry or Registers of Scotland. When the property is mortgaged, no land certificate is issued; instead a charge certificate is issued to the lender

Land charges registry A government department in Plymouth where rights over, and interests in, unregistered property are recorded; charges are registered against the name of the owner, not the property concerned

Landlord The owner of a property who grants a lease or sub-lease of the property; also known as lessor or reversioner

Land Registry A government department (head office in London and district registries in various other places in England and Wales) where details of properties with a registered title are recorded

Lease The charter setting out the terms and conditions of the leasehold

Leasehold Ownership of property for a fixed number of years granted by a lease

Leaseholder The person to whom a lease is granted (i.e. the person who buys a flat); also known as a lessee or tenant

Lessee see Leaseholder

Lessor see Landlord

Local land charges register A register kept by the local authority, containing charges of a public nature affecting the property, which is consulted when a local search is made

Local search An application made on a duplicate form, to the local authority for a certificate providing certain information about a property in the area. Also denotes the search certificate itself. Loosely speaking, a local search also includes the answers given by the local authority to a number of standard enquiries, made on another special form

Management company A company set up by the landlord or the tenants to manage the services provided and attend to repairs in a block of flats

Marriage value The notion that when the tenants buy the freehold they are obtaining a benefit of the increased value of the freehold and the leaseholds being together

Merger The purchase of the landlord's freehold by a tenant

Missives The written offer and subsequent letters between the solicitors of the buyer and the seller (Scotland)

Mortgage Loan for which a property is the security. It gives to the lender (mortgagee) certain rights in the property, including the power to sell if the mortgage payments are not made

Mortgage deed The document setting out the mortgage conditions

Mortgagee One who lends money on mortgage, such as a building society, bank, local authority, insurance company or private lender

Mortgagor The borrower (whose property is security for the loan)

NHBC scheme This is a form of insurance cover/building guarantee available on most newly constructed houses and flats

Negative covenants Covenants restricting one party from doing something; for example, using the premises for certain purposes

Negative equity Where the sale of the property will not generate sufficient funds to discharge the mortgage debt

Negligence Breach of a legal rule which imposes a duty of care on any person who ought to foresee that his or her act or omission could cause loss or injury to another

Notice to complete A notice served by either the buyer or the seller if completion does not go ahead on the agreed date because of delays by the other. It then becomes a term of the contract that completion will occur within a reasonable period of the notice and that time will be of the essence for both parties

Nuisance The legal duty not to unlawfully interfere with someone's use or enjoyment of land

Official search An application to an official authority (such as a local authority, the Land Registry or the land charges registry), to find out some relevant facts about a particular property

Option A contractual right to buy something (e.g. a new lease or the freehold)

Overreaching The ability, by paying the purchase money collectively to two trustees (legal owners), to get free of a co-owner's interest in the flat

Overriding interests Rights which are enforceable against a property, even though they are not referred to on the register of the property at the Land Registry

Parcels The part of the lease which describes the property which is being leased

Periodic tenancy A lease which is not fixed term (i.e. a tenancy from week to week or month to month)

Positive covenants Covenants which compel one party to do something; for example, to pay rent or to insure

Possession Procedure whereby a landlord goes to the court to evict a tenant or other lawful residential occupier

Pre-emption The contractual right to have first refusal (e.g. when the freeholder decides to sell the freehold)

Preliminary enquiries See Enquiries before contract

Premium Capital sum (the purchase price) paid for a long lease; also the payments to insurers for insurance cover

Privity of contract The contractual relationship between the original landlord and the original tenant

Privity of estate The relationship between the current landlord and the current tenant

Protocol A standardised procedure (and preferred practice) for conveyancing introduced by the Law Society; intended to simplify and quicken the (pre-contract) process

Purchaser The buyer

Quiet enjoyment An implied covenant that the landlord shall not unlawfully interfere with the tenant's enjoyment of the flat

Reddendum The part of the lease which states the ground rent payable and when it is to be paid

Re-entry Landlord lawfully retaking possession of a property with a court order on forfeiture

Register In the case of a property with a registered title, the record for that property kept at the Land Registry, divided into the property, the proprietorship and the charges registers

Registered title Title or ownership of freehold or leasehold property which has been registered at the Land Registry, with the result that ownership is guaranteed by the state

Registers of Scotland Where records of titles under Sasines or land registration schemes are kept

Relief Redress or remedial action sanctioned by law; for example where the tenant's lease is allowed by the court to continue despite the fact that the landlord has obtained a judgment for forfeiture

Remedy The means of legal redress

Rent-to-mortgage Scheme allowing council tenants to count their rental payments as contributing to the purchase of the flat

Repair Renewal or replacement of part of a building

Repayment mortgage Loan on which part of the capital and interest are paid back by regular instalments throughout the term of the loan

Reservations Rights set out in a lease as being kept by the landlord over the property he or she has let; the converse of easements and usually of similar nature

Reserved property Parts of the building or garden which the landlord keeps under his or her control

Restrictive covenant A covenant which restricts the use of the premises

Reversion An interest in a property which will eventually return to the original owner (or successors) after the period in which another person holds the property comes to an end; loosely used to denote the freehold

Reversioner See Landlord

Right to buy Right of council tenants to buy the rented flat in which they live

Sasines Register System of title registration prior to introduction of land registration

Search An enquiry for, or an inspection of, information recorded by some official body, such as a local authority, the Land Registry or the land charges department

Secure tenant An individual who occupies as his or her only or principal home a property of which the landlord is a local authority, a county council, a housing association or one of a few other public-sector landlords

Security of tenure The right to remain in possession after the original contract has expired

Service charges The cost paid periodically to the landlord or the management company for the services provided to the tenants

Severance The conversion of a joint tenancy into a tenancy in common

Solicitors' property centres Organisations run by solicitors on a co-operative basis providing details of all properties being sold by solicitors in the area (Scotland)

Specific performance Equitable remedy amounting to an order that a reluctant party complete the contract (i.e. performs what has been agreed)

Stamp duty A tax payable to the government on some deeds and documents, including deeds of transfer, conveyance or assignment of property at a price above (at present) £60,000; deeds and documents cannot be used as evidence or registered at the Land Registry unless they are properly stamped

Standard security A mortgage document (Scotland)

Statute An Act of Parliament

Statutory A right or obligation arising from a statute or subordinate legislation made under it

Subject to contract Provisionally agreed, but not so as to constitute a binding legal contract; either the buyer or the seller may still back out with no legal consequences, without giving any reason

Sub-lease A lease carved out of another lease, necessarily for a shorter period, created by a person who has only a leasehold interest in the property

Sub-tenant Tenant who leases property from a landlord who owns a leasehold, not a freehold, interest in that property. It is possible for a chain of tenancies to be built up running from the freeholder (the head landlord) to his or her tenant and down to a subtenant, then to a sub-sub-tenant, and so on. Each tenant becomes the landlord of his or her own sub-tenant down to the last link in the chain – the tenant in actual occupation

Superior Original developer of the land or estate-owner; person a flat- or house-owner pays feuduty to (Scotland)

Superior landlord Someone with a higher interest than the tenant's immediate landlord; if A, a freeholder, grants a 99-year lease to B, and B then grants a 21-year lease to C, the superior landlord is A

Surrender The selling or giving up of the lease to the landlord

Survivorship (right of) The right of a surviving joint tenant to acquire automatically on death the interest of a deceased joint tenant

Tenant The person to whom a lease is granted (word is interchangeable with lessee)

Tenants' association A body which is representative of the tenants and recognised as such by the landlord; the importance of such associations lies in the collective bargaining power the members have in relation to the landlord

Tenants' management company A company formed by tenants to manage the block or estate; such a company usually acquires the freehold to the property

Tenants in common Two (or more) people who together hold property in such a way that, when one dies, his or her share does not pass automatically to the survivor but forms part of his or her own property and passes under his or her will or intestacy (this is in contrast with what happens in the case of joint tenants)

'Time is of the essence' A term in the contract indicating that stated time limits must be observed; if a party is late in performing a contractual obligation where time is of the essence, the other party is released from his or her corresponding contractual obligation. Completion time can be made 'of the essence' in a contract for the sale of land by either party serving a 'notice to complete'

Title Ownership of a property

Title deeds Documents going back over 15 years or longer which prove the ownership of unregistered property

Transfer A deed which transfers the ownership of a property, the title to which is registered at the Land Registry (as opposed to the deed used where the title is unregistered)

Trust An arrangement whereby the legal ownership of property is vested in trustees on behalf of the real owners, the beneficiaries

Trustee A person in whom the legal ownership of property is vested, but who holds it for the benefit of someone else (called a beneficiary)

Trustees for sale People who hold property as trustees on condition that they should sell the property, but usually with a power to postpone doing so indefinitely if they want to

Trust for sale Where there is co-ownership the co-owners hold under a trust to sell the property (which can be postponed indefinitely) and account to the beneficiaries for the proceeds of sale

Underlease see Sub-lease

Unities (the four) Possession, time, title and interest: the necessary ingredients of a joint tenancy

Unregistered land Property, the title or ownership of which has not been registered at the Land Registry

Upset price The price set for a flat above which offers are invited (Scotland)

Vendor The seller

Waste An act by the tenant damaging the interest of the landlord in the property

ADDRESSES

Association of British Insurers
51 Gresham Street
London EC2V 7HQ
0171-600 3333

Campaign Against Residential
Leasehold Abuse (CARLA)
c/o 6 Pye Corner
Castle Hedingham
Essex CO9 3DE
(01787) 462787

Chartered Institute of Arbitrators
24 Angel Gate
London EC1V 2RS
0171-837 4483

Federation of Private Residents'
Associations
62 Bayswater Road
London W2 3PS
0171-402 1581

Incorporated Society of Valuers &
Auctioneers
3 Cadogan Gate
London SW1X OAS
0171-235 2282

Insurance Ombudsman
Insurance Ombudsman Bureau
City Gate One
135 Park Street
London SE1 9EA
0171-928 7600

Lands Tribunal
48/49 Chancery Lane
London WC2A 1JR
0171-936 7200

Lands Tribunal for Scotland
1 Grosvenor Crescent
Edinburgh EH12 5ER
0131-225 7996

Law Society of England and Wales
113 Chancery Lane
London WC2A 1PL
0171-242 1222

Law Society of Scotland
26 Drumsheugh Gardens
Edinburgh EH3 7YR
0131-226 7411

Leasehold Enfranchisement Advisory
Service
8 Maddox Street
London W1R 9PN
0171-493 3116

Leasehold Enfranchisement
Association
10 Upper Phillimore Gardens
London W8 7HA
0171-937 0866

National House Building Council
Buildmark House
Chiltern Avenue
Amersham
Buckinghamshire HP6 5AP
(01494) 434477

Ombudsman for Corporate Estate
Agents
Beckett House
4 Bridge Street
Salisbury
Wiltshire SP1 2LX
(01722) 333306

Royal Institution of Chartered
Surveyors
12 Great George Street
London SW1P 3AD
0171-222 7000

Solicitors Complaints Bureau
Victoria Court
8 Dormer Place
Leamington Spa
Warwickshire CV32 5AE
(01926) 822007/8/9

INDEX